FRACTIONAL MONEY

NOTE TO 1988 REPRINT

Fractional Money, by Neil Carothers, here reprinted, is one of the most elusive, yet most valuable source references in the numismatic field. In several hundred pages, the author discusses in detail the economic conditions, legislative acts, and other events which led to the production of various coins from the earliest federal issues through the 20th century, to the time of the book's publication.

While many numismatic references detail coins, die varieties, and other numismatic attributes, relatively few give the why and wherefore of how such coins came to be. Carothers' discussion of economic conditions and the resultant effects on coinage and coinage distribution stands today as the definitive work on the subject. Likewise, other chapters in the book will prove invaluable to the dedicated numismatist and researcher.

In presenting this reprint to the present generation of collectors, Bowers and Merena Galleries has made it possible to acquire for a reasonable price a volume which was apt to cost $75 or more in original form, if indeed a copy could be located.

SILVER QUARTER
1836

SILVER HALF-DOLLAR
1806

SILVER DIME
1827

SILVER HALF-DIME
1837

COPPER CENT
1796

COPPER HALF-CENT
1811

NICKEL-COPPER
CENT
1857

SILVER-COPPER
3 CENT PIECE
1851

BRONZE 2 CENT PIECE
1864

SILVER 20 CENT PIECE
1875

NICKEL-COPPER
3 CENT PIECE
1873

HISTORIC U. S. FRACTIONAL COINS

FRACTIONAL MONEY

A HISTORY OF THE SMALL COINS AND FRACTIONAL PAPER CURRENCY OF THE UNITED STATES

BY

NEIL CAROTHERS

Professor of Economics and Director of the College of Business Administration, Lehigh University

NEW YORK

JOHN WILEY & SONS, Inc.

London: CHAPMAN & HALL, Limited

1930

Reprinted In 1988 By:

Bowers and Merena Galleries, Inc.

Box 1224

Wolfeboro, New Hampshire 03894

PRINTED IN U.S.A.

PRESS OF
BRAUNWORTH & CO., INC.
BOOK MANUFACTURERS
BROOKLYN, NEW YORK

Reprinted in 1988 by:
Bowers and Merena Galleries, Inc.
Box 1224
Wolfeboro, NH 03894

ISBN 0-943161-12-6

To My Mother
ASENATH WALLACE CAROTHERS

FOREWORD

This book is the outcome of an extensive study made when I held a fellowship in economics in the graduate school of Princeton University. I had undertaken research work in the field some years earlier, primarily, it might be said, in self-defense. As an instructor in money and banking I had found myself on the defensive before any inquiring and intelligent student, for the reason that the existing works on our financial history offered no adequate explanation of the laws, policies, and events which have made the story of our silver coinage. The book has grown out of the effort to discover the unknown facts of United States coinage history. That it developed, virtually, into a complete history of United States coinage is merely a testimony to the importance of the long neglected small coins.

I finish the work with a feeling of kinship to the proverbial Teutonic research worker of whom it was said that he could go down deeper, stay down longer, and come up muddier than any other of his kind. More than a thousand periodicals and government documents have been worked through in an effort to obtain original data.

To the reader who would question so extended a treatment of the history of silver coins the reply would be that in this history will be found the explanation of many of the major events in the financial history of the United States. Even so, in the interests of brevity many interesting details have been omitted and two important chapters, one discussing the quantity theory as it relates to fractional money and

vii

the other telling the story of fractional currency in the Confederacy, have been eliminated in their entirety.

The critical tone which pervades the book results from a reluctant but inevitable recognition of the necessity for criticism. I can not bring myself to gloss over the errors and condone the inefficiency that have marked the administration of our coinage throughout its long history.

I am under obligation to many for helpful suggestions and for courteous aid in the search for material. The work was begun under the guiding hand of Professor E. W. Kemmerer, and the final form owes much to his patient and thorough scrutiny of the entire manuscript. Professor Frank A. Fetter and my colleague, Professor H. M. Diamond, have also given much in time and labor to the tedious task of critical reading. My colleague, Dean C. M. McConn, has made valuable suggestions in connection with certain chapters. It should be emphasized, however, that none of these is responsible for the judgments of men and measures presented in the book. In innumerable ways my wife, Eileen Hamilton Carothers, has been helpful and encouraging.

NEIL CAROTHERS

December, 1929.

CONTENTS

CONTENTS

APPENDICES

FRACTIONAL MONEY

CHAPTER I

INTRODUCTION

THE MEANING of "small coins"—Definition of fractional currency—
Functions of fractional currency—Fiduciary coinage—Subsidiary and minor
coins—Characteristics of fiduciary coins—Importance of fractional currency

The story of United States currency has been told in
various general treatises on finance and in many special
studies. The works of Sumner, Laughlin, Watson, White,
Dewey, and Hepburn present the fundamental facts. But
the supposedly larger questions of monetary standards and
metallic ratios have so absorbed the attention of currency
historians that they have neglected the development of the
small coins which constitute the medium of exchange in petty
transactions.[1]

The expression "small change" or "small coins" is loosely
used to refer to those less valuable denominations of the
currency which are used to effect exchanges of goods and
services in retail trade and minor economic transactions.
These small coins are contrasted with the money of larger
denomination that serves as a medium of exchange in more
important transactions or as a reserve in credit operations.
It is impossible to draw a sharp distinction between the two

[1] There is no adequate history of United States coinage, and none which
gives even an outline of the facts of fractional currency history.

types. A coin of large denomination may be used in the purchase of an article of little value, whereas a number of small coins may serve in a transaction involving goods of considerable value. In time of currency disorganization small coins have been substituted for coins of much greater size, whereas coins and notes of large denominations have upon occasion taken the place, in some degree, of small change. Differences in legal tender quality between large and small units of currency do not constitute an essential difference of monetary character or function. These legal tender differences are, for that matter, of recent development. Nor do physical differences in design, metallic materials, or bullion values cause differences of monetary character. Our copper cents and silver dollars are alike in deriving their currency values and functions chiefly from sources other than their metal values.

There are, however, material differences of function between the currency of retail trade and the money of larger denominations used in more important transactions, and it is desirable to find a line of demarcation between the two types. From the standpoint of United States currency this line should be drawn at the value of one dollar, even though the silver dollar has been for many years a "small change" coin. Coins and paper notes of a value less than one dollar are best described by the term "fractional currency." For the purposes of this study the term will be used to include all money of this value that has been used by the people of the United States, whether its material was precious metal, base metal, or paper, whether it was of foreign origin, colonial issue, national government issue, or private manufacture, and whether it was of standard money quality or subordinate character.

Fractional currency occupies a very important place in economic life. Its primary function is to serve as a medium of exchange in the petty exchanges and minor transactions of everyday affairs. These transactions make up a very large part of the total volume of trade. A second function of fractional currency is its service in payments of large sums with fractional remainders. Always an important service, this second function has become increasingly important with the development in our day of keen competition in retail price quotations. A third function, derived from the other two but none the less distinct, is that of "making change" in transactions in which a purchaser offers currency of large denomination in payment for an article or service of small value. A quarter-dollar may be used in payment for a cigar, or it may be used in making change for a ten dollar note offered by the purchaser of the cigar. In this third function small change serves to extend the range of usefulness of large denominations of currency. This use is exemplified most strikingly, perhaps, in the operations of such institutions as the change-booths of city transportation companies.

The essential characteristic of the small change currency of the present day is its fiduciary nature. It is credit currency, in the form of paper notes or of coins lacking the value as metal which they have as money. Legislation, in one way or another, maintains their fiduciary value in terms of standard money. Fiduciary coins have been defined as "coins whose money value is greater than the market value of the principal metal by an amount more than sufficient to cover the expense of coinage." Simply expressed, this means that fiduciary coins are those whose value as money exceeds their value as metal plus the costs of alloy and minting. If the silver in a half-dollar costs thirty cents and the costs of alloy and minting are five cents the coin is fiduciary by fifteen cents. This definition, which expresses the common understanding, is not satisfactory. The one vital feature of fiduciary coinage is the difference between its money value and its metal value. A coin is fiduciary when its money value exceeds its bullion value, regardless of the costs of minting. The costs of coinage, a fiscal item charged off the treasury books at the time of issue, are unknown to the public and have no bearing on the circulation value, the metal value, the melting point, or the export point of the pieces in circulation. A half-dollar is a fiduciary coin so long as its metal value is less than fifty cents, whether it cost the government one cent or ten cents to mint it. In fact there have been instances in American history of fiduciary silver coins whose combined metal value and coinage costs exceeded the money value. They were fiduciary none the less. The reference to the principal metal in the definition cited is likewise unsatisfactory. The metal value of any coin derives from its entire metal content. In the case of many fiduciary coins there is no principal metal. The metal value of the copper-nickel cent of Civil War times was almost equally divided between nickel and copper. Fiduciary coins should be defined as coins whose money value is greater than their metal value.

In most countries the small change currency consists of various denominations of fiduciary coins made of silver, of a base metal, or of alloy compounds of base metals. The base metals most commonly used are copper, nickel, aluminum, tin, and zinc. The coins are nearly always fiduciary by an amount considerably greater than the costs of coinage. Consequently there is a seigniorage profit involved in their issue, and free coinage by individuals directly or through the government is impracticable. Modern nations have, therefore, made the production and issue of fiduciary coins a government monopoly, the coins being sold to the public for other types of currency. Issued in this way, the coins will go into circulation only where there is public need for small change, and over-issue is improbable.

It is customary for the government to redeem the coins at the original issue price or to accept them in payment for government dues, not only to provide for the unlikely contingency of redundancy but also to enable the holders of worn coins to dispose of them without undeserved loss. A provision for legal tender is not an absolute essential, but it is desirable, in that a limited legal tender power prevents disputes and uncertainty in the payment of debts.

In summary it may be said that fractional coins in a properly administered system are fiduciary coins, manufactured on government account, sold for standard money at prices well above their bullion values, redeemable at the option of the holders at their issue prices, and endowed with a limited legal tender power.[2] There is no difference whatever between silver coins of this character and coins of copper, bronze, nickel, or other metals. It is customary, however, to distinguish between silver coins of this type and those not made of precious metal, the term "subsidiary" being used to designate fiduciary silver coins and the term "minor" to describe those made of the base metals. As a means of classification this usage is convenient and helpful. The not uncommon use of the term "token money" to distinguish fiduciary coins from standard money is unsatisfactory. In fact, as Professor Kemmerer has pointed out, the use of the word "token" to describe fiduciary coins is misleading, since it conveys the idea that the coins are not money but mere substitutes for money.[3]

[2] The principles governing fiduciary coinage are considered in detail in Chapter XXI.

[3] Kemmerer, Money and Credit Instruments, 33. American economists use these terms with an unfortunate lack of discrimination. The use of "token" as a synonym for "minor," to distinguish minor coins from subsidiary, is especially bad. It makes a distinction between minor and subsidiary coins that does not exist. For an example of this usage see Edie, Principles of Economics, 499.

To render efficient service fractional currency should possess certain physical attributes. The denominations should be in such number that exchanges over a wide range of prices may be effected with a minimum of mechanical operations and mathematical calculations, but the number should not be so great that there are coins of nearly equal values. The denominations should accord with some decimal scale that makes change operations easy and arithmetical computation simple. The content and design of the coins should be based on considerations of economy, convenience, and attractiveness. Failure to provide for one or another of these physical qualities has frequently been a cause of public annoyance.

Economists and historians have not given subsidiary and minor coins the attention they deserve. Economically, small change is a highly important instrument of commerce. Historically, conditions arising in the development of the fractional currency have had a decisive influence in determining the course of United States finance. Failure to recognize these facts has led currency historians to misinterpret major events in our currency history.

The disappearance of a nation's standard money is a disaster entailing widespread loss and suffering. The collapse of the monetary systems of Europe in the World War caused untold injury. But the problem of a disappearing standard currency is met by the issue of a paper money substitute, and in dire need the business world can turn to commodity exchanges, bullion contracts, or transactions in terms of foreign currencies. Exchanges can be made. But the consequences of a breakdown in the fractional currency cannot be greatly mitigated. Barter exchanges and credit transactions are impracticable in small trade. The only recourse is the issue of emergency substitutes of paper or cheap metal, and such issues are invariably attended by economic loss and public inconvenience. In the final analysis it was the debased condition of the small coins in England that led to the establishment of the gold standard in that country. It was the precarious situation of the small change currency of France that brought about the formation of the Latin Monetary Union. It will be shown subsequently that a like condition in the United States determined the course of American currency history.

The history of the fractional currency of this country is interwoven with that of the standard coinage. In large measure the story of the fractional coins is the story of the silver dollar. It will be necessary in the course of this book to review and analyze the various governmental measures and policies, long familiar to students of finance, that have affected the standard currency. The discussion of these matters will be confined to those phases that have a definite relation to the development of the fractional currency.

Chapter II

THE ORIGIN OF SUBSIDIARY COINAGE

Development of fractional currency—Mediaeval small coins—Billon coins—Fractional coins in England—English silver legislation—Lord Liverpool's plan—The first subsidiary coinage.

It is a commonplace of economic history that the standard currency of the present day is the result of a long and irregular evolution from a less valuable to a more valuable medium of exchange. This evolution has been chiefly a result, though likewise a cause, of the general economic development from a primitive extractive economy, through stages of agriculture and handicrafts, to the modern industrial régime. The standard money has been evolved from crude commodity currencies, through various copper, bronze, iron, and silver media, into the highly developed gold and gold-exchange standards of today.

The small change currencies have had a development corresponding to that of the standard coin. When copper came to be the medium in the more important transactions, shells, salt or other commodities were the money of the minor exchanges. In turn, when silver came to be the standard, coins of copper and other base metals became the currency of small trade. And finally the dominance of the gold standard has relegated silver to the position of a subordinate currency material. The so-called "limping standard" of the United States and France, under which the silver dollar and the five-franc piece are by a legal fiction treated

8

as standard coins, is merely a transitional development in this downward evolution of silver. The gold-exchange standards of India and the Philippines, under which silver is still the major circulating medium, likewise represent a stage in the elimination of silver as a standard currency. In the relatively short space of two centuries the colonies and the United States passed through the stages that mark the evolution of money from primitive times.

Western Europe emerged from the Middle Ages with a crude sort of bimetallic standard. There was free coinage at the royal mints for both gold and silver, but it was a free coinage unlike that of our day. Coinage was a royal right, and as such it was made the instrument of extortion. Abuse of the coinage prerogative is an outstanding feature of the currency history of Europe in the Middle Ages. These abuses took the form of excessive seigniorage charges for coinage, deliberate debasements of the coins by increasing the proportion of alloy at the expense of the gold or silver, reduction of the total weight of the coins without a change in their legal values, and general enactments increasing the legal tender values. These measures were not always for the benefit of royal revenues. They were frequently instituted in the hope that they would prevent the exportation of coin or resuscitate a failing bimetallic system. From 1300 to 1700 the coinages of the leading countries of Western Europe were repeatedly debased. The debasements in England were less frequent and less flagrant than those of France and Spain.[1]

The mediaeval small coins were made of silver, of base metals, and of compositions of silver and base metals. The base metal coins were usually made of copper, brass, or bronze. The smaller silver coins were merely subdivisions

---

[1] See Shaw, History of the Currency, 84, 319; Palgrave, Dictionary of Political Economy, Vol. 1, 498–500.

of a larger silver standard unit.   They differed in no respect save size from the standard coin.   They had the same standard character, legal tender faculty, and percentage of alloy. The royal ministers and mint-masters realized at a comparatively early date that debased silver coins and coins of base metal mixtures were in character somewhat different from standard coins, but the possibility of coining small silver pieces on government account and maintaining their values by limitation of supply was not recognized.[2]   There was, apparently, no conception of a single gold standard with a subordinate currency of silver.

In the debasements of the gold coins it was the common practice to substitute silver or copper.   The usual outcome was a "reform" of the coinage system by the establishment of a new standard unit containing the amount of gold to which the adulterated coins had been reduced.   Nearly all the modern gold units of Europe are the descendants of larger coins gradually reduced by debasement.   In the silver coins copper or other metals were added until in some cases the percentage of silver became negligible.   Silver pieces that had been adulterated in this fashion were known in France as "billon."[3]   Eventually the word was used to refer to any brass, bronze, or copper coin that contained a trace of silver.   Economic forces laid some restraint on the debasement of the larger coins, but there was hardly any check on the adulteration of small silver pieces.   The profits

---

[2] Monroe, in Monetary Theory before Adam Smith, traces the slow evolution of this conception.   Fiduciary coins of various kinds were in circulation in Europe for more than 2,000 years before their nature was clearly understood.   Fiduciary bronze coins were issued in Sicily four centuries before the time of Christ.   The famous statement of Gresham's law in Aristophanes' Frogs referred to fiduciary bronze coins of Athens.   For an interesting account of coinage in ancient times see Burns, Money and Monetary Policy in Early Times.

[3] The English spelling was generally "billon," the Spanish "vellon."

from "billon" coinage were a material item in the royal revenues. Even base metal coins, whose issue was from an early date a government monopoly, were occasionally debased by arbitrary increases in legal tender value.

It is one of the curious facts of this period that base metal coins were not frankly and openly fiduciary. Every government could have made and sold them as useful coins for domestic currency. But the copper and brass coins came into circulation disguised as silver pieces, with metallic values supposedly equal to their face values. It was a fixed opinion of the time that all coins must contain gold or silver. Long before there was any English copper coinage the royal mint was trying to provide small change by issuing tiny silver pieces in the denominations of three farthings and of one half-penny. Copper farthings were not authorized until 1613, and there were no copper pennies until 1797.

One consequence of this condition was a scarcity of small coins. Before the time of Shakespere tavern-keepers and tradesmen were making private tokens for small change. For more than two hundred years such private tokens were in general circulation in England.[4] They were commonly made of mixtures of copper, tin, and lead. Some were made of leather. The first official copper coins were issued by Lord Harrington under a patent from James I. They were farthing pieces, so small that eight of them would be required to equal our present-day cent piece.

The billon coins and many of the silver coins of the Middle Ages were fiduciary. But they were fiduciary only because government proclamations could for a time maintain them at fictitious valuations. Their circulation was established by compulsion and there was no limitation on their issue. All coinage from the mints was in theory standard coin of the realm. The right of the crown to make

[4] See Nicholson, Treatise on Money, Chapter IV.

arbitrary and inequitable valuations of the currency was not successfully questioned.

England first discovered the principles underlying a sound small currency system. As early as 1445 the legal tender of a debased silver half-penny was limited to 12 pence in a total payment of 20 shillings.[5] The Harrington copper pieces of 1613 were made receivable by the people "only with their good liking." In 1666 all seigniorage charges on gold and silver coinage were abolished, and this wise action was reinforced by the removal of restrictions on the export of the coins.

First in the inauguration of these important measures, England was also first to discover that the problem of a satisfactory currency for retail trade could be solved by the application of principles governing the value of fiduciary coin, principles that had hitherto been demonstrated only through dishonest or mistaken debasements of the coinage. The discovery was accidental and was the culmination of a series of inadequate and temporary currency measures.

During the greater part of the eighteenth century the legal bimetallic ratio was favorable to the export of silver. The full-weight pieces were melted or exported. The small change currency consisted of pieces of private issue and worn, clipped, or counterfeit silver coins whose bullion values were so low that exportation was not profitable. Toward the end of the century the market ratio fluctuated widely, with the result that at times the gold coins of full weight were exported or subjected to clipping. In 1774 the gold coins were called in for recoinage. With the silver currency in a degenerate condition it was probable that underweight silver coins would be imported and exchanged for the new gold coins. It was decided, therefore, to restrict the field

[5] Breckinridge, Legal Tender, 38. In 1577 France made billon legal tender for one-third of any payment below 100 sols.

of circulation of the silver currency. A law was passed limiting the legal tender of silver coin to 25 pounds and prohibiting the importation of underweight silver pieces.

These measures are among the most important in monetary history. Instead of following the time-hallowed practice of changing the legal ratio of coinage, Parliament sought to maintain the circulation of both metals by separating their functions and creating a field of usefulness for each. Bimetallism was not abandoned, but the silver coins, all of them worn below their nominal weights, were to be used in minor transactions.

The legal ratio, 15¼ to 1, was still unfavorable to silver, and none of the metal was brought to the mint. In 1778 a temporary rise in the market value of gold brought the market ratio to the legal ratio, and a small amount of silver was presented to the mint for coinage. A continuance of this market situation would result in a large silver coinage and ultimately drive out the gold coin. A committee on the state of the currency recommended that the mints should be closed to silver, suggesting that the suspension of coinage should be temporary, pending a final decision as to coinage policy. In June, 1798, Parliament stopped the coinage of silver. By this measure and the earlier statute limiting the tender of silver coins England had adopted the single gold standard.

The law was admittedly temporary, and the problem of silver coinage was still unsolved. In 1805 Lord Liverpool presented to the king his famous proposal for the establishment of a permanent gold standard.[6] With great clarity and force he urged the impossibility of bimetallism and the superiority of gold as the standard metal. He presented a plan which he had worked out to provide for silver coins.

[6] For the story of this chapter in English monetary history see Liverpool, Coins of the Realm, and Shaw, History of the Currency.

The weights of the coins were to be reduced to a point at which their bullion values in terms of gold would be less than their circulation values. The legal ratio was not to be changed. Silver bullion owners would receive the same amounts in coin that they had been obtaining, but the coins would be smaller. The difference was to be taken by the government as seigniorage. Lord Liverpool reasoned that there could be no excessive issue of silver coins. The owner of bullion would take silver to the mint only when there was a need for small change, and the volume of coinage would be adjusted to the requirements of trade. Because they would be worth more than their bullion values the coins would not be exported. They could not displace gold because their legal tender power would be limited.

The outstanding feature of the plan was the recognition of the principle that the value of coins depends primarily on the quantity in circulation rather than the bullion content. The quantity theory was widely known, but it had not been proposed as the basis of a currency system.[7] Lord Liverpool had seen the practical operation of the principle in the continued circulation of silver pieces worn beyond all semblance of legal coins.

Liverpool's plan did not provide for a practicable fiduciary coinage system. The fundamental feature of subsidiary coinage was lacking. The silver coins were not to be made on government account and sold to the public for gold. Free coinage was not abolished, and all the practical difficulties of bimetallism were inherent in the plan. It would work perfectly whenever the market ratio happened to coincide with the legal ratio. Under those conditions both gold and silver would be coined in adequate volume, and the silver coins would be perfect instruments of retail trade. With the legal ratio unfavorable to silver, however, the owners of

7 See Laughlin, Principles of Money, Chapter VII; Monroe, Chapter XIX.

silver bullion would suffer a loss when they presented it for coinage. There could be no coinage of silver until the extreme need for small change was sufficient to outweigh this inevitable loss. If the ratio should be unfavorable to gold the coinage of that metal would cease and the country would be flooded with the new silver coins, regardless of the limitation on their legal tender.

Lord Liverpool's proposal was an attempt to graft a fiduciary silver coinage on a bimetallic system, and it was defective. He recognized, rather vaguely, that there were imperfections in his plan. He said that it might become necessary to suspend the free coinage of silver or even to make silver coinage a government monopoly. In this tentative suggestion he had touched the vital feature of subsidiary coinage. Had he urged coinage on government account as the first essential of his plan, his place among the great figures in the development of monetary science would have been established.

In 1816 Parliament adopted Liverpool's plan.[8] All the outstanding silver was called in for recoinage. The law provided that a royal proclamation should at a later date open the mint to the free coinage of silver at the old bimetallic ratio. At this ratio the mint price of silver was 62 shillings for each Troy pound. The bullion owner was to continue to receive 62 shillings. But the pieces were to be reduced in weight about 6 per cent, so that a Troy pound would produce 66 shillings in the new coins. The government was to take the 4 shillings as seigniorage.

Since the ratio was still unfavorable to silver there could be no extensive coinage under the law. The recoinage of the old silver pieces, however, resulted in the issue of a quantity of the new coins. When the supply of old coins was ex-

[8] A copy of the law is in the International Monetary Conference Report of 1878, 373. See also Burns, 286.

hausted the mint officials continued the issue by purchasing silver in the open market, coining it, and selling the coins for gold. This practice, not provided for in Liverpool's plan, made silver coinage a government monopoly. The proclamation providing for free coinage was never issued, and the mint continued to produce the new pieces and sell them to the public at a profit to the Treasury. Eventually, more than a generation later, the practice was confirmed and made permanent by law.

Without intending to do so England had established a permanent gold standard and had, in a roundabout way, after forty years of experimental legislation, accidentally arrived at a subsidiary coinage system, the first in history.

The story of England's development of subsidiary coinage has special significance for the student of United States currency. This country, under conditions not unlike those in England, struggled with the problem of silver coinage for sixty years, the last thirty with England's successful system before it as a model. In the end the United States adopted this same system, with much the same failure to understand it and much the same intention to consider it a temporary expedient. In both countries it was the crying need for an adequate small change currency that led to the gold standard and a subsidiary silver currency. The painful experiences of the United States in developing the system will be described in subsequent chapters.

CHAPTER III

FRACTIONAL CURRENCY IN THE COLONIES

MONETARY conditions in the colonies—Legal tender laws—The shilling standard—Commodity currency—Wampum—Spanish silver coins—The Spanish dollar—Paper money—Fractional coins of Spain and other countries—Scarcity of small coins—Copper coins—The Massachusetts silver coinage—Fractional notes—Currency in the non-British colonies—Currency difficulties of the colonists—Preservation of English reckoning—Monetary terms.

The history of colonial currency is a confused record of primitive methods of exchange, nondescript currency materials, transitory standards, arbitrary legal enactments, and ill-advised issues of paper money. The colonists came from countries in which a satisfactory currency was unknown. Even in England, where the evils of debasement were eliminated before 1700, there had never been an adequate national currency. The primary cause was the defective operation of bimetallism. There was in Europe no conscious adherence to the bimetallic philosophy as it is understood today, with a predetermined plan to adopt a coinage ratio and maintain it against all opposing forces. The idea was rather to modify the legal ratio whenever particular circumstances appeared to call for such action. Silver, since it was the more common metal, was the primary standard, while gold, although it was also the standard metal, was coined at whatever ratio to silver the whim or advantage of the occasion dictated. As a result of shifting values and incorrect ratios, discrepancy of ratios between neighboring coun-

17

tries, and irregular supplies of bullion, every country suffered the consequences of alternating plenty and scarcity of coins. Every country encouraged the circulation of whatever foreign coins it could entice into its territory. The circulating medium everywhere was an indescribable pot-pourri of gold, silver, copper, tin, brass, and bronze coins.

Under the conditions a stable, uniform currency was an impossibility. There was hardly a conception of such a currency as an ideal. Such principles of money as were known to the small minority of educated men were drawn from the Mercantilist philosophy. The immigrants to the British plantations brought with them no understanding of monetary science. This fact explains much in the history of colonial currency, and it excuses errors of policy that have been criticized by writers of later generations.

The colonists brought little money, and they found no gold or silver mines. They were forced to resort to barter. Gradually they came to use as the general media of exchange certain commodities that were widely acceptable and possessed in some degree the important qualities of durability and portability. In time it became necessary to regulate these commodity currencies, and the colonial legislatures made certain of them a legal tender for private and public debts. Some of the statutes merely designated the commodities which should pass current as money. Others were comprehensive legal tender statutes, specifying the physical qualities the currency should possess and fixing its value in terms of British money.[1]

The method of selecting from a number of commodities those that should have a legal tender power developed a type of legal tender law unlike that of the mother country. In England all money from the mint was legal tender with-

---

[1] For examples of the two types of laws see Bronson, Connecticut Currency, and Felt, Massachusetts Currency.

out statute because it was coin of the realm, the king's issue, whereas legal tender in the colonies was a matter of special enactment, and no commodity possessed the quality until it had been conferred by law. The colonial practice naturally resulted from the scarcity of British coins, the absence of domestic coins, and the diversity of commodity currencies.[2]

The English colonists used the British money of account, reckoning all values in terms of pounds, shillings, and pence. They consistently applied the English terminology to the various commodity currencies and to the foreign coins which eventually came into circulation. English coins, however, were scarce, and trade with England was not sufficiently extensive and continuous to preserve a fixed value between the colonial commodity currencies and the standard coins of the home country. In the course of time the commercial values and consequently the currency values of the commodities used as money diverged from the actual values of the English coins which they were supposed to equal. There was no longer a correspondence between the value of the actual English shilling and the nominal shilling which the commodity currency represented in commerce and in law.

Thus the shilling came to be a mere nominal value, depending on the fluctuating ratings assigned to the commodity currencies. These ratings varied from colony to colony. Beaver-skins, the common currency of New York and Connecticut, might have a legal value of 9 pence in one colony and 8 pence in the other. In each the shilling was a nominal unit, serving as a local measure of values and basis of monetary calculations. Each colony chose for itself the shilling

[2] Miss Breckinridge, in Legal Tender, 16, 52, presents the doubtful view that colonial and English legal tender doctrines were, because of this difference of application, essentially different in principle, the English theory holding all money to be a tender unless otherwise declared, the American theory only that money which had been so designated. Laughlin, in Principles, Chapter XIII, accepts this view.

and pence valuations of the sundry coins and commodities upon which it conferred legal tender. This practice is the outstanding feature in the history of colonial currency. It influenced the currency development of the United States long after the achievement of independence.

The commodities most widely used as money were the staple products of colonial economy. Corn, cattle, and wool were used in New England. In Maryland and Virginia tobacco was the chief currency. Lumber and tobacco were common means of payment in New York.[3] Beaver-skins, since they commanded a ready market in England and were durable and portable, were everywhere acceptable and were a common currency in New England, New York and Pennsylvania. In the Carolinas debts were paid with rice, pitch, corn and other commodities. In the case of commodities such as rice and tobacco, which could be graded as to quality and preserved in storage, the colonists created a currency of warehouse receipts. The comparative excellence of this paper currency contributed to the prosperity of the southern colonies.

Traffic with the Indians led to the use of wampum currency in most of the colonies. Under various local names— wampum, peage, sewant, peake, and roanoke—it was a legal tender from Massachusetts to Virginia.[4] Wampum, made of polished black and white sea shells in strings of varying lengths, was an unsatisfactory currency. It was fragile, not easily portable, and subject to artificial coloring. It was a general medium of circulation in the seventeenth century,

[3] For references to the commodity currencies see Bronson; Felt; Fernow, Coins and Currency of New York; Bruce, Economic History of Virginia, Vol. 2; Mereness, Maryland; Bullock, Essays in Monetary History; Weeden, Economic History of New England.

[4] Weeden's Indian Money and Woodward's Wampum are interesting histories. See also Scharf, History of Maryland.

and New York continued to use it well into the eighteenth century.

Coin was scarce in the colonies, but it was not entirely lacking. Every ship from England, Holland, France and Spain brought a small quantity of coins, and a brisk trade with the West Indies was bringing a steady stream of silver to the Atlantic ports. By 1700 "country pay," as the commodity currency was called, was giving way to coin payments in towns, although it remained the common currency in rural sections. The coins were a heterogeneous collection. Gold coins from England, France, Portugal, and Arabia were common. The silver coins were from Mexico, Peru, Spain, Holland, England, Germany, France and Sweden. A South Carolina legal tender statute of 1701 named nine varieties of silver coins and four varieties of gold.[5] The proportion of English coins in the total was very small.

The predominant coin throughout the colonies was the Spanish piece-of-eight, or eight-real piece, known variously as the peso, the peso duro, the piastre, the piece-of-eight, and the Spanish dollar. The colonists always referred to it as the Spanish dollar. This famous piece, fairly entitled to rank as the greatest of historic coins, came from the Spanish mints in Mexico, Peru, and Spain. The Spaniards had established mints in Mexico in 1535 and in Peru in 1621. Early in the seventeenth century a stream of silver from these mints began to pour into the trade of Europe and America.[6]

---

[5] South Carolina's First Paper Money, in Sound Currency, Vol. 5.

[6] Sixteenth century coins from the Joachimsthal in Bohemia were called "Joachimsthalers" or "thalers." This was corrupted to "dalers" in Sweden and "dollars" in England. The Spanish peso was equivalent to the German "reichsthaler," and the English transferred the name "dollar" to the Spanish piece. The word is still in colloquial use in England after three hundred years. It occurs four times in Shakspere. The Spanish dollar was the world's chief coin from 1600 to 1800. From it have been derived the present

For two hundred years Mexico and Peru provided the greater part of the world's currency. The majority of the coins went to Spain and from that country were distributed to all parts of the world.

The colonies received Spanish coins chiefly from the West Indies. The islands had no mints, but they enjoyed a flourishing trade with the mainland and with European countries. The English colonies along the Atlantic coast received additional supplies of Spanish coins from the French and Spanish settlements along the Gulf of Mexico, while pirates and other maritime adventurers brought coin to various Atlantic ports.[7]

The Spanish dollar of the seventeenth century had a legal weight of about 388 grains of pure silver, roughly equivalent to 4 shillings and 6 pence. In 1738 the weight was reduced to 382.85 grains. The crude state of the art of coinage and the difficulty of administrative control by Spanish authority combined to cause irregularities in the coinage of the Mexican and Peruvian mints.[8] The dollars in circulation in the colonies were of widely differing pure silver contents. The mint weights were of little consequence. No full-weight coins were in circulation in any event. Clipping and sweating were widely practiced, and such coins as escaped this treatment were picked out for shipment to England. The Spanish coins were everywhere acceptable "by tale," without regard to their weight or condition. Before

standards of nearly all the countries of North America, Central America, and the West Indies, as well as Japan and the Philippines. With its Mexican successor, it has been the chief coin of China for two centuries. See Chalmers, History of the Currency, 390–394. Shaw's History of the Currency gives a fascinating account of the consequences in Europe of the stream of dollars from America.

[7] See Chalmers, 5; Carroll, Historical Collections of South Carolina, Vol. 1, 86; Long, History of Jamaica, Vol. 1, 19.

[8] The mint weights of the Spanish dollar are a vexed problem. See Sumner's Spanish Dollar and the Colonial Shilling.

1650 Connecticut, Massachusetts, and Virginia had passed laws making Spanish coins a legal tender. From that time on, the "dollars of Mexico, Sevill and Pillar" were the first consideration in the currency statutes of all the colonies.

The currency value of the Spanish coin had to be adjusted to local commodity currencies that had steadily depreciated in actual purchasing power. The colonies did not attempt to adjust the legal valuations of declining local currencies to the actual value of the British shilling. If Pennsylvania beaver declined in purchasing power from 9 pence to 6 pence, the only result was a greater discrepancy between the metal shilling of England and the nominal shilling of Pennsylvania. The colonial currencies gradually lost all relationship to the standard money of the mother country. But the Spanish dollar was a concrete metallic entity, worth 4 shillings and 6 pence in English coin, and it received a rating in local currencies in accordance with its value in the London markets. Thus we find in the colonies the apparent paradox of legal ratings as high as 2 shillings for the English silver shilling and 8 shillings for a Spanish dollar worth 4 shillings and 6 pence. The valuations of the dollar varied not only from colony to colony but also from time to time in the same colony. By 1700 they had crystallized into permanent ratings, varying from 5 shillings in Georgia to 8 shillings in New York.

These diversities of valuation did not prevent the movement of coin from colony to colony, nor did they restrain the exportation of coin to England. Although they were a cause of confusion in reckoning, they did not restrict commerce between colonies. Contracts between residents of New York and Philadelphia, for example, stated whether payment would be made in "New York currency" or "Pennsylvania currency," and the amount in Spanish dollars was adjusted accordingly. The discordant ratings made transactions awkward, but they worked no material injury in the early colonial period. With the growth of foreign commerce and inter-colonial trade they became a source of endless confusion and developed customs of accounting and reckoning that were to retard the progress of a national coinage until the period of the Civil War. In 1704 and 1707 Parliament attempted to control the valuations by proclamations forbidding a higher rating than 6 shillings, but the order was nullified by private agreements in business and by colonial statutes that rated the dollar by weight.

In 1690 Massachusetts issued Treasury bills to pay military expenses. These notes were the first government paper money issued in Europe or America.[9] Other colonies followed suit, and paper money became the chief medium of exchange in the colonies. The bills were ostensibly issued to meet a deficiency in coins, each colony holding that it was deprived of a metallic currency by an unfavorable balance of trade or by over-valuation of the Spanish dollar by its neighbors. In fact the notes were issued to meet ordinary expenses of government, to replace old issues with "new tenor" bills, or to encourage new projects of various kinds.

The colonies differed in the extent to which they surrendered to the temptation to issue notes. Massachusetts, New York, and New Jersey greatly over-issued at times, although their excesses were less than those of Rhode Island and South Carolina. The remaining colonies were more moderate, and inflation, depreciation, and repudiation played a minor part in their currency histories. Paper money was

---

[9] In 1685 a French official in Canada paid local troops with promises written on the backs of playing cards, and "card money" in imitation of this odd currency was later issued by the French government for use in Canada. See McLachlan, Money of Canada, 12. There are many histories of colonial paper money. Among the best are Davis, Currency and Banking in Massachusetts Bay; Hickcox, History of the Bills of Credit; McFarlane, Pennsylvania Paper Currency; and Potter and Rider, Bills of Credit of Rhode Island.

never the sole medium of exchange for long periods. The colonists always had certain amounts of coin in circulation, and metallic money always returned with the periodic repudiation of outstanding issues of paper. By acts of 1751 and 1764 Parliament suppressed the issue of legal tender paper money. A few colonies showed an inclination to evade the prohibition by issuing various kinds of treasury notes and loan bills.

Fractional currency has been defined in an earlier chapter as money of a less denomination than one dollar. Inasmuch as the Spanish dollar of the colonies became the silver dollar of the United States, it is proper to apply the term fractional to all the small coins of the colonies, despite the fact that the nominal standard unit was a shilling whose value in terms of our present-day currency ranged from 12 to 20 cents. The colonists themselves made no distinction whatever in law or business between the large gold and silver coins and the small silver pieces of retail trade. They had no standard monetary unit by which other coins could be measured. The double standard existed, but it was given little attention. Gold coins were given a legal rating in terms of shillings and pence. Silver coins were also given legal values. The mathematical ratio between the two valuations was the bimetallic ratio. There is little evidence to show that diversity of valuations and discrepancy of ratios in the various colonies affected the movement of coins. The conditions of commerce and the character of the coins in circulation were alike in discouraging bullion operations, and legal ratios were of small importance. All coins, from the smallest fractional silver piece to the Portuguese gold coins, were standard money in the colonies.

The Spanish dollar was divided into eight reales or reals, usually written as "rialls" or "ryalls" in the colonial records. The fractional coins were the four-real piece, the double-real, the real, the half-real, and the quarter-real. The half-real was in Spanish a "medio," the quarter-real a "cuartino." The values of these fractions varied, of course, with the legal ratings given to the Spanish dollar. In New York a real was a shilling. In Massachusetts it was 9 pence, in Pennsylvania 11 pence. The Spanish fractional coins were produced in great quantities in the Mexican mints. They gradually drifted into the colonies and became much the largest element in the metallic currency. In the payment of a debt of 294 pounds in Boston in 1705 the creditor received 107 pounds in Spanish dollars. The remaining 187 pounds were paid with 5,625 double-reals and reals, most of them much reduced by wear.[10]

The general course of commerce was such as to give the colonies a favorable balance with the West Indies and an unfavorable balance with England. There was a general tendency for coin to flow to the colonies from the islands. In the West Indies the smaller Spanish fractions were scarce. The half-dollar, double-real, and real were common, as was "the base pistorine" so often mentioned in the colonial records. This "pistreen," as Jefferson called it, was a debased two-real piece that was coined in the home mints of Spain. The bulk of the shipments to the colonies consisted of dollars and half-dollars, but great numbers of double-reals, reals, and pistorines were forwarded. Few medios were imported and apparently no cuartinos.[11]

In addition to the Spanish fractions the colonists had uncertain quantities of small silver coins from other countries. The legal tender laws which rated the Spanish dollar always referred to the smaller silver coins, most frequently with a phrase, "other Spanish moneys in proportion," that became

---

[10] Sumner, Coin Shilling of Massachusetts Bay, 409.

[11] Chalmers' History of the Currency is the best authority on the West Indies currency.

a stereotyped part of such statutes. But they frequently included a provision for the English shilling and six-pence and the French crown and livre, and occasionally for silver coins from Holland, Sweden, or Germany.

It is abundantly evident from the records that the quantity of this small silver coinage was insufficient for retail trade.[12] In 1691 William Penn urged prospective settlers to convert one-third of their possessions into coin. A writer of 1701 declared that in the Southern colonies the people were forced to the necessity of "carrying Sugar and Tobacco upon their backs to barter for little Common Necessarys." Weeden states that the colonists in New York had hardly any small change currency except wampum. The scarcity was most acute in the denominations below the value of six-pence. The smallest coin in wide circulation was the real, whose currency value varied from 7½ pence to 1 shilling and whose metal content was greater than that of the six-penny piece. A petition to Parliament in 1701 declared that "the least piece of money commonly current in the Islands and Colonys upon the Continent of America is Seven Pense halfepenny, being an 8t part of a piece of Eight." It was a common practice to cut Spanish dollars into quarters, eighths, and sixteenths, and this "sharp change" or "cut money" was freely acceptable in all parts of the country.

The scarcity of small silver would have been felt less severely if there had been a plentiful supply of copper coins, but these coins were less common than silver. The Mexican mints coined copper maravedis in the eighteenth century, but copper coins did not reach the colonies from Mexico or the

---

[12] References to scarcity of coins of all kinds, gold, silver, and copper, appear by hundreds in the colonial records. See especially Chalmers, 10; Felt, 42; Gould, Money and Transportation in Maryland, 36; Weeden, Early Rhode Island, 17; Hickcox, Historical Account of American Coinage, 9, 17; Crosby, Early Coins of America, 139–143.

West Indies.[13]   Copper pennies were not coined in England until the time of the Revolution, and the supply of half-pence and farthings was hardly sufficient for English domestic needs.   In 1645 a Virginia statute declared that a "quoine of copper would be most beneficial to the Colony."   More than sixty years later the same colony passed a law which rather naively declared a legal tender for copper coins provided the mother country should send such pieces to the colony.   Mereness states that Maryland had practically no copper coins in the colonial period, and Jefferson said that copper coins had never circulated in Virginia.

Copper coins were scarce everywhere, but the New England colonies had relatively large supplies.   Immigrants usually brought some copper coins.   Parliament occasionally granted to some adventurer a patent authorizing a copper coinage for the colonies.   The most ambitious of these projects was that of William Wood, who was authorized in 1722 to make for Ireland and the colonies pennies and half-pence of an odd mixture of copper, tin, and zinc, with a silver proportion of one in four hundred.   The coins were unpopular in Ireland, partly because of anonymous attacks by Dean Swift, and the patent was withdrawn before a great number of the pieces reached the colonies.   In 1681 New Jersey gave a legal tender standing to "Patrick's pence," which were copper coins brought over by an Irish tradesman. There is one authentic case of private copper coinage in the colonial period.   Copper was discovered in Connecticut, and a large number of three-penny copper pieces were coined in 1737 and 1738.   There are fugitive references to various coins that were probably special importations for colonial use, among them the Carolina and New England coins of

[13] Del Mar, History of the Precious Metals, 347. For other references to copper coins see Bruce, Vol. 2, 500; Washington, Writings of Jefferson, Vol. 2, 136; Mereness, Maryland.

1694 with the elephant design and a tin coin of the date
1685. There are occasional indications of the circulation
of tradesmen's tokens. The Massachusetts legislature of
1701 prohibited the issue of such "pieces of brass and tin."

England made no effort to provide a general circulation
of gold and silver for the colonies and but little effort to
supply a small change currency. The one large shipment in
the colonial period was made in payment of a debt and not
in pursuance of a currency policy. This shipment to Boston
in 1749, covering the costs of a military expedition,
amounted to 17,000 pounds sterling. It consisted chiefly of
Spanish dollars, but there was also a quantity of small silver
and copper coins. There were 10 tons of copper coins, with
a currency value of 2,000 pounds. Lord Baltimore undertook to provide a silver currency for Maryland in 1659.
Approximately 2,500 pounds in underweight shillings, groats,
and six-penny pieces were forwarded, each "householder
and freeman" being required to exchange sixty pounds of
tobacco for ten shillings in coin.[14]

Unable to persuade the mother country to set up colonial
mints, some of the colonies attempted to establish them
without sanction. Virginia, Maryland, and New York passed
futile statutes with this end in view. Only Massachusetts
succeeded. The need for fractional currency in the colonies
is demonstrated by these attempts at a domestic coinage.
There were no mines and no bullion in the colonies, and a
mint could not increase the total currency. It could only
withdraw current coins and convert them into new pieces.

---

[14] The small coins referred to in this chapter are described in Crosby's
Early Coins of America. See also Dickeson, American Numismatic Manual;
Sumner, Coin Shilling of Massachusetts Bay. The earliest coin produced in
England for use in America was probably the Sommer Island "hog" coin of
1612, referred to in Capt. John Smith's "Historie." The elephant coins were
doubtless originally produced for use in the Orient.

The objective of these proposed mints was the creation of small coins.

This fact is brought out in the history of the Massachusetts Mint. The coinage was confined to shillings, 6 penny, 3 penny and 2 penny pieces. The bullion supply was found in the current circulation of foreign coins. The Massachusetts coins were very popular in all the colonies and were made legal tender in such remote places as the island of Barbados. In an effort to keep the coins at home Massachusetts was driven to an expedient which has significance for the student of subsidiary coinage. The legal tender of the "pine tree" silver was deliberately raised to a point much above the ratings of the corresponding English and Spanish silver coins, with the overvaluations on a sliding scale that gave the smallest coins the highest ratings. The law which set these ratings, that of 1671, limited the tender of the 2 and 3 penny pieces to 10 shillings. We see in these measures an inchoate understanding of fiduciary currency principles and a recognition of the desirability of preventing such currency from encroaching on the standard money. The remarkable character of the measures is evident when it is remembered that England did not recognize these same principles until almost a century and a half later, the Congress of the United States not until 1851.

It was apparently the intention of the colonists to confine their paper notes to large denominations. The earlier issues had a minimum denomination of 5 shillings, and some of the colonies never issued bills of less value than 1 shilling. In a number an ingenious device was adopted to provide small fractions without issuing small notes. This was the issue of notes in odd sums. In New York, for example, there were notes for 1 shilling, 1 shilling and 9 pence, 1 shilling and 6 pence, and 1 shilling and 3. By the process of making change the notes could be used in payments of 3, 6, or 9

pence.[15]   With excessive issues notes of large denominations
fell to very small values, just as the paper currencies in
Europe in our time fell to the smallest fractional values, and
all coin disappeared.   When the "old tenor" notes were
withdrawn it was necessary to issue fractional notes for small
change.   In 1722 Massachusetts issued notes for 1, 2 and
3 pence and again in 1744 circulated notes of 2, 4, 6, and 9
penny denominations.   In colonies which did not issue small
notes the larger denominations were sometimes torn into
halves and quarters.

The discussion of colonial currency to this point has been
confined to the history of the settlements under English control.   There is a marked similarity in the currency history
of the French, Spanish and Dutch settlements.   In all of
them the colonists adopted local commodity currencies, used
foreign coins indiscriminately, suffered from scarcity of currency, petitioned the home governments to send coins, and
passed legal tender laws like those of the British plantations.[16]   And in all of them the settlers clung to the standards and the terms to which they had been accustomed at
home.   New Netherlands had guilders and stivers as the
money of account.   The Swedish settlers on the Delaware
used dalers and skillings.   In the French settlements on the
Gulf of Mexico livres, picaillons, and sous were the money
of account despite the predominance of Spanish coins.   The
Louisiana settlements received at least one large shipment
of French copper and silver coins.   They also went through
a period of excessive issues of paper money, followed by the
circulation of "playing card money" in small denominations,

---

[15] See Davis, 149; McFarlane, 77; Phillips, Paper Money of the American
Colonies; Hickcox, History of the Bills of Credit.

[16] The records of the currencies of the non-British colonies are meagre.
See Dickeson, American Numismatic Manual; Del Mar, History of Money in
America; Historical Collections of Louisiana, Vol. 5; McLachlan, Money of
Canada; Robertson, Louisiana under Spain.

somewhat like the very early paper notes of Canada already referred to. It is worth noting that these French fractional notes were issued in the Spanish denominations of 25, 12½, and 6¼ sous, to correspond with the double-real, real, and medio.

In the century and a half before the Revolution the colonists tried every device that gave promise of increasing the circulating medium. They used commodities ill-adapted to the purpose, adopted the Indian wampum, accepted every kind of coin, over-rated metallic money, and finally turned to the novel expedient of government paper money. It is difficult in this day to visualize a commerce, even of a primitive type, carried on with the miscellaneous instruments of the colonial period. Some authorities take the view that the colonists had little excuse for overvaluing coin or issuing paper money, and they cite contemporary writers to prove that the supply of coins was reasonably satisfactory before the era of paper money.[17] In a general sense this point of view may be approved. As a thesis it may be accepted that a nation has the kind of currency it deserves. A country lacking both mines and mints can obtain an adequate currency if it goes about the matter intelligently. If the colonists had refused clumsy substitutes a reasonably satisfactory currency of coins would have been assured. But it would have been obtained at a high cost in reduced imports of goods and slower economic progress. Conditions were unfavorable to the development of an efficient currency. England was separated from the colonies by many miles in distance and many days in time. The majority of the arriving immigrants were miserably poor. The Spanish coins reached the colonies by circuitous routes from far distant mints, and the flow of these coins from the West Indies was offset by a constant drain of money to the mother country.

[17] For example, see Bullock, Essays, 14.

The "moderate amount of specie" which the colonists were said to have could not have been large. The few estimates of the actual quantity in the records of the time are untrustworthy, since they necessarily represent conjecture rather than statistical knowledge.[18] Evidence of scarcity is to be found in the incessant complaints in contemporary literature, as well as the many petitions asking Parliament to forward coins and to set up colonial mints. Even more significant was the use by the colonists of such makeshifts as commodity money, wampum, and government paper money, three currencies unknown to their experience in England.

The fact stands out in the colonial records that the small currency available for retail trade was inadequate. The colonists contrived to carry on the major activities of commerce by means of gold coins, large silver coins, warehouse receipts, credits established in London, and direct barter. But the need for small change was never satisfactorily met. The price level was lower then than now, and retail trade was on a petty scale. The colonists were ever in need of small coins for local trade, traveling expenses, and payment of wages.

It is likewise clear that the Spanish silver coins in the colonies greatly exceeded the total volume of English coins of all kinds, gold, silver, and copper. The metallic standard, in whatever sense there was a standard, was the Spanish dollar. Yet the colonists in the English settlements persistently held to the English standard and the English reckoning. In all the paper money issues for three-quarters of a century there were only two in terms of Spanish money, and these

---

[18] For estimates of colonial coin see Davis, Colonial Currency Reprints, Vol. 2, 327; Lee, New Jersey, Vol. 1, 244; Fernow, 300; Felt, 26. The oft-quoted statement of a traveler that in 1698 Pennsylvania had more coin than England is merely a testimony to the conditions in England, where there was an acute scarcity of coins.

two, one in Maryland and another in New York, were insignificant temporary emissions.   Using one kind of money in exchanges and another kind in calculations and accounts is a confusing practice at best.   In the colonies it was especially difficult because the English and Spanish systems were not easily reconciled.   The Spanish dollar, divided into half-dollars, quarters, and eighths, was not easily adjusted to the pound, divided into 20 shillings of 12 pence each.   Neither system was decimal.   A shilling from the British mint was not a shilling in any colony.   In Georgia it was 1 shilling and 3 pence, in Massachusetts 1 and 6, and in New York 2 shillings.   A Spanish real was 1 shilling in New York, 9 pence in Virginia, and 11 pence in Pennsylvania.   Colonial ratings of British half-pence were not always in accord with their actual values as British coins.   Accounts were always kept in shillings and pence.   The children of the colonists were taught to convert the Spanish coin values into English moneys and to know the diverse ratings in neighbor colonies. The few journals of the period customarily published tables of conversion rates.

The preservation of the English reckoning had important consequences after the establishment of the nation.   One interesting result was the development of a peculiar nomenclature that has left its impress even to this day.   The real was valued at 1 shilling in New York in the entire colonial period. When a national coinage was adopted the real was the equivalent of 12½ cents, and the people of New York used the term "shilling" to designate this value.   Long after the Spanish coins had disappeared "two shillings" was the common designation of the quarter-dollar.   In Pennsylvania the real was worth 11 pence and the medio 5½ pence, and the two coins were referred to respectively as "eleven-pence" and "five-pence."   The two terms were corrupted to "levy" and "fip."   In later years the two United States coins most closely approximating these values were the dime and half-dime, and for generations Pennsylvanians called a dime a "levy" and a half-dime a "fip."[19]

Two terms of colonial origin are in common use today. The English settlers referred to their small silver coins as "bits." The Spanish real was the equivalent of the English "six-penny bit." Both in the West Indies and on the mainland the real was popularly known as a "bit." In 1703 William Penn said that "Our Single and Double Bitts or Royalls are like our old clipt thin sixpences, they want ⅓ of the value they goe at, a great abuse." And eighty years later Jefferson referred to the medio as a "half-bit." The United States quarter-dollar of a later day was equal to two reals, or two "bits," and in the South the usage survived. The Southern and Western custom of calling a quarter-dollar "two bits" has the sanction of two centuries behind it. With the exception of the word "dollar" the term is the oldest in American usage. The word "picayune" is a corruption of "picaillon," the name of the small silver coin of Louisiana. It was transferred to the Spanish medio and later to the half-dime. Down to the period of the Civil War "picayune" was the common name of the five-cent piece in many sections of the South. Through an odd custom of referring to a trivial article as "not worth a picayune" the word is now incorporated into our language, although it no longer refers to a coin.

The currency experiences of the colonists left their mark on later generations. The indiscriminate use of foreign coins accustomed the people to the use of any available currency. The shifting legal tender valuations bred a misconception of the functions of government in the control of currency. In the entire period there was little progress in the development

---

[19] An interesting discussion of colonial nomenclature is found in White's *Archaic Monetary Terms of the United States.*

of monetary theory. The decimal system as applied to coinage was unknown, the principles of fiduciary coinage unthought of. Apparently the colonists did not consider the possibility of a uniform standard money. England's niggardly policy in dealing with colonial currency was shortsighted. With a domestic mint enjoying the support of the mother country the colonists might have created from miscellaneous foreign pieces a fairly satisfactory local currency. The mother country might have done much in the way of shipments of coin or special coinages for the colonies. For two hundred years England's attitude was arbitrary and unsympathetic.

CHAPTER IV

THE REVOLUTIONARY PERIOD

THE CONTINENTAL paper money—Adoption of the dollar standard—Fractional notes—Coins in the Revolutionary period—Copper coinage by the states—Private coins.

The colonies had hardly retired their bills of credit and resumed specie payments when the outbreak of war brought new problems. Long before the Declaration of Independence the issue of paper money was adopted as the chief means of financing the war. It is unnecessary to discuss here the effects of this policy on prices, credit, industry, and social welfare. Issue succeeded issue, with the inevitable results in the form of depreciation, expulsion of coin, financial collapse, and repudiation. The bills took three forms. One type was issued by the Continental Congress in its own name and for its own purposes. The second type was issued with the guarantee of Congress for the benefit of particular colonies, or states, as they came to be called at this time. A third type was issued by the different states on their own responsibility. Notes of all three types depreciated to vanishing point values.

The form in which these notes were printed is the outstanding feature of the Continental paper money. The resolution of June 22, 1775, which authorized the first emission provided that the notes should be payable in "Spanish milled dollars or the value thereof in gold and silver." Circumstances had forced Congress to adopt a new standard. As

a working basis it was impossible to adopt any other currency than the Spanish dollar. The nominal shilling standard was a variable throughout the country, worth one sum
in Spanish coin in one state, another sum in others. The
only currency common to all the states was the Spanish
dollar.

This departure from the practice of a century and a half
was highly important. It was an official declaration that the
actual standard of the country was the silver dollar of Spain.
From that time to the present day the accounts of the government have been kept in dollars.[1] Apparently the measure had no immediate influence on private accounts or general business practice, but it undoubtedly made the people
familiar with valuations and calculations in terms of dollars.
The notes issued for state purposes with the guarantee of
Congress were sometimes in terms of dollars, but more often
in shilling currency. But the issues of individual states were
always in terms of shillings, and after the Continental notes
disappeared the states continued to issue in shilling currency.
The states still clung to the old standard, even after separation from the mother country.

In February, 1776, the scarcity of coins led Congress to
include in an issue of new currency 1,000,000 dollars in
fractional notes. In November 500,000 dollars more were
authorized, although the records fail to make it clear that
this second lot was ever issued. These small notes were in
terms of Spanish dollar fractions, with the denominations
based on an awkward adaptation to the shilling currency of
Pennsylvania. In that state and in Maryland the legal rating of the dollar was 7 shillings and 6 pence, or 90 pence.
Congress, directing the government from Philadelphia,
adopted the Pennsylvania valuation for the small currency
and divided the dollar into multiples of one-ninetieth. The

[1] See Journal of the American Congress, Vol. 1, 124; Vol. 2, 36.

denominations were ⅑, ⅙, ⅓, ½, and ⅔ of the dollar.[2] In Pennsylvania a note for ⅑ of the dollar was 10 pence in local currency, a note for ⅔ was 60 pence or 5 shillings.

The denominations selected could not be reconciled with the coins which had been in circulation. There were no Spanish coins lower than the half-dollar that corresponded with the fractional paper notes. The rating of 90 pence to the dollar fitted the shilling valuations of two states only. In the others it was impossible to convert the notes into even amounts in local currencies. Pelatiah Webster, writing in 1791, calculated the issues of Continental currency in terms of dollars, eighths and ninetieths, a curious combination of the Pennsylvania standard and the Spanish denominations.[3]

The individual states exercised their own discretion in fractional denominations. Some of them issued the notes in shillings and pence, choosing all the units from 1 penny to 10 pence. Others elected to issue fractions of the Spanish dollar, adjusting the denominations to their own valuations. States that rated the dollar at 96 pence, such as New York, chose denominations of 1/16, ⅛, ¼ and ½ of the dollar. In the New England states the fractions of the Continental notes were adjustable to the local dollar rating of 72 pence, and these states issued notes in the denominations of the Continental fractions, although the differences in the rating of the dollar were such that ⅑ of a dollar was 10 pence in

[2] For details of the Continental issues see Haseltine, Description of the Paper Money; Phillips, Paper Money; Breck, Historical Sketch of Continental Paper Money.

[3] Webster, Political Essays, 501. Pennsylvania and Maryland used Webster's notation. In New York and North Carolina accounts were in dollars and seventy-seconds. The copper pieces issued as 1/100 of the dollar that appeared later in the Continental period were valued in English terms. The Massachusetts "cent" was accepted as 2/3 of a penny. There is no indication in the records that decimal notation in money accounts was used.

Continental money, 8 pence in New England local issues. Georgia chose the convenient but diverse fractions of ⅒, ⅕, ¼, ½ and ⅔ of the dollar, the combination including fractions that fitted her own 5 shilling rating and three other prevailing valuations.

The depreciation of the notes was so rapid that their denominations had no practical significance, but they illustrate the problem of diversity of standards and valuations with which the country struggled in its financial operations. In the country as a whole there were in circulation fractional notes issued in denominations of 1, 2, 3, 4, 5, 6, 7, 8, 9, and 10 pence and ¹⁄₁₆, ⅒, ⅑, ⅛, ⅙, ⅕, ¼, ⅓, ½ and ⅔ of the Spanish dollar, an assortment of units probably without parallel in currency history. The government was resolutely keeping its accounts by the awkward system of dollars and ninetieths. The money of account in private transactions was universally the shilling, with five different ratings in thirteen states. The actual currency was depreciated paper issued in terms of six standards.

With the final collapse of the paper currency in 1781 and the military success of the Continental armies "hard money" reappeared in circulation. Contemporary estimates of the metallic currency at the beginning of the war are probably conjectural. Whatever the amount, it had entirely disappeared. During the war years certain amounts of coin had come into the country, not only from the West Indies but from Europe. Some was obtained from France by loans, and other amounts were brought by French or British troops. It seems improbable that the vanished coins had been exported. It is more probable that they were hoarded. The government conducted its operations almost entirely with paper money. In 1779 the total metallic currency falling into the hands of the government officers was less than 75,-000 dollars. In 1781, when coins were again in circulation,

Hamilton estimated the total coin holdings of the country at 6,000,000 dollars.[4]

The depreciation of the Continental currency eventually drove out the copper coins. The public accepted paper money as a substitute for the larger gold and silver coins, but the inconveniences of fractional notes for small trade were so great that both the state governments and individuals attempted to maintain a circulation of copper coins. In the period from 1774 to 1783 there were many private projects of coinage, some of them sanctioned by the state authorities, and coin collections of today contain many specimens of copper, brass, bronze, and tin coins of Revolutionary times, with a few pieces of silver. Two of these coins are of peculiar interest. One, a large silver coin with the inscription "Continental Currency 1776," bears a close resemblance to our standard silver dollar. It was only a pattern piece, made by some individual experimenter. The other coin is a copper piece bearing the inscription "Massachusetts I C L M." Crosby believed the device to mean "1 cent lawful money." This interpretation, although plausible, is obviously speculative. Massachusetts did not authorize a state coinage until 1786. None the less it is possible that this pattern piece represents the first use of the word "cent" as the name of a coin and the first attempt at a decimal coinage system.[5]

The end of the war and separation from the mother country permitted the states to experiment with coinage. Under the Articles of Confederation, adopted in 1778, the Continental Congress had the exclusive right to regulate "the alloy and value of coins struck by their own authority,

[4] See Hamilton, Works, Vol. 1; Sumner, Financier and Finances of the American Revolution.

[5] Crosby devotes 200 pages to the various private and state coinages of the Revolutionary period. For the coinages of the New England States see also American Journal of Numismatics, Vol. 53.

or by that of the respective states." This clause prohibited the individual states from setting a valuation on coins of their own minting, but it left them free to undertake every kind of coinage. The brief interval between the Declaration of Independence and the adoption of the Constitution was the only period in which a colony or state had the right of coinage.

Many of the states availed themselves of the privilege. New Hampshire had undertaken the coinage of a few copper pieces in 1776, even before the Articles of Confederation. Vermont in 1785 granted to one Harmon a patent for the coinage of copper pieces of 160 grains weight, later authorizing a reduction to 111 grains when it was discovered that other states were making smaller coins. New Jersey granted to three petitioners the privilege of coining 10,000 pounds of copper, the coins to weigh 150 grains and to be legal tender at 15 to the shilling. This legal tender provision was a direct violation of the coinage clause in the Articles of Confederation, as were similar provisions in other states. It exemplifies a curious belief that was to appear time and again in the coinage history of the country over the next seventy-five years. This was the notion that copper coins were not money in the ordinary meaning of the term, that general statutes regarding money did not apply to copper pieces. It was a survival from the days when it was believed that all coins should contain gold or silver.

In 1785 Connecticut granted to four petitioners a patent for the coinage of copper pieces of 144 grains, the state to receive 5 per cent of the total issue. The coins were to have no legal tender "except for the purpose of making even change." This little provision deserves notice, for it is unique. So far as the writer knows, it is the only instance where a legal tender statute specifically recognizes the necessity of providing for some certain method of paying "odd sums" with fractional remainders.

The coinage projects of Massachusetts were especially ambitious. In 1786 the legislature established a mint and provided for the coinage of gold, silver, and copper. The plans for gold and silver coinage were never realized, but two copper coins were minted in large quantities. One was a "cent," weighing 150 grains and valued at ⅟₁₀₀ of the Spanish dollar, the other a half-cent of proportionate weight and value. This Massachusetts •cent piece was the first official coin on a strictly decimal basis in history. As will be shown in the next chapter, credit for its adoption belongs not to Massachusetts but to the national government.

The copper ·coins of Connecticut and New Jersey were produced in large quantities and were popular at home and in neighboring states. All the states either coined copper pieces or made arrangements for their production, some of them abandoning their plans when they learned that the mints of their neighbors sufficed to supply their needs. South Carolina was the only state to undertake a coinage through a foreign country. In 1785 a contract was made with Charles Borrell under which he was to have silver and copper pieces coined in Switzerland to the value of 30,000 pounds. Apparently the coinage was begun, but no pieces were ever brought into the country.

The coinage of the various states had to compete with a large volume of private coins and tokens that came into circulation after 1783. Some were imitations of the state coppers, circulated by individuals who could manufacture them at a profit. Others were of original design and nameless origin. Probably the largest proportion were importations from England, many of them coined in the Birmingham mint of the famous mint-master Boulton. They were

of varying weights and differing designs, some commemo-
rating the independence of the colonies or the union of the
states.   One type was an underweight imitation of the British half-penny.   Many bore a likeness of Washington.
Apparently all the imported coins were English in denomination, most of them of half-penny value.   Commercial firms
in the coast cities bought them in England, imported them,
and made a profit by putting them into circulation at their
face values.   As the coins did not bear the name of the
importer they could not be returned for redemption or exchange.   A few pieces, circulated for advertising purposes,
bore the names of merchant firms.

   These private coins flooded the currency and became a
matter of universal complaint.   They were especially trouble-
some in the Atlantic cities.   More than forty tons of one
design are known to have reached New York.   Rhode Island,
New York, Pennsylvania, and New Jersey passed laws prohibiting their circulation, and other states passed various
restrictive measures.   The popular dislike of these "debased
tokens" was undoubtedly the cause of the first efforts to
establish a national coinage.   To what extent it was a cause
of the strong prejudice against all copper money that prevailed to the Civil War period is a matter of conjecture.

   The people did not understand the character of these
copper coins.   They objected to them on the ground that
they were inferior in weight to genuine British half-pence
and to their own state coins.   The weight of the private coins
was immaterial.   The genuine coins of England and the
copper pieces of the various states were also fiduciary, circulating at values above their metal values.   Most of the
states were insufficiently supplied with small change, and a
reasonable quantity of the "base Birmingham coppers"
would have filled a currency need.   The real injury lay in the
unrestricted volume, which was aggravated by the concen-

tration in certain cities. They were paid for with gold and silver coins, and their excessive circulation resulted in the loss of silver coins that were badly needed.

Spanish silver was slowly coming into general circulation, through the reappearance of hoarded coins and the importation of fresh supplies from the West Indies. The amounts were not adequate. Copper coins were more than plentiful, but "sharp change" was still used for larger exchanges. None of the states succeeded in establishing a coinage of silver. An Annapolis goldsmith named Chalmers set up a mint in 1783 and coined a number of 6 penny pieces.[6]

The war period marked an advance in currency theory and practice. The issue of the Continental notes in Spanish dollars established a new basis of accounting and inaugurated the struggle to eliminate the English shilling standard. The control of note issue by the central authority, even if only partial, brought concretely before the people the possibility of a unified currency, and experience with state issues of paper and state coinages showed the desirability of a single control. In the closing years of the war period thoughtful men in the new nation were searching for some plan that would give the country a workable monetary system.

[6] This is one of the very few instances of private silver coinage in American history.

CHAPTER V

THE FOUNDATIONS OF UNITED STATES COINAGE

REPORT of Robert Morris on coinage—Details of the plan—Gouverneur Morris and the decimal system—Objections of Thomas Jefferson—Jefferson's plan—The Grand Committee's plan—Resolution of 1785—Plan of the Board of Treasury—The Mint Ordinance of 1786—First United States coinage.

The coinage system of this country grew out of the activities of a small group of statesmen of the period after the war. The leading figures in this group are Robert Morris, Gouverneur Morris, Thomas Jefferson, and Alexander Hamilton. There was no attempt to create a national coinage during the war, although various proposals to establish a coinage of Continental copper pieces had been considered by the Congress.[1]

In January, 1782, Congress directed Robert Morris, Superintendent of Finance, to prepare a report on the values of foreign coins. Morris took advantage of the occasion to submit a report, already prepared, in which every phase of the coinage situation was discussed, the building of a national mint was urged, and an original plan of coinage was proposed. This report was essentially the work of Gouverneur Morris, who was the assistant of Robert Morris.[2] Both men had long been interested in the problem of

[1] See Smythe, Life of Franklin, Vol. 7, 381.

[2] Sparks, Life of Gouverneur Morris; Washington, Writings of Jefferson, Vol. 1. The report is in the International Monetary Conference Report of

coinage.   Six months before the time of the report they had summoned an expert named Dudley from Boston to work out plans for a mint.

The report proposed an elaborate coinage plan, in which there was to be a single silver standard, with a seigniorage charge of 3½ per cent.   The standard monetary unit was to be wholly new.   With the exception of South Carolina, still in the throes of excessive paper money issues, the different states retained the old Spanish dollar valuations of 5 shillings, 6 shillings, 7 shillings and 6 pence, or 8 shillings. In any section of the country the dollar was worth 60, 72, 90, or 96 pence.   The least common multiple of these four figures is 1440.   One quarter of a grain of pure silver was almost exactly $\frac{1}{1440}$ of the Spanish dollar.   Morris chose this quarter grain as the basis of his system.   He called it the "unit" or "quarter."

The coins proposed were as follows:

Coin	Material	Number of Quarters	Weight
"mark"	silver	1000	250 fine grains
"quint"	silver	500	125 fine grains
"cent"	silver	100	25 fine grains
"eight"	copper	8	not stated
"five"	copper	5	not stated

It should be noted that these proposed coins were unlike any coins of Spanish or English standard.   The largest coin, the "mark," was to be a new piece.   With allowance for the seigniorage charge it would be worth about 73 per cent of the Spanish dollar, in terms of our present day coinage about 70 cents.   The smallest silver coin, the "cent," would be worth about 7 cents.

The ingenuity of the plan is obvious.   Any sum in Brit-

1878.   Robert Morris states that he went to the lodgings of Gouverneur Morris "to examine the plan we had agreed on."   The two men were not related.

ish pence from 1 penny to 8 shillings could be expressed in an even number of "quarters," and any Spanish coin from the cuartino, or quarter-real, to the dollar was likewise convertible. The current Spanish coins would have the same values in quarters in all the states. Any ordinary transaction, whether in Spanish coins or English currency, could be effected in terms of quarters. The copper pieces, the "eight" and the "five," were so designed as to be easily adjustable to the current valuations of state cents and English half-pence. The "eight" would be a half-penny in six states. In the other states the "five" would be ⅓, ¼, or ⅕ of a penny.

Morris had presented one of the most remarkable currency plans ever proposed. It was his idea to abandon completely both the Spanish coinage and the English reckoning, to establish an entirely new standard coinage, and to adopt a decimal system of accounting. To accomplish these objectives it was necessary to create a currency that would be interchangeable with the Spanish coins, convertible into English currency terms, and quite different from either type of money. It was not possible to eliminate Spanish coins if the proposed coins should be less adaptable to the British reckoning or to eliminate the British accounting if the new coins should be similar to the dollar and its fractions.

Morris' plan met these conditions admirably. It was complex, difficult to understand, and revolutionary in character, but it was inherently sound. There was one defect. The unit of the system, the quarter, was very small. Morris proposed that accounts be kept in quarters, cents of 100 quarters, and marks of 1,000 quarters. Translated into terms of the present day, it was a proposal to keep accounts in dollars, dimes, and mills. The plan did not include a coin of 10 quarters, equivalent to our present day value of 1 cent. In his proposed copper pieces Morris had failed to insist on a completely decimal system, yielding on this one point to the temptation to create coins like those in circulation. If he had included a copper coin of the value of ¹⁄₁₀₀ of the mark, the plan would have been practically without flaw.³

Gouverneur Morris' connection with the decimal system has been misunderstood. Historians have thought that he introduced decimal reckoning in the United States.⁴ The practice of decimal notation had been slowly displacing the duodecimal and vigesimal system in Europe ever since Stevin de Bruges in his sixteenth century pamphlet La Disme proposed the decimalization of coins and measures. Jefferson, writing at this time, said that everyone had learned decimal arithmetic "as a school-boy." What Morris did was to propose a decimal system of coinage and to point out convincingly its superiority to every other system.

In a resolution of February 21, 1782, Congress approved the report and directed Morris to draw up his plans for a mint. Various difficulties prevented immediate action, and it was more than a year before Dudley presented pattern pieces of the proposed coins, among them a silver "mark," a silver "quint," and a copper "five." As Robert Morris says in his diary, this was the first coinage struck by authority of the union of the states. He presented the coins to Congress and suggested that a committee be appointed to consider his plans for a mint.

³ Buried among the records of the government is an unsigned report which appears to contain the original plan drawn up by Gouverneur Morris before the "alterations and amendments to my satisfaction" to which Robert Morris refers. It differs from the official plan only in the fact that the copper coins were on a decimal basis. See American State Papers, Finance, Vol. 1, 103.

⁴ See Roosevelt, Gouverneur Morris, 90; Fiske, Critical Period of American History, 270. Roosevelt and McMaster credit Morris with various currency developments which can hardly be ascribed to him.

Meanwhile Jefferson had been considering the proposed system. In a letter to Gouverneur Morris he indorsed the decimal system, but emphatically criticized the small "quarter" unit of the Morris plan. He objected to the denominations of the coins on the grounds that they were not like those of the pieces in circulation. This latter objection indicates that Jefferson did not understand the Morris plan, which had for its primary purpose a new coinage which would drive out the Spanish coins. In his reply to Jefferson Morris accepted the criticisms in part and agreed to certain changes in his plan. If he had been able to make clear what his system contemplated and how it would work his arguments could hardly have failed to convince. He did point out that Jefferson's rival plan would fail to drive out either the Spanish coins or the English reckoning. But his statements were so technical that they must have bewildered members of Congress. The terse and lucid presentation of Jefferson was more convincing, and the Morris report was rejected.[5]

Jefferson presented a comprehensive coinage plan. He preferred the double standard at the current market ratio, which he thought was 15 to 1. He urged the adoption of the Spanish dollar as the standard unit, with its subdivisions on a strictly decimal basis. He admitted that his smallest coin, $\frac{1}{100}$ of the dollar, could not be adjusted exactly to any state valuations of the current coin, but maintained that the discrepancy between this coin and the nominal "penny" of the different states was unimportant. He thought that the current Spanish dollars averaged about 365 grains of fine silver, and he chose this weight as the standard unit. He proposed the coinage of the following pieces:

[5] For the records of the plans and the reports of Morris and Jefferson see International Monetary Conference Report of 1878 and Washington's Writings of Jefferson, Vol. 1.

Coin	Material	Fine Weight, Grains
10 "units" or dollars	gold	243⅜
"unit" or dollar	silver	365
half-dollar or "5 tenths"	silver	182½
"fifth" or "pistreen"	silver	73
"tenth" or "bit"	silver	36½
"twentieth" or "half-bit"	silver	18¼
"hundredth"	copper	not stated

This plan had the advantage of simplicity. The unit had long been familiar. It had the disadvantage of a basic decimal unit, the "hundredth," that would not fit into the prevailing system. There was an error in the calculation of the unit weight. The current Spanish dollar was 6 or 7 grains heavier than the weight proposed. And there was an inherent defect in the character of the unit itself. The proposed silver coins above the "tenth" would be exactly equal to Spanish coins, and the Spanish currency would continue to circulate. The English accounting would not disappear. A Grand Committee, with one member from each of the thirteen states, approved Jefferson's plan. Although a coinage system was not actually established for many years, this plan was the foundation of United States coinage. At a later date Jefferson said that he had originated the system "which now prevails."

In May, 1785, the Grand Committee presented Jefferson's plan with certain amendments and refinements of detail.[6] A seigniorage charge of 2 per cent on both gold and silver was recommended, and the fine silver content of the silver unit was set at 362 grains. With the seigniorage charge the mint weight of the standard dollar would be approximately 370 grains, at which figure it was close to the average weight of the Spanish dollar. The committee dropped Jefferson's "fifth" or "pistreen" in favor of a quarter-dollar. The objective of the change is not clear. Span-

[6] International Monetary Conference Report of 1878, 445.

ish pistorines and French livres were in circulation at a value of one-fifth of the dollar, but the Spanish double-real and the English shilling, worth a quarter of the dollar, were more common. The question of the relative desirability of the two denominations was not finally settled for a hundred years.

The committee was concerned over the matter of copper coins. They had hopes that the "hundredth" would displace the "base British half-pence" and stop "the commerce in vile coin" which, they estimated, cost $30,000 annually. They remedied Jefferson's oversight in omitting a weight for the hundredth, choosing 131 grains as a weight which would make it "6 per cent better" than the English coins and yet give the government a profit on coinage. The committee proposed a new coin, a copper "two-hundredth." Morris had objected that the hundredth was too large a value to serve as the smallest coin current. Jefferson had replied that a rural population would not use a coin of very small value. The more advanced the civilization, he said, the smaller the currency unit acceptable to the people. The committee accepted the view of Morris.

On July 6, 1785, Congress formally resolved that the country's coinage system should be decimal, with the dollar as the standard unit. This marked the first official adoption of decimal coinage in any country. Robert Morris resigned in 1784, and the working out of the mint plan was entrusted to a Board of Treasury of two members. These two proceeded to a new survey of the coinage problem, finally submitting three alternative plans, with widely different silver dollar weights, a double standard ratio of 15.6 to 1, and weights for the copper coins that varied in accordance with the size of the dollar.[7]

[7] For a copy of the report see the appendices in Watson, History of American Coinage.

A feature of their report was the introduction of new names for some of the proposed coins. The gold coins, which were to bear an eagle design, were to be called "eagles." Jefferson's "tenth" was to be called a "disme," and his "pistreen," selected in this plan instead of the Grand Committee's quarter-dollar, was to be a "double-disme." The word "cent" was substituted for "hundredth" and "half-cent" for "two-hundredth." There was to be a nominal unit of 1/1000 of the dollar, to be called a "mille," and accounts were to be kept in dollars dismes, cents, and milles.

The words "eagle," "disme," and "mille" were new. Gouverneur Morris had called one of his proposed silver coins a "cent," and both McMaster and Roosevelt credit him with the introduction of the word. On the other hand, Alexander Hamilton said in 1791 that it had long been familiar in America. In the preceding chapter it has been noted that the letter "C" on an obscure coin of 1776 may have meant "cent." Morris had used many original names in his various reports and notes, but "mille," "disme," and "eagle" were not among them. Morris was conversant with Latin and French, as was Jefferson, who had, however, used English terms for his coins.[8]

Whatever their origin, the terms mill, dime, and eagle were first used in the report of the Board of Treasury. They were eventually incorporated into our currency terminology. It is an odd fact that the names of our coins came neither from the Spanish coins which were the familiar currency for two centuries nor from the English terms which were universally used for an equal time. The word "dollar," an English corruption of a German word, was unknown to the Spaniards as a name for their peso. In the history of United States coinage only one other word has been added to the list presented by the Board of Treasury, and that word,

[8] See McMaster, Vol. 1, 195.

"nickel," is only a colloquial term for the 5 cent piece. The word "penny" is still employed as a name for our cent piece, although it is an inaccurate term. Its use goes back to this Revolutionary period. Jefferson's hundredth, or cent, was roughly equivalent to a currency penny in New York, where the Spanish dollar was 96 pence.

Congress considered the report on August 8, 1786, indorsed one of the three plans submitted, and directed the Board to prepare a plan for a mint. The report they presented recommended a mint, but was devoted chiefly to discussion of the evils of debased foreign copper coins. On October 16, 1786, Congress passed the famous Mint Ordinance.[9] The measure confirmed the coinage plan already approved, provided for officials of the mint, and contained detailed provisions regarding copper coins. Depositors of gold or silver bullion for coinage were to purchase cents and half-cents to the amount of 5 per cent of their deposits. Copper coins were to be receivable for government dues in the same proportion. After September, 1787, no foreign copper coins were to circulate, and the state copper pieces should be valued only at the rate of 1 cent for each 172 grains. Like all the other reports and resolutions of this period, the Mint Ordinance had little tangible result, but it marked another step in the direction of a national system. The provision relating to foreign copper coins was the first instance of federal assumption of the right to prohibit the circulation of any sort of coin, and the provision regarding the state coinages was an aggressive exercise of federal power. It virtually outlawed the state copper coins, since none of them weighed 172 grains.

The importance of the Ordinance is illustrated by the action of Massachusetts in connection with its proposed gold, silver, and copper coinage, described in the preceding chap-

[9] International Monetary Conference Report of 1878, 450-453.

ter. The law providing for this coinage declared that a mint was necessary because Congress had by resolution of August 8 established a standard of coinage for the various states.[10] The state legislature evidently thought that Congress would specify the details of the coinage system and leave each state free to provide such coins as it needed. The Massachusetts law was passed on October 16, 1786, which happened to be the same day on which Congress passed the Ordinance definitely declaring and exercising its right to demonetize the coinage of any state.

The Ordinance resulted in the issue of a few cents and half-cents, the first official coinage of the United States. They were made by a private coiner under contract. On July 6, 1787, Congress adopted a design for the coins.[11] "United States" was to be stamped in a circle and inside this the legend "We are one." On the other side was the inscription "Mind your business." The coins are widely known to collectors, sometimes under the name "Franklin penny," because Franklin is supposed to have suggested the motto.

Further progress was halted while the country struggled with the problem of an organic plan of government. As finally adopted in 1789 the Constitution dealt only briefly with coinage. Congress was given the power "to coin money, regulate the value thereof, and of foreign coin." The individual states were forbidden to coin money, issue paper money, or declare anything but gold and silver a legal tender. This last prohibition, aimed at the old bugbear of foreign copper coins, was unwisely framed. The states should have been forbidden to pass any type of legal tender law. The failure to determine precisely the rights of the states in this sphere was to cause disturbance at a later day.

The adoption of the Constitution placed on Congress

[10] A copy of the Massachusetts law is in the New York Public Library.
[11] See Watson, 25; McMaster, Vol. 1, 403.

the responsibility for the immediate establishment of a national coinage. The country was using a foreign currency, long familiar and in some respects efficient, but unsatisfactory in condition and quantity. There were five standards of value and reckoning in a small nation of thirteen states. A national coinage was the one means by which the diversity of standards could be eliminated. The work of the Board of Treasury, the Grand Committee, the two Morrises, and above all Thomas Jefferson had laid the foundations. The double standard, a Spanish dollar unit, a decimal system, and a copper coinage of cents and half-cents were accepted features of any system the new nation should establish.

Chapter VI

THE ESTABLISHMENT OF THE COINAGE SYSTEM

Mint report of Alexander Hamilton—Details of the plan—Establishment of national coinage by Congress—Details of the law—Hamilton's relation to the national coinage establishment—Copper coinage amendments of 1792 and 1793—Legal tender law of 1793.

In April, 1790, the House of Representatives directed Alexander Hamilton, who was Secretary of the Treasury, to prepare a plan for a mint. Hamilton's report, presented in January, 1791, was a remarkably comprehensive discussion of the problems of money of his day.[1]

He recommended the double standard at a ratio of 15 to 1, with the standard unit of silver equal to the current Spanish dollar. The exact weight of the standard silver unit was arrived at by clever reasoning. The Spanish dollars in circulation, passing "by tale," were so worn that selection of an average weight was hazardous. An assortment gathered at random had shown an average pure silver content of 371 grains. An earlier essay by Morris had given 373 grains. In dealings between merchants it was customary to give the dollar a gold valuation of 24¾ grains. If the market ratio was 15 to 1, as Hamilton thought, the average weight of the Spanish dollar, by the verdict of skilled traders, was 15 times 24¾ grains, or 371¼. Hamilton recommended, accordingly, that the fine weight of the

[1] The report is in the Annals of Congress, 1st Cong., Vol. 2.

gold unit be fixed at 24¾ grains, the silver unit at 371¼. The silver unit of the United States would thus be a new coin, unlike any Spanish dollar ever minted, but very closely approximating in weight the actual coins in circulation.

The British as well as the Spanish standard of fineness in gold coins was 11/12. The 24¾ grains in the gold unit was divisible by 11, and Hamilton recommended for both gold and silver coins a proportion of 11 parts pure metal to 1 part alloy. The gross weight of the gold unit would be 27 grains, of the silver coin 405 grains. With no recognition of the important fact that the Spanish dollar actually contained a proportion of alloy higher than 1/12 he recommended that the new silver coins be made to resemble the Spanish pieces.

Hamilton devoted much space to the question of a seigniorage charge, displaying an unusual grasp of a difficult subject but reasoning obscurely at times. His general attitude was unfavorable, and he objected to the high rates suggested in earlier reports on the grounds that they would discourage coinage. He grudgingly conceded that he was "inclined to an experiment" with a rate of ½ of 1 per cent. This charge should be levied only when the depositor of bullion received his coins immediately. If he had to wait, there should be no charge.

Earlier reports had recommended the coinage of a number of denominations. Hamilton wanted only two gold coins, two silver coins, and two copper pieces. Of the two gold coins, a $10 piece and a $1 piece, the latter was not to circulate. It would be sufficient to coin 50,000 pieces in order to familiarize the people with the standard gold unit. The two silver coins should be the dollar and the "tenth" or "disme." Hamilton thus failed to choose between the Grand Committee's quarter-dollar and Jefferson's "fifth" or "double-disme." The restriction on the number of coins was in the interests of economy. Intermediate silver coins could be added, he said, if experience indicated a need for them.

Hamilton's aversion to "debasement" in any form showed itself in his references to copper coins. He recommended a weight of 264 grains for the cent and 132 grains for the half-cent. At such weights the coins would hardly be fiduciary. As Hamilton said, their money value would "about correspond with the value of the copper and the expense of coinage." In his attitude toward these coins he was less progressive than his predecessors, the Board of Treasury and the Grand Committee having recommended coins of much less weight. Hamilton said that the advantage of having "the intrinsic value" equal to the money value outweighed the consideration of profit. He shared the belief of Morris and the Grand Committee that any material reduction in weight would result in duplication of the coins by private coiners. He admitted that the cent would be inconveniently large, and suggested that the amount of copper could be reduced and a trace of silver added, as in "the billion money of France." It would be necessary to adopt this type of coin if a fall in the price of copper should make the pieces more valuable as money than as metal. In this part of the report, more than in any other, Hamilton was unenlightened. He agreed with Morris, as against Jefferson, that a half-cent coin was desirable, but on the grounds, reminiscent of mediaeval economics, that small coins enable the poor to buy cheaply and therefore "labor for less." [2]

Hamilton had definite views as to nomenclature. He objected to the names recommended by the Board of Treas-

---

[2] Morris, Jefferson and Hamilton all held the theory that prices are lower when there are very small coins in circulation. There is an element of truth in this doctrine, but it represents in the main a confusion of cheapness of goods with small purchases of goods.

ury. The foreign derivation of "mille," "cent," and "disme" would make them unpopular. Jefferson's "unit" was preferable to "dollar" and his "tenth" to "disme." "Mille" and "cent" might be acceptable, since they were shorter than "thousandth" and "hundredth."

His recommendations in regard to the major problem of eliminating foreign coins were admirable. For one year, while the mint was getting under way, the circulation of foreign coins should be unrestricted. In the second year the silver coins of Spain and the gold coins of three countries should be allowed to remain. In the third year these particular pieces should be legal tender only at their bullion values. After the third year all foreign coins should be outlawed. It might be well, he said, to give the President power to continue the circulation of Spanish coins beyond the three year limit.

Hamilton's motives in recommending the double standard were made a part of the controversy over bimetallism that raged in the three decades before 1900.[3] Hamilton undoubtedly preferred the single gold standard, on the grounds that gold was the more stable metal, but he recommended the double standard because he believed that a single standard would be "liable to all the objections which arise from the comparison of the benefits of a full, with the evils of a scanty circulation." He was, of course, mistaken. A double standard does not of itself bring a larger quantity of currency.

Hamilton's selection of the double standard was in fact forced upon him by the fractional currency situation. In common with all statesmen of his time, he thought of all coins as standard coins. He could not visualize a non-standard fiduciary silver coinage. Lord Liverpool's tentative and incomplete plans for a subsidiary coinage were still

[3] See, for example, Laughlin, Bimetallism, Chapter 2.

a decade in the future. Hamilton, as he saw it, had to choose between the double standard and the single silver standard, and he chose the former. The double standard was adopted by the United States because there was no other known system which would provide a fractional silver currency and at the same time create a gold currency for major transactions. Robert Morris, who recognized the difficulties of bimetallism, had advocated the silver standard.

Congress approved Hamilton's report and by resolution of March 3, 1791, ordered the establishment of a mint. The vote on the measure disclosed much opposition to a national coinage. The leading spirits in the new republic were strongly in favor, but there was opposition both in Congress and among the people. The vote in the House was 25 to 21. The probable factors were state jealousy of federal activities, resentment of the constitutional prohibition of paper money issues, objection to the cost of a mint, and the feeling that Spanish coin was a satisfactory currency.[4]

The matter dragged through another period of months. In October the Senate appointed a committee to consider the mint project and present a bill. The chairman of the committee was Robert Morris. It fell to the lot of the man who had first proposed a national coinage to work out a plan which had been chosen in preference to his own. In December Morris introduced a bill. Of its progress through the Senate there is little record. It is clear that it was debated at length and amended in a number of ways.[5] In January, 1792, the Senate passed the bill and sent it to the House, which overwhelmingly voted out a clause providing for a likeness of the President on the coins. With

---

[4] See Journal of the House, 1st and 2nd Cong., 402; Writings of Madison, Vol. 1, 551.

[5] Journal of the House, 1st and 2nd Cong.; Journal of the Senate, 2nd Cong., 1st session.

this eliminated the House passed the bill by a vote of 33 to 22. The Senate at first refused to surrender its plan for a portrait of the President on the coins, but finally yielded. The law was signed by President Washington on April 2, 1792.[6]

In the fundamental features the law followed the plans of Hamilton. In details it diverged widely. The double standard at a ratio of 15 to 1, a gold unit of 24¾ fine grains and a silver unit of 371¼ grains, a seigniorage charge of ½ per cent if the depositor received his coins immediately, and a copper cent and a half-cent with the absurdly large weights of 264 and 132 grains were provided for, just as Hamilton had recommended. The provisions for alloy and for individual denominations of coins departed widely from Hamilton's recommendations, and there was no provision whatever for his excellent proposals regarding the continued circulation of foreign coins.

The law provided for gold coins in denominations of $10, $5, and $2.50. The silver coins were to be the dollar, half-dollar, quarter-dollar, disme, and half-disme, with fine and gross weights proportional to their values. Hamilton had recommended an alloy proportion of 1/12 in all the gold and silver coins, and the law provided for this alloy in the gold coins. But the silver coins were given a gross weight of 416 grains per dollar, making the proportions 179 parts copper to 1485 parts silver. The silver coins were to have the clumsy fineness of 1485/1664.

The only explanation of this awkward figure is to be found in a brief statement in one of Madison's letters to the effect that it was derived from an assay of the current Spanish dollars.[7]   Hamilton himself was probably responsible

---

[6] Appendix G contains copies of all the important laws of the United States that have dealt with fractional currency.

[7] Writings of Madison, Vol. 1, 551.

for this departure from his plan. It has been noted that he wanted the new silver dollar to resemble the Spanish coin. The alloy in the Spanish dollar was legally 1/12, but in the mints of Mexico and Peru the coin had been persistently debased, sometimes to the point where the copper content was more than 1/10. The dollars in circulation with a weight of 371 grains in fine silver had a gross weight between 415 and 416 grains. If the new United States silver dollar was to have this gross weight the copper proportion would have to be much greater than 1/12. Confronted by the alternative of rejecting Hamilton's 1/12 alloy or creating a coin smaller than the Spanish dollar, Congress elected to increase the alloy, giving the new dollar a weight of 416 grains instead of 405. The unwieldy alloy was a mistake. The difference in appearance between a 405 grain dollar and a 416 grain coin is slight. It is questionable whether there was any great advantage in having the coins similar, whereas a convenient alloy in minting was an important matter. This was apparently recognized at the time, as Madison says that some members of Congress voted against the bill because of the alloy provision.

The legal tender provisions, referring only to gold and silver coins, declared that all the coins, from the $10 gold piece to the silver half-disme, should have unlimited legal tender power. The legal tender of worn coins, a matter not considered by Hamilton, was provided for. Such coins were to be a full tender, but at values proportionate to their weights. There was no provision for redemption of any sort of coins. Under these conditions the legal tender law meant that gold and silver coins, no matter what their condition, would remain in circulation indefinitely. There was no reference in the law to foreign coins. Hamilton's carefully worked out plan for driving out Spanish coins was entirely ignored.

The provisions for copper coinage were rudimentary. The two copper coins were named and assigned their respective weights. There was no provision for their coinage or their issue. So far as the law read, they were to be standard coins, with free coinage for any persons who should bring copper to the mint. The question of their legal tender quality was ignored.

The law declared that the official money of account in the United States should be dollars, dismes, cents, and milles. This was not a command to the people that they use this method of accounting. It was a suggestion to the public, as well as an official pronouncement that the government would use the decimal system in all its transactions. It was probably thought that private business would be influenced by the official example.

If allowance be made for the undeveloped state of monetary science in that day, the law of 1792 may be regarded as a practical and efficient measure. But there were serious defects and omissions. The Senate committee had materially changed Hamilton's plans, and most of the changes had been for the worse, especially in respect to the silver coin alloy and the circulation of foreign coins. The failure to attack the problem of Spanish coins jeopardized the whole plan for a national coinage. The provision for legal tender of gold and silver coins in proportion to the metal remaining in them was impractical. Merchants could not weigh coins received in trade. In time the currency would decline in physical condition, with no remedy provided by law. The clumsy fractional alloy in the silver coins was simply an error of judgment, while the failure to provide a working plan for copper coinage was a gross oversight.

Historians customarily credit Hamilton with the creation of our national coinage. Consideration of all the circumstances leading up to the law of 1792 reveals that Hamilton's task was that of selection rather than creation. Years before Hamilton's report Jefferson had convinced everyone that the silver dollar of Spain should be the country's unit. The double standard was urged by Jefferson and indorsed by the Congress of the Confederation. The decimal system had been formally adopted in 1786. The ratio of 15 to 1 had been suggested by Jefferson in 1784. The denominations of the coins were adopted by the Senate committee as the Grand Committee outlined them in 1785, and not as Hamilton recommended. It was Hamilton's problem to merge the conflicting recommendations of earlier reports into a concrete plan of coinage. This he did with conspicuous ability.

Some of the defects in the law were immediately obvious. Within a month the copper coinage clause was radically changed. The amendment provided for the coinage of cents and half-cents on government account, authorized the purchase of a small quantity of copper, and directed the issue of the pieces to the public through the Treasury. When the coinage of cents and half-cents reached a total of $50,000, the Treasurer was to make a public announcement and six months after the date of this proclamation the currency of all other types of copper coins should cease. The penalty for offering other copper pieces after this date was to be a fine of $10 and confiscation of the coins. The amendment implied that United States copper coins were legal tender, but there was no specific statement to that effect.

A few months later the copper coin provisions were again amended. The law had adopted the weights urged by Hamilton, although it should have been obvious that a copper cent two-thirds as large as the silver dollar was impracticable. Voight, the first mint engraver, had made some specimen cents and half-cents, and they were so clearly unsatisfactory that he made patterns of "the billion coins of

France" to which Hamilton had referred. They were the "silver-centre cents" so highly prized by modern collectors. The piece weighed about 60 grains and contained, according to Jefferson, about three-quarters of a cent's worth of silver in a center plug. Congress considered the two specimens and chose to reduce the weight of the copper pieces. The amendment, passed in January, 1793, made the weight of the cent 208 grains, of the half-cent 104 grains. Congress thus rejected Hamilton's theory of copper coinage before the mint was established.

The question of foreign coin was also raised immediately. A committee was appointed in May, 1792, but it was not until February, 1793, that a bill could be put through. In that month the first of many legal tender statutes was passed. It declared that the gold coins of certain countries should be legal tender for certain amounts in proportion to their metallic contents. The effect of this was to make foreign gold coins legal tender no matter how worn they might be. The Spanish silver coins, which were the primary currency of the country, were treated differently. The Spanish dollar, with its fractions in proportion, was to be legal tender if it weighed 415 grains. A similar provision was made for the silver crowns of France. Three years after the mint should begin coinage all foreign coins except Spanish silver should cease to be a tender. It was provided that after coinage should begin the Treasury should turn over to the mint for recoinage all its foreign money receipts except the Spanish silver pieces.

The provisions of this law were inferior to the measures proposed by Hamilton. They gave little promise of driving out any type of foreign coins, and they actually provided for the indefinite circulation of Spanish silver. The provision of legal tender for the Spanish coins if they weighed as much as 415 grains to the dollar is difficult to understand. New coins from Mexico and Peru were above this weight, but the pieces in circulation were much worn. Under a strict interpretation of the law a large proportion of the current coins had no legal standing. The provision was impractical. The impossibility of weighing coins in retail trade meant that the entire mass of Spanish coins would be accepted as legal coins. The law as a whole was a compromise between a policy that would quickly create a real national coinage and one that would make foreign coins the sole medium of exchange.

It is, of course, a matter of speculation to dwell on the course that Congress might have taken, but it is interesting to consider how the new system could have been immediately established. It would have been possible to choose, deliberately, as the standard United States silver dollar a coin somewhat below the weight of the Spanish dollar, make this dollar full legal tender, and open the mint to free coinage. Hamilton's gold coin ratio of 15 to 1 could have been retained. At first glance this appears to be a debasement scheme. It would, however, have worked no injustice. The effect would have been to bring most of the Spanish coins immediately to the mint. No class in the community would have been injured, not even the very small group of creditors holding obligations payable in Spanish dollars. The new system would have been firmly established, and sixty years of currency disturbances and difficulties would have been avoided.

The law of 1792, with the three amendments that followed shortly thereafter, established the monetary system of the United States. Out of the complex currency conditions in which it was entangled the country had evolved a real national system, and this was accomplished despite state mistrust of federal activities, widespread preference for Spanish coins and English reckoning, and general unfamiliarity with monetary principles.   The system adopted had deficiencies that were to cause serious troubles in the future, but it was sound in fundamentals.   It was superior to any system of coinage that had been developed by any other nation.

Chapter VII

FROM 1792 TO THE LAW OF 1834

ESTABLISHMENT of the mint—Illegal coinage of silver—Copper coinage amendment of 1795—Reduction of copper coins by Washington—Difficulties of the coinage system—Recoinage of foreign currency—Coinage of silver dollar stopped—Unpopularity of copper coins—Legal tender of foreign coins —Fractional bank-notes—State of the coinage—Retention of old terms and reckoning—Slow progress of decimal system—Neglect of the currency by Congress—Proposals for improvement.

The law of 1792 did not specifically assign jurisdiction over the currency to the Treasury department, although the wording of the statute implied this arrangement. Washington turned it over to the Department of State, probably because he wished the coinage to be administered by Jefferson, who had acquired in Europe a wide knowledge of coinage methods. In 1795 control was transferred to the Treasury, primarily as the result of a letter from Hamilton to Washington in which he criticized the mint administration and insisted that the currency was a matter of Treasury control.[1]

The mint, located at Philadelphia, began operations on a small scale before the end of 1792. The first Director was David Rittenhouse, a man of high scientific attainments. Having failed in an effort to bring from Europe various experts, especially a Swiss coiner named Drost, Jefferson employed Voight, who shortly thereafter presented the copper and billon pattern pieces already referred to. Condi-

[1] Hamilton, Works of Hamilton, Vol. 5, 71.

tions were unfavorable. Among the handicaps were primitive mint machinery, inexperienced officials, and limited supplies of bullion. The regular coinage of copper was begun in 1793, of silver in 1794, and of gold in 1795.[2]

The first coinage of silver was in open violation of the law. Rittenhouse naturally objected to the clumsy fractional alloy of copper. The copper proportion of 179/1664 was inconvenient in mint operations, and the excessive percentage of copper, almost ⅛ of the coin, would in Rittenhouse's judgment make the pieces "too black." Anticipating the passage of the amendment of the law which he had requested, Rittenhouse altered the legal weight by increasing the amount of pure silver in the coins to the proportion of 9⁄10, making the fine silver content 374¾ grains instead of 371¼.

The alteration, which changed the coinage ratio from 15 to 1 to 15⅛ to 1, was an unauthorized change in the legal standard of coinage. The alloy provision in the law was a mistake, but the obvious way to correct the error without a new statute was to reduce the percentage of copper. Reducing the copper proportion to 1⁄10 would have given the dollar a gross weight of 412½ grains, the weight adopted by Congress many years later. Such a change would have been unauthorized but harmless. As it was, the depositors of bullion were deprived of about 1 cent on every dollar coined. The one large private depositor of the period, a man named Vaughan, was mulcted of $2,200, a con-

---

[2] The coinage of gold and silver was delayed by the inability of the assayer and the chief coiner to furnish the $10,000 bond required. The amount was reduced by a law of March 3, 1794. Washington himself presented some of his own silver plate to the mint in 1792 and a few dimes were turned out. The first depositor of silver bullion was the Bank of Maryland, which in July, 1794, presented a volume of French coins which produced more than $80,000. See Snowden, Ancient and Modern Coins, 107, and Stewart, History of the First United States Mint.

siderable sum in that day. When he discovered his loss, he appealed to Congress for reimbursement, but without success. De Saussure, Rittenhouse's successor, continued the unauthorized coinage, and the practice was not stopped until Boudinot became Director in November, 1795.[3]

There was no domestic supply of copper, and importations were irregular. Copper pieces of state coinage and of foreign origin continued to circulate. A New York firm imported large quantities of Birmingham coppers in 1794 and 1795.[4] On March 3, 1795, the copper coinage provisions of the law of 1792 were again amended. The Secretary of the Treasury was directed to transport cents and half-cents to the important towns at government expense and the President was empowered to reduce the weights of the copper coins whenever it would be "for the benefit of the United States." This clause marked an advance in the progress of fiduciary coinage. While its immediate objective was to enable the Treasury to reduce the weights when the price of copper made the coinage unprofitable, the provision permitted the Treasury to make the coins fiduciary if it chose. The reluctance of Congress to go far in this direction was shown in a restraining clause forbidding the President to make the reduction more than 48 grains to the cent.

On December 27, 1795, Washington reduced the weight of the cent to 168 grains and of the half-cent to 84 grains.[5]

[3] The history of this unauthorized coinage can be traced through the Annals of Congress, 3rd session, and American State Papers, Finance, Vol. 1. For doubtful interpretations see Bolles, Financial History of the United States, Vol. 2; Watson, 229.

[4] Hickcox, Historical Account of American Coinage, 84.

[5] Richardson, Messages and Papers of the Presidents, Vol. 1, 191, and Vol. 10, 78. Washington did not issue the proclamation until Jan. 26, 1796. This has led historians to give 1796 as the year in which the copper coins were reduced. The Treasury's own publication, "Information respecting

The coinage of copper increased thereafter, and in 1799 the total coinage had reached the sum of $50,000. Under the law of 1792 the Treasury was at this point to issue a proclamation prohibiting the circulation, after six months, of any copper coins except pieces from the United States mint. For some reason the proclamation was not issued, despite two letters from Director Boudinot to the President calling attention to the matter. The proclamation would have served to clarify the legal status of the coins, uncertain at that time and for many years after.

The unauthorized copper pieces gradually disappeared, probably without loss to the holders, since copper was much needed for industrial uses. The costs of minting went down with the increased coinage after 1795, and United States cents and half-cents became genuine fiduciary coins. In 1800 there was a net profit of $5,000 on their coinage, and in subsequent years there was usually a small margin of seigniorage. The copper coinage was thus the first national currency to have its own field of use, without competition of foreign coins. Even here the conditions were far from satisfactory. Congress made no permanent provision for a supply of copper until 1800, and the law of that year, so formulated that its exact meaning is obscure, limited the purchases of copper in such a way that the coinage could increase only when the price of copper declined. The figures indicate that the coinage exceeded the amounts permitted by the law.[6] The copper cent had been reduced from the original weight of 264 grains to 208 grains, and again to 168 grains. It was still too large for convenient handling, and it was very unpopular. Its circulation was

United States Bonds, Paper Currency, and Coin," fails to give the year correctly.

[6] Appendix D and Appendix E give the figures for United States silver and minor coinage from 1792 to 1927.

confined to the largest towns of the North. As for the half-cent, it was rejected by the entire population. Jefferson's contention that only an urban population would use a very small coin was vindicated.

The hopes of Jefferson and Hamilton that a domestic coinage would displace foreign gold and silver were not realized in their time. The coinage was very small, and the mint was regarded as a costly failure. The expenses of operation were nearly $300,000 for the first $3,000,000 produced, representing a heavy burden on the Treasury. Bills providing for the abolition of the mint were introduced in 1800 and 1802, one of them passing the House.[7] It was the plan of the abolitionists to depend on foreign coins for a gold and silver currency and to have the copper pieces made by Boulton, the English coiner.

Many circumstances hindered the coinage. The mechanical equipment of the mint was poor. The machinery for rolling, cutting and impressing, run by horse power, was crude. The use of steam power machines was urged upon Congress by successive secretaries and directors from 1795 to 1836. The failure of Congress to appropriate funds for the purchase of gold and silver bullion in advance of deposits was fatal to prospects of successful coinage. The depositor of bullion had to wait weeks and even months for his coins. The law provided for immediate exchange of coin for bullion, at a charge of ½ of 1 per cent, but in practice this was impossible. The system of coining deposits separately was very expensive. One large appropriation for the purchase of gold and silver bullion would have permitted coinage in bulk, and exchange of the coins for depositors' bullion would have furnished a continuous fu-

[7] Annals of Congress, 7th Cong., 1st sess., 1248. See also American State Papers, Finance, Vol. 1, 615, 632, 741. The removal of the capital to Washington in 1800 raised the issue of the desirability of abolishing the mint.

ture supply, reduced the costs of operation, and brought in a revenue from the seigniorage charge. Petitions from various officials urged Congress to provide a bullion fund. As early as 1797 a House committee reported that the mint could not succeed without such a fund.[8]

The legal tender laws discouraged the recoinage of foreign pieces. A Spanish dollar of 415 grains was by law of the same value as the United States dollar of 416 grains. Spanish coins weighing 416 grains could be recoined at a profit, if the delay in coinage were ignored, but it was more convenient and more profitable to file or sweat the coins down to 415 grains or less. Coinage for private depositors of foreign coins or bullion was negligible in amount.

The law of 1793 required the Treasury to recoin all the foreign money except Spanish silver that was received in government operations. The Treasury did not obey the law. The postal and customs offices were widely scattered, and it was not practicable to ship coins to Philadelphia. Fiscal operations were carried on chiefly through the United States Bank, in which receipts were deposited. The Treasury never adopted the practice of delivering its foreign money receipts to the mint, but an arrangement was made for an initial delivery of $10,000 in foreign coins by the Bank, with additional deliveries to be made from time to time. The Bank finally adopted the practice of sending foreign coin receipts to the mint when the machinery was idle through lack of private deposits. Occasionally it had French crowns or other silver pieces recoined on its own account. In the first forty years of the mint's existence much the largest part of the coinage was for the first and second United States Banks.[9]

General economic forces were also unfavorable to coin-

---

[8] American State Papers, Finance, Vol. 1, 473, 494.

[9] American State Papers, Finance, Vol. 1, 503, Vol. 2, 19, and Vol. 4, 225.

age progress. The ratio of 15 to 1, very close to the world's market ratio when Hamilton selected it, was out of line before the end of the century. By 1799 the ratio in Hamburg and London was 15¾ to 1. At this rate it did not pay to take gold bullion to the mint. Gold was not imported when the balance of trade brought metal to the United States. The coinage of silver exceeded gold coinage each year save one in the period from 1805 to 1834. Gold coinage did not cease, however, small supplies of bullion coming from Mexico, the West Indies, and in later years from Georgia and North Carolina. Market reactions to metal values were not sensitive in that day, and the coinage of gold continued in the face of an adverse ratio. But United States gold was not a general medium of circulation after 1800, and after 1825, when a dollar in gold had reached a value of $1.02 in silver, it ceased to circulate entirely.

In the West Indies the United States silver dollar was accepted as the equivalent of the Spanish dollar. There was a small profit in exporting American dollars, exchanging them for Mexican and Spanish dollars of larger silver content, and recoining the foreign pieces. It was the first of the "endless chain" type of phenomena that has at intervals disturbed our national finances. In 1806 Jefferson put a stop to the practice by directing the mint to coin no more silver dollars.[10] The order remained in force thirty years, and the United States dollar, not in general circulation before 1806, was virtually unknown from 1792 to 1836. Many half-dollars went to the West Indies after the coinage of the dollar was prohibited.

With no gold coins or silver dollars in circulation the half-dollar was the desirable coin for major transactions,

[10] See Watson, 74. Jefferson had no constitutional authority for such action.

bank reserves, and payments abroad. The coins did not circulate widely. They went from the mint to the Bank of
the United States. The Bank distributed them to its own
vaults, to other banks, and to brokers who exported them.
A Senate committee of 1830 reported that United States
silver coins were regarded as so much bullion and were "lost
to the community as coins." They estimated that of the
$25,000,000 in silver coined since the opening of the mint
only $14,000,000 remained in the country, and of this
amount $2,000,000 was in the reserves of the Bank.[11]

The coinage of quarters, dimes, and half-dimes, as contrasted with the half-dollar, was negligible from 1792 to
1834. In nineteen years of this period there was no coinage
of quarter-dollars, in thirteen years no coinage of dimes,
and in twenty-six years no half-dimes. The total number
of quarters, dimes, and half-dimes coined before 1830 was
less than one piece for each person in the country in that
year.

The half-dollar coinage was relatively large, increasing
steadily from an annual average of about $500,000 in the
early years to an average of $2,000,000 after 1825. These
figures are significant, for they measure the failure of the
national coinage system in the first forty years. The ratio
was favorable to silver, and yet the only considerable coinage was in half-dollars that did not circulate. Mint conditions were primarily responsible. The officials, anxious
to increase the coinage and reduce expenses, discouraged
depositors who asked for small silver coins. Because there
was no bullion fund the depositor had to wait while the
mint coined his bullion, and the coinage of half-dollars could
be accomplished more quickly and more cheaply. Year
after year the mint directors apologized for the scarcity
of small silver coins with the explanation that only by coin-

------

[11] Senate Executive Documents, 21st Cong., 1st sess., no. 19.

ing half-dollars could the mint take care of the silver bullion presented. The reports indicate that the directors refused to coin small pieces except at times when a falling off in deposits made it convenient.

The copper coins were not an important auxiliary of the silver pieces. The cent piece was not popular. It circulated only in the towns. The half-cent failed to find a place anywhere. It was not coined at all in the years from 1811 to 1825. It is doubtful whether the bulk of the fairly steady output of cents went into circulation. It was the custom of the Treasury to send the copper pieces, packed in casks, to the various government offices. Copper was a rare metal, imported only from England, and at times the market price rose to a point where the copper pieces were worth more as metal than as coin. At such times industrial concerns would buy the coins by the cask and melt them for commercial use.[12] Manufacture and trade in that day were not adjusted to small margins of profit, and cent and half-cent values, despite the low price level, were almost unknown.

As a result of these adverse conditions the country lacked a satisfactory retail currency. The scarcity, especially marked in the war and depression era from 1812 to 1820, prevailed in the entire period to 1834. Complaints of scarcity were incessantly made.[13] The small trade coins of the country were a variegated lot of silver and copper pieces, including Spanish small silver coins, English, French and Dutch silver pieces, United States fractional silver, and United States copper coins. The Spanish pieces were much the largest element. The statistical records of the time are meagre. It was estimated by the Senate finance committee

[12] Annals of Congress, 14th Cong., 1st sess., 694.
[13] See International Monetary Conference Report of 1878, 679; American State Papers, Finance, Vol. 1, 503, Vol. 2, 456, and Vol. 3, 530.

in 1830 that the total of Spanish silver in circulation was $5,000,000. If this figure is used in conjunction with the mint reports on coinage and the Treasury reports on re-coinages, it is possible to estimate that the total circulation of coins below the half-dollar was in 1830 less than 25 cents per capita, an amount entirely inadequate to meet the needs of trade.

It was the scarcity of small change that the mint was clearly obligated to meet. For major transactions there was a sufficient if unstable currency of United States Bank notes, private bank-notes, Spanish dollars, and United States half-dollars. The people had suffered from scarcity and diversity of small change for two hundred years. What they needed above all else was a quantity of clean, new, and uniform small coins. At a large annual expense the mint was turning out half-dollars that did not circulate. It was doing almost nothing else.

The legal tender of foreign coins was renewed in 1806, 1816, 1819, 1823, 1827, and 1834. According to each of the laws the legal tender of all foreign coins except Spanish pieces was to expire after three years. The language of the statutes is so confusing that careful analysis fails to reveal the exact intentions of Congress. The law of 1806 specifically declared that *Spanish dollars and their fractional parts* were full legal tender, but no subsequent law ever referred to the fractional coins. After Mexico and Peru achieved independence the Spanish coinage was continued, but the designs and names were no longer those of Spain. After 1830 Mexican coins predominated over Spanish in the United States, just as the Mexican dollar superseded the Spanish piece-of-eight in China and the Philippines. But none of the legal tender statutes of the United States ever made Mexican fractional coins a tender. In 1857 the Director of the Mint ruled that no Mexican or Spanish fractional coins were legal tender after 1834. It seems probable that the intention of Congress was to make all of them a tender.[14] During the entire period the public believed that they were.

A banking mania took possession of the country in the first quarter of the century. From 1810 to the Civil War the notes of state banks were the major element in the currency, the outstanding circulation being two to four times the estimated quantity of coin. There was no domestic coin between the 50 cent piece and the $2.50 gold coin, and there was in general circulation no coin of any sort larger than the Spanish dollar. The banks filled the vacancy with notes, the majority in denominations of $1 and $5.[15] Fractional notes were issued at an early date, Massachusetts banks putting out 25 cent notes in 1805. In the depression following the War of 1812 specie payments were suspended and metallic money disappeared. The issue of fractional notes became general, and for many years bills for 5, 6¼, 10, 12½, 20, and 25 cents were in circulation throughout the country. The volume of these issues will never be known. In the bank statements of the period issues were not reported by denominations, all notes below $5 being recorded as "small notes."

The notes of "wild-cat" banks were redeemed with difficulty. Those issued by reputable banks were redeemed only in part, as some of them drifted into remote regions from which they did not return. It was widely recognized that small bank-notes were undesirable. By 1830 many states had restricted the issues to minimum denominations of $1,

[14] It is the impression of many historians that foreign coins of all sorts were legal tender in this period. See White, Money and Banking, 33. Many current gold and silver coins were not included in the legal tender provisions. There was no specific mention of any type of fractional coin after 1806.

[15] See Dewey, State Banking before the Civil War, and Gouge, Short History of Paper Money.

$2, or $5. Enforcement of the laws was lax, and there was no way to prevent the notes of one state from circulating in another. Niles' Register reported in 1820 that small notes were disappearing in the populous sections, but thirteen years later Gouge declared that they were more common than silver coins.

Besides Spanish silver and fractional bank-notes the people used a variety of substitutes for domestic small coins, some of them derived from colonial experience. Municipal governments, transportation companies, and mercantile concerns issued fractional notes in times of scarcity. The city of Albany had issued small notes in 1792, before the national coinage was begun. McMaster says that in the war period after 1814 the city of New York alone issued $190,-000 in 1 cent, 3 cent, and 6 cent "change-bills," while the state of North Carolina issued a total of $80,000 in fractional notes. Another expedient was the "cut-money" of colonial days, which was, apparently, refused in the towns but readily accepted in frontier settlements. Where the laws against fractional notes were enforced it was not unusual to circulate fractional parts cut from $1 notes.[16]

The writers of the time ascribed the scarcity of small coins to the currency of notes issued by banks and private parties. There was, however, a scarcity of coins in regions where small notes were not common, and this scarcity of coin existed after small notes had been suppressed. In fact the small note issue was not large enough to meet the actual need. There was only a small profit in their issue, and no profit at all if they were regularly presented for redemption.

---

[16] For references to various kinds of fractional notes and substitutes for coins see Niles' Register, Vol. 18, 42; Gouge, Inquiry into Principles, 21; Numismatist for Jan., 1913; Bankers Magazine for July, 1853; McMaster, Vol. 4, 296–298. The practice of cutting large coins into crude fractional pieces, common in this period, had been known since the early colonial period.

The issue of fractional paper currency and the use of such makeshifts as "sharp-change" and torn scraps of notes were due to the failure of the government to provide small coins.

A study of the fragmentary records available indicates that in the period from 1800 to 1834 there was a steady drain of gold from the country and a small increase in the circulation of silver coins. The increase in silver pieces was not commensurate with the growth of population, which was rapid, and there was a heavy circulation burden on the Spanish coins. As already explained, it was feasible to clip Spanish coins to the legal weight of 415 grains, and coins far below this weight were accepted without question. The silver coins of Mexico and Spain entered into circulation in a degenerate condition and once there they could not be withdrawn, either by redemption, by export, or by recoinage into United States coins. The Senate report of 1830 said that the entire coin currency was depreciated from 6 to 20 per cent, the smaller coins showing the greater losses. Storekeepers habitually accepted coins in any state of depreciation, protecting themselves against losses from the receipt of hopelessly worn coins by a general increase of prices for their goods.

There was a slow evolution in currency terminology and reckoning in the period down to 1830. The colonial practices were gradually giving way. The methods of state banks and mercantile concerns were influenced by the dollar-and-cents accounting of the Treasury and the United States Bank. Banks adopted the decimal system almost from the beginning, and their notes were always issued in dollars and cents. Newspapers quoted prices in shillings and pence for many years after 1792, but the advertisers who quoted in dollars and cents predominated after 1800.[17]

[17] The quaint almanacs of the period printed tables of state valuations of shillings and pence until about 1800. See Massachusetts Register for 1803.

The decimal system made slow progress with the people at large. The continued circulation of Spanish coins was responsible. These coins had been valued in British terms for two centuries. They were still called by the old names —bit, levy, fip, or shilling. A real was worth 12½ cents, but it was a shilling to a New Yorker. In every state 10 reals should have been $1.25, but it was 7 shillings and 6 pence in Virginia. In private transactions accounts were usually in terms of shillings and pence. Long after it had become the rule to express written and printed quotations in United States monetary terms the people thought in terms of English money.

Even where United States terms were used, decimal denominations were unusual. Prices of 5 and 10 cents were rare. The common price quotations were 6¼, 12½, 18¾, 25, 37½, 50, 62½, and 75 cents.[18] Decimal fractions came in very slowly, quotations taking such forms as $1¼, $3⅝, and $5⅞. There is, for example, no decimal quotation in the Philadelphia North American for April 3, 1839. The government encouraged the use of Spanish fractions by receiving and paying out worn coins that should have gone to the mint and by adjusting the postal system to Spanish denominations. Postal rates for certain distances were 6¼ cents, 12½ cents, and 18¾ cents. Contemporary critics considered this practice a major obstacle in the way

In 1797 the Farmers Almanack changed its price from "4 shillings per dozen, 6 pence single copy" to 75 cents and 10 cents. Porcupine's Gazette in 1798 advertised a razor strop at 5 shillings, 7 pence, ½ penny. The Weekly Herald of New York was quoting nearly all prices in dollars and cents in 1804.

[18] Greeley's Whig Almanac was priced at 12½ cents until 1858. Harris' Pittsburgh Intelligencer was 6¼ cents a copy in 1841. In the New York Herald issues in 1852 there were such quotations as 6 shillings, 37½ cents, 62½ cents, and $9¾. The New Orleans Picayune in 1852 quoted articles at 18¾ cents and 37½ cents.

of decimal reckoning.[19] The dollar mark, a matter of course in our day, was slowly coming into use. The origin of this symbol, still a matter of popular tradition, has been ascribed to the pillars of Hercules on the Spanish dollar or to a combination of the letters representing the United States or "Uncle Sam." While it might easily be a converted form of the Spanish symbol for the Spanish dollar, it is more probable that it is a combination of the letters "ps," for pesos, first used by a government clerk in 1788.[20]

The state of the currency was an inevitable drag on business. In everyday transactions it was necessary to make calculations in three currencies, one decimal, another based on eighths, quarters and halves, and the third on twelfths and twentieths. The condition of the coinage and the banknote circulation was a matter of discussion in Congress, in current periodicals, and in public petitions and memorials. It is not possible to acquit Congress of negligence in dealing with the situation. From 1795 to 1834 Congress passed no law improving the condition of the currency, although its own committees joined with the Mint directors and the Treasury secretaries in urging year after year the building of an efficient mint, the establishment of a bullion fund, the alteration of the silver coin alloy, and the outlawing of foreign coins. The coinage was involved in a vicious circle. Spanish coin could not be driven out until the mint provided domestic coins in abundance. But the mint, already a heavy burden on the Treasury, would require large outlays before it could become useful. Congress had the option of abolishing the mint or making it a success. It did neither, choosing to renew the legal tender of foreign coins and to ignore the vital problem of domestic coinage.

[19] Sparks, Life of Gouverneur Morris, Vol. 1, 180; McMaster, Vol. 7, 109.
[20] See Cajori, Evolution of the Dollar Mark. For an interesting rival explanation see Snowden, Ancient and Modern Coins, 92.

Laughlin describes the forty years before 1834 as the silver period in United States history. As a matter of fact it was a period of nondescript currency, made up of bank-notes, underweight foreign gold coins, foreign silver coins of many varieties, and domestic fractional silver coins. Adverse conditions prevented the circulation of adequate quantities of silver as well as gold. It was not a silver period except in the sense that a mixture of foreign and domestic silver coins served inadequately as a reserve for bank-note issues.

Congress failed to see the simple, obvious, and immediate solution of the problem. At any time from 1792 to 1834 the application of the subsidiary coinage principle to the quarter, dime, and half-dime would have revolutionized the currency situation. The copper coins were demonstrating in a small way the possibilities of fiduciary coinage, and in England there was after 1816 an example of successful subsidiary coinage on a national scale. But members of Congress as a group were not familiar with monetary principles. No Director of the Mint or Secretary of the Treasury from 1792 to 1850 recommended a subsidiary coinage or indorsed the English system.

Here and there individual officials showed a clear perception of monetary principles. As early as 1800 a House committee reported that the melting and exportation of domestic coin could be prevented only by "debasement," but they could not bring themselves to recommend so doubtful a measure. In January, 1816, Representative Root, speaking in the House, declared that the current coins were so deficient that they were "hardly accepted by servants in taverns" and recommended as a first step in reform the reduction of the copper cent from 168 to 96 grains, the establishment of a $1 legal tender limit for copper coins, and the passage of a stringent law against private manufacture of

copper coins. Having been made chairman of a committee
to draft a law, he requested Director Patterson to pass upon
his proposals, to which he added a provision for the coinage
of 2 cent and 4 cent fiduciary copper coins. Director Patterson and Secretary Dallas rejected all the proposed measures, even that which determined the uncertain legal tender
status of the copper coins.

In January, 1819, Representative Lowndes presented to
the House an elaborate and able report on the currency
situation, in which he said that the one way to insure a
domestic coinage of silver was to establish a heavy seigniorage charge. He introduced a bill to reduce the weight of
all the silver coins from 371¼ to 356⅖ grains per dollar.
The difference of 14.85 grains was to be taken by the government as seigniorage. The legal tender power of the
quarter, dime, and half-dime was to be reduced to $5. For-
eign coins were to have their legal tender faculty withdrawn. This plan, lacking the fundamental feature of coinage on government account, was practically identical with
the British measure of 1816, with the same confusion of
subsidiary coinage and bimetallism, but its adoption at this
time would probably have resulted, as in England, in the
eventual establishment of the gold standard with a perfect
subsidiary silver system.

Secretary Crawford, in his well-known report of 1820,
recommended the coinage of a mixture of copper and silver,
such as had been "adopted in other countries with great
advantage." He replied to critics who had said that "the
public would scarcely submit to the circulation of a coin
so worthless" with the statement that the people already
accepted coins of any sort, however base. If, as critics
feared, the coins should be imitated, a combination of zinc
and silver would defy counterfeiters. Crawford's proposals
represented both sound principles and antiquated theory.

His coins were merely "the billion" pieces that had caught the fancy of Hamilton, but he clearly intended the pieces to be fiduciary.

The 1830 report of the Senate Finance Committee discussed the currency problem at great length and graphically described the monetary customs, difficulties, and needs of the time.   Special attention was given to the physical condition, legal status, and relative quantities of the various types of coin.   The committee attributed the failure of domestic coinage to the laws making foreign coins a legal tender.   They pointed out the error which made United States coins legal tender even if they were badly worn.   The committee was impatient with the failure to establish the status of copper pieces.   "Our copper coins are either legal money, or they are not," they declared.   The report was accompanied by a bill which provided for a reorganization of all the legal tender statutes.   Legal tender was to be withdrawn in the case of all foreign coins and all domestic coins worn as much as 4 per cent.   Copper coins should be legal in payments to 10 cents, and United States half-dollars, quarters, dimes, and half-dimes should be legal tender only in payments up to $5.   Some of these proposals were of uncertain merit.   Others were excellent.   The limitation on silver coins was intended to force the use of gold in large transactions.   Gold was worth at the time about 3 cents per dollar more than silver.   Congress rejected the bill in its entirety.

These proposals of Root, Lowndes, Crawford and the Senate committee have been outlined in order to illustrate the very gradual development of an official understanding of subsidiary coinage.[21]   No one of the four plans was

[21] The proposed measures of Root, Lowndes and Crawford are to be found in American State Papers, Finance, Vols. 1 and 3. Root's interesting and able speech is in the Annals of Congress, 14th Cong., 1st sess., 694. The Senate report is Sen. Exec. Doc. no. 19, 21st Cong., 1st session.

complete, but each one exemplified a growing realization of the impossibility of national bimetallism in a rigid form and each one, in one way or another, showed a conception of the possibilities of reducing the silver or copper coins to a subordinate and fiduciary basis. A selection of the best features of the four proposals, even if they had been applied only to the quarter, dime, and half-dime, would have given the people the small currency which the growing trade of the country so much needed. Congress rejected every feature of every plan proposed.

CHAPTER VIII

THE LAWS OF 1834 AND 1837

THE CURRENCY problem—The subsidiary coinage bill of 1832—The law of 1834—The law of 1837—Currency scarcity of 1837—Private copper coins—Improvement in silver currency conditions—Views of historians—Recoinage of foreign currency—Special ratings of Spanish coins.

From 1829 to 1834 the question of currency reform was constantly agitated. Forty years after the establishment of the mint the coinage system was a discreditable failure. There were three elements in the problem, the circulation of bank-notes issued by a host of state banks of every degree of financial integrity, the disappearance of gold as the result of an adverse coinage ratio, and the continued circulation of a non-decimal foreign silver coinage of degenerate condition. The bank-note question and the problem of gold coinage were, perhaps, of the more fundamental importance, but the problem of the fractional currency was more immediately pressing and more intimately bound up with the customs and daily life of the people.

Many reports and proposals grew out of the general discussion, some of them of much historical interest. Secretary of the Treasury Ingham, Cashier White of the Bank, Director of the Mint Moore and various committees of Congress presented their views. White and Ingham, officially representing the attitude of the Treasury, favored the single silver standard, in all probability because they could devise no other plan which would insure a small silver cur-

88

rency. The Senate Finance Committee, of which Sanford was chairman, gave up its plan for changes in the legal tender statutes and turned its attention to the bimetallic ratio. Its members unanimously indorsed the double standard. In the last month of 1830 the committee introduced a bill changing the ratio from 15 to 15.9 to 1 by reducing the fine weight of the gold dollar to 23.35 grains.[1] The House "Select Committee on Coins," of which Representative White of New York was chairman, presented a well-written report likewise approving bimetallism but contending that the proper ratio was 15.62½ to 1. The bill which the House committee presented, as well as the Senate committee's bill, went over to the succeeding Congress. In the course of the next year the House committee twice introduced a bill calling for the double standard at their ratio of 15.62½.[2]

Early in 1832 White's committee was in some way converted to the theory of fiduciary coinage and introduced a bill calling for a unique system of subsidiary coins, not only of silver but also of gold. There were to be only two standard coins, a $10 gold piece and a $1 silver coin. All other coins of both metals were to be subsidiary, heavily reduced in weight and coined from bullion owned by the mint. The subsidiary gold coins, which were to be legal tender to $10, would yield the government a seigniorage of more than 5 cents per dollar. The silver half-dollar, quarter, dime, and half-dime, limited in tender to $5, were to contain 360 grains of fine silver per dollar, which would give a seigniorage of about 3 per cent.

Two years later the committee still favored this double

---

[1] Senate Bills and Resolutions, 21st Cong., 1st sess., 49.

[2] In 1834 White's committee presented a report which contained all the important documents from 1830 to 1834. It is widely known to students of finance as House Exec. Doc. no. 278, 23rd Cong., 1st session.

subsidiary plan. On February 19, 1834, an improved and
expanded bill was introduced.[3] The ratio of the standard
coins was altered to 15.62½, the proposed subsidiary gold
and silver coins were made receivable for government dues,
the alloy in both types was fixed at ⅒, and the copper coins
were given a legal tender value to 10 cents.

Although this bill was never enacted into law, it is worth
while to examine it. The committee believed in bimetallism
but recognized the difficulty of the problem of keeping both
metals in circulation. To insure this concurrent circulation
they had decided to establish a fiduciary coinage of both
gold and silver. Under the plan the owner of standard
gold or silver coins could buy at face value at the mint his
choice of fiduciary gold coins 5 per cent below the standard
or silver small change 3 per cent below. The market ratio
at this time and for a generation after was close to the proposed legal ratio of 15.62½, and for thirty years from
the time the bill was first introduced neither gold nor silver
subsidiary pieces of the proposed coinage could have been
melted or exported at a profit.

The proposal of a subsidiary coinage of gold borders
on the fantastic. In the absence of a provision for redemption in standard gold coin, the purchase of sub-standard
gold pieces of limited tender would have been hazardous.
In practice such purchases would have been negligible, although the legal right to buy such coins would have been
at worst a harmless if novel arrangement. But the subsidiary silver provisions were admirable. The committee
presented with the bill a report which gives the best exposition of the principles of subsidiary coinage ever published
in a government document in this country. This is all the
more notable in view of the fact that the theory was but

[3] The three bills are in House Bills and Resolutions, 22nd Cong. 1st sess.,
no. 603, and 23rd Cong., 1st sess., no. 313.

little understood. In discussing the reform of the currency in earlier reports Secretary Ingham, ex-Secretary Gallatin, and Director Moore had condemned the English subsidiary system and displayed a whole-hearted misunderstanding of its character. In the face of this authority the committee recommended a thoroughgoing subsidiary plan. Adoption of the plan would have anticipated the law of 1853, driven out the Spanish silver coins, and altered the financial history of the country.

The bill was read twice and considered by the House in Committee of the Whole. The high standing of White and other members of the committee would probably have assured its passage. When it came up for final disposition in June White suddenly withdrew the bill and introduced a substitute in no way resembling it. It contained nothing relating to subsidiary coinage, alloy, legal tender, or mint improvements. There were only two provisions. One of these, a minor item, dealt with seigniorage charges, providing that if depositors of bullion received their coins within 40 days they should pay a charge of $\frac{1}{2}$ per cent. The essential provision reduced the weight of the standard gold dollar from $24\frac{3}{4}$ grains of fine metal to 23.2 grains. This changed the coinage ratio from 15 to 1 to 16.002 to 1. Despite the bitter opposition of a few members the bill was forced through both houses. It became the law of June 28, 1834.[4]

The forces behind the passage of this measure have never been clearly revealed. In five bills and four reports White had recommended the ratio of $15.62\frac{1}{2}$, and he was fully aware that a ratio of 16 to 1 would be a false adjustment. There were at least three influences favorable to such an adjustment. Eastern commercial interests wanted gold re-

---

[4] For the debate see Benton, Abridgement of Congressional Debates, Vol. 12, 383, 496, 508.

stored to circulation for general business purposes and for foreign trade. Southern interests wished to encourage the gold mines of Georgia and North Carolina, which in the five years preceding had become the chief source of such gold coinage as the mint produced. Jones, a Georgia member of the House, boasted that he had persuaded White to introduce the bill, and before a year was out Congress established mints in the two states. And there was political pressure for a gold coinage to drive out the notes of the Second United States Bank and hasten the destruction of that ill-fated institution. The only argument advanced at any point was the statement that Spain had a 16 to 1 ratio. In fact this ratio was a failure in Spain, and leading countries such as France had a ratio of 15½.

From a legal standpoint the law was a debasement of the currency by approximately 3 per cent. From the standpoint of the fractional coinage it was an egregious blunder. By giving gold a higher value as coin than it could command in the arts Congress had deliberately provided for the cessation of silver coinage. It had virtually adopted the gold standard without any provision for a small change currency. Adoption of the gold standard with a subsidiary silver system attached would have been excellent. A transparent pretense of maintaining the double standard was inexcusable. The law was inspired by crassly partisan motives.

The old gold unit weighed 27 grains, with a fine weight of 24¾ grains and an alloy proportion of 1/12. The new unit was to have a fine weight of 23⅕ grains and a gross weight of 25⅘ grains. Expressed as a common fraction, the alloy was 13/129 of the weight of the coin, a fraction that cannot be converted into a common decimal. The law had been so hastily framed that the alloy was thus a clumsy fractional percentage, like that which had been the bane of mint operations in silver coinage since 1792.

The old gold coins were worth more than $1.05 in terms of the new dollar, and such amounts as were in bank reserves and other hidden stores were brought out for re-coinage. They were not the only supplies. From the day of its passage the law of 1834 affected the whole course of trade and finance. Payments from Europe, formerly made in silver, were now made in gold. Gold sovereigns from Europe began to arrive in large numbers. Gold from Mexico and South America was now coined and put into circulation. The output of the mines in Virginia, Georgia, and North Carolina, at least half of which had formerly gone abroad in bars, now went to the mints. The average annual gold coinage from 1825 to 1834 was about $400,-000, and none of this had gone into circulation. In six months of 1834 the coinage amounted to $4,000,000, all of which went into circulation. The objectives of the framers of the law were fully realized.[5]

The fractional alloy proportions of 13/129 in the gold coins and 179/1664 in the silver coins were a great inconvenience, and in 1836 Director Moore wrote to Congress urging that they be changed. He also made a strong plea for various mint improvements that had been provided for in the subsidiary coinage bills of 1832 and 1834, urging especially the creation of a bullion fund and a statutory recognition of the cent and half-cent, which had been coined for thirty-nine years under the authority of a proclamation by Washington.

A House committee made these recommendations the occasion for a thorough reconsideration of the whole coinage system. While the committee failed to realize that the law of 1834, with its ratio undervaluing silver, made a provision for a new silver coinage system inevitable, it did recognize the necessity for improving the small change currency. The

[5] See Laughlin, Bimetallism, Chapter 3.

bill presented by the committee included a provision for subsidiary coinage on a very tentative basis.[6]   The dime and
half-dime were to be reduced about 3 per cent, coined from
government bullion, and sold to the public.   They were to
be legal tender in payments to $1.   The bill passed the
House and went to the Senate, where a committee indorsed
it and added a clause reducing the weights of the copper
coins and making them a tender to 10 cents.   When the
measure again reached the House that body struck out all
the provisions relating to the copper coins and the subsidiary
silver coins.   Once more Congress refused to pass a measure in every way excellent and desirable.

As finally passed January 18, 1837, the law was a complete revision and codification of all the mint and coinage
laws, one of the two statutes of this kind in the country's
history.   There were 38 clauses, covering the matters of
legal standards, seigniorage, mint charges, legal tender,
mint procedure, tolerance in coin weights, and accounting
methods.   Reforms sorely needed since the opening of the
mint were provided for.   Most important was the creation
of a bullion fund of $1,000,000, with which the mint was
to buy bullion for the manufacture of coins in advance of
deposits by owners.   The seigniorage charge of $\frac{1}{2}$ per cent
for immediate deliveries of coin was abolished.   The mint
was directed to give depositors the denominations they preferred if it was possible to do so.   A copper purchase fund
was created, and the copper coins of Washington's proclamation were made statutory.

The alloy in both gold and silver coins was brought to
10 per cent.   In the silver coins the copper content was
reduced $3\frac{1}{2}$ grains, bringing the gross weight of the silver
dollar from 416 to $412\frac{1}{2}$ grains without a change in the

[6] House Executive Documents, 24th Cong., 1st sess., Vol. 3, and House
Bills and Resolutions, 24th Cong., 1st sess., no. 529.

fine weight of 371¼ grains. The alloy in the gold coins
was determined in a different way. The weight of 23.2
grains in the act of 1834 had been selected as the nearest
one-decimal approximation to a 16 to 1 ratio, the one de-
sired by those responsible for that law. The gross weight
of 25.8 grains made the closest approximation to a 10 per
cent alloy. The natural procedure in reforming the alloy
was to reduce the copper until it was ⅑ of 23.2 grains, but
this proportion cannot be expressed as a common decimal.
The House committee solved this difficulty by raising the
fine gold weight to 23.22 grains, which was ⁹⁄₁₀ of the gross
weight of the 1834 coin. This altered the legal ratio from
16.002 to 15.988 and presented the unique spectacle of a
change in the standard money of a nation to meet a problem
in arithmetic. Materially the change involved an appreciation in the standard of only ¹⁄₁₂ of 1 per cent. The gold and
silver dollar units created by the law of 1837 have not since
been changed.

The crisis of 1837, coming shortly after the passage of
the law, still further demoralized the fractional currency and
created an acute shortage of coins of all kinds. Copper
pieces of many varieties appeared, issued by individuals and
by corporations. The currency scarcity only partly explains
the large volume of these private copper coins. Many were
issued for purposes of advertisement or political propa-
ganda. The political tokens are quaint and curious relics
of our currency history, the majority exemplifying the spirit
of scurrilous and bitter partisanship of the time of Andrew
Jackson. The absence of the name of the maker on hundreds of the varieties known to collectors indicates that
great numbers were issued primarily for profit. Almost
all of them were smaller than the cents from the mint. A
button factory in Waterbury, Connecticut, issued many
thousands, and the volume in Baltimore reached such pro-

portions that Federal officers took steps to prosecute private coiners under the provisions of the long-forgotten law of May 8, 1792. Fractional notes were also issued in large amounts by individuals, concerns, and banks.[7] In Philadelphia the circulation of notes in denominations from 5 cents to $2.00 was estimated to be $1,000,000. Both Philadelphia and Baltimore issued municipal notes, the latter city putting out more than $100,000 in one month. Before 1839 both the copper coins and the fractional notes were disappearing, and the cities were redeeming such of their notes as were presented. Only a few private copper coins or small notes appeared in circulation after 1840.

The anonymous issues of private coins could not be redeemed. Eventually they went to the melting pot at a loss to the holders. Notes issued by the cities were redeemable, but many were lost or destroyed in use. The notes issued by corporations could usually be redeemed, but in many cases dissolution of the concern or removal to a new address made redemption impossible. In 1839 New York prohibited the circulation of small notes, and thousands were left in the hands of the public.

The legal status of this private copper and paper currency illustrates the uncertainty of Federal powers in monetary matters in all the period prior to the Civil War. The old copper coinage measure of 1792, outlawing private copper coins, was to be in force only after the issue of a proclamation the Treasury had failed to promulgate. A drastic anti-counterfeiting law was passed in 1806, but it was specifically limited to gold and silver imitations. The federal government had created no legislation by which it could pre-

---

[7] For details of the issues of coins and paper notes see Falkner, Private Issue of Token Coins; Low, Hard Times Tokens; Niles' Register, Vols. 53 and 65; Raguet's Financial Register, Vol. 1; Philadelphia Public Ledger for Oct. 23, 1837.

vent counterfeiting of cents or the private coinage of genuine cent pieces. Nor was there any Federal restraint on
the private issue of notes. Only the good will and good
sense of the state governments prevented notes of banks and
corporations from driving out all metallic currency.

The denominations of the fractional notes of the panic
period showed that the decimal system was gradually coming into its own. As compared with the notes of the 1812
period, they indicate definite progress in eliminating Spanish
denominations. All the notes were now issued in cents, and
the majority were in the United States denominations of 5,
10, and 20 cents. On the other hand, many notes issued by
concerns in the less populous sections were still in denominations of 6¼, 12½, and 25 cents.

The crisis of 1837 only temporarily diminished the unprecedented flow of gold coins from the mints. For forty
years after the establishment of the 16 to 1 ratio a gold
dollar was worth less than a silver dollar. In the first half
of this period the market ratio was never higher than 15.93
to 1, and the average was close to 15.7. While a discrepancy
between legal ratio and market ratio was not at that time
the immediate and conclusive force it is today, it was inevitable that the coinage of silver should be discouraged.
No foreign debtor sent silver in payment after 1834. The
United States had no productive silver mines. Inevitably
the false coinage ratio would stop silver coinage and drain
the country of the coins already in circulation.

Eventually the overvaluation of gold did these very
things. The time came when the owner of silver bullion
lost 3 cents in every dollar if he had it coined at the United
States Mint, and silver coinage ceased. But this time was
nearly a generation later. Currency historians have thought
that the law of 1834 immediately drove out the silver coins
and placed the country on a de facto gold standard. Upton,

who has been widely quoted, declared that "$50,000,000 at once disappeared." Inasmuch as the total coin in the country in 1832, both gold and silver, was by estimate of the mint director and other authorities about $30,000,000, the absurdity of this statement is obvious. A few historians have noted that the scarcity of silver did not become acute, but none has recognized the fact that the laws of 1834 and 1837, despite their misguided ratio provisions, greatly improved the condition of the silver currency and gave the country the largest supply of fractional money it had ever known.[8]

The prevailing view is an interesting example of *a priori* reasoning from the premise that Gresham's law operates immediately and with full force whenever two moneys of unequal values are made equally good in payment of debts. Gresham's law is one of the immutable forces in economic life, working now as it did when Aristophanes first observed it. Given a material difference between coinage ratio and market ratio, the cheaper metal will go to the mint to the exclusion of the other, provided, however, that there is free play in the choice of metals and public knowledge of conditions. There is always a margin of delay and indifference, and the rapidity of the process is governed by many collateral influences. The primary factor is the actual disparity in the ratios, but there are other elements such as mint charges, the expense of gathering and shipping coins, the denominations of the coins, the extent of bullion trading, the location of bullion supplies, legal restrictions, and the general sophistication of the people.

The ultimate destruction of the silver coinage was postponed by a combination of forces. The first of these was the extraordinary coinage of gold, which immediately al-

See Bolles, Vol. 2, 511; White, Money and Banking, 35; Holdsworth, Money and Banking, 27; Upton, Money in Politics, 175.

tered the silver circulation. Silver had long borne a double burden, serving both as a retail currency and as a standard money in banking and general financial operations. The larger silver pieces, Spanish dollars and half-dollars and United States half-dollars, were buried in bank reserves. The new gold coins were now substituted for these silver pieces, which immediately appeared in circulation.

A more important factor was the flow of silver coins and bullion into the country. The long period of revolutionary disturbances in the Latin-American countries before 1825 had greatly restricted the output of silver. About 1830 the Mexican mines were revived on a large scale, and Mexican silver flowed into the United States regardless of the unfavorable ratio. Such figures as are available indicate that from 1834 to 1843 the imports of silver coin and bullion actually exceeded the exports by about $20,000,000.[9] Instead of declining in the face of an adverse ratio silver coinage showed a remarkable increase. The coinage of silver dollars, resumed now after a suspension of thirty years, and of half-dollars, almost the only tangible result of the mint's existence to this time, was very small. With great numbers of gold coins in circulation, there was little need for these two silver coins. But the coinage of quarters, dimes, and half-dimes reached proportions hitherto unknown. More of these pieces were coined in the four years after 1834 than in the previous history of the mint. The average annual coinages of the three pieces had been, respectively, about $18,000, $22,000, and $9,000. In 1839 the respective figures were $208,000, $239,000, and $113,000. In 1838 the branch mint at New Orleans devoted itself wholly to the making of dimes.

Mint improvements will partly account for the silver coin-

[9] See Hunt's Merchants Magazine, Vol. 10, 376; Senate Reports, 53rd Cong., 2nd sess., no. 235; United States Statistical Abstract for 1887, 42.

age. In 1831 a new mint at Philadelphia was completed, and in 1836 steam power was introduced. The law of 1837 abolished seigniorage charges and created a bullion fund which enabled the mint to accumulate great stocks of coins in all denominations. For the first time silver coinage was free, gratuitous, and immediate. The mint no longer discouraged depositors who asked for small coins, and business interests were more than willing to suffer a slight loss on bullion ratios in return for a supply of fresh new silver coins of convenient sizes.

The new coinage would have served little purpose if the pieces had been hoarded or exported. But they remained in circulation. At first glance this appears to be an economic anomaly. But the disparity in the ratios was not large. During most of the period from 1834 to 1850 the silver dollar was worth about $1.01 in gold.[10] A large majority of the Spanish coins were reduced by wear much more than 1 per cent. As for the new United States pieces, there was little profit in systematic collection for export when the costs of the transaction averaged around 1 per cent.[11] When payments were made abroad it was profitable to send silver, and the larger coins of Mexican and United States minting were culled out and exported. The advantage of silver shipments, offset by the higher costs of handling, disappeared entirely if the pieces were underweight. There were cross-currents in bullion movements, with a large influx of gold from Europe, a considerable domestic production of gold, an extensive importation of silver from Mexico, and a steady outflow of silver to England.

In any event the country had for the first time a fairly satisfactory fractional currency. The scarcity of small

[10] See Appendix F.

[11] There is one fugitive reference to the costs of shipping silver, in Senate Report no. 104, 33rd Cong., 1st sess., estimating it at 1 per cent.

change that had existed since colonial beginnings was relieved, and the clumsy substitutes of the past disappeared. A legal ratio favorable to silver before 1834 had given the country a negligible amount of domestic silver coins; an adverse ratio after that date was accompanied by an unprecedented coinage of silver. In 1843 Eckfeldt and Dubois, in their coinage manual, made the following statement: "It is a remarkable fact, however, that our gold and silver coins have ever since that date passed concurrently, without premium either way." Seven years later a New Orleans paper said the country was "tolerably well supplied" with silver change.[12] For more than a decade after 1834 bimetallism was fairly successful in the United States. It was unsuccessful before and after that period.

In 1844 the Treasury adopted a general policy of recoining foreign coins received in government business, although the post offices and customs offices did not rigidly follow the procedure. It was merely a compliance with a law that had been ignored for nearly fifty years. The Treasury did not make the law's distinction between Spanish coins and other foreign pieces, but recoined all foreign pieces received. Since the general effect was to eliminate Spanish coins and English reckoning, the policy was beneficial, but in one respect it was undesirable. It resulted in the withdrawal of coins too worn for exportation or melting and their recoinage into new quarters and dimes that would tend to be driven out by the adverse ratio. The recoinage reduced the available fractional currency.

The Treasury contrived to effect this recoinage at the expense of the public. It has been noted that the legal status of Spanish and Mexican coins was ambiguous. It is doubtful whether the pieces below the dollar had any legal

---

[12] See Eckfeldt and Dubois, Manual of Gold and Silver Coins, 143; Hunt's Merchants Magazine, Vol. 10, 245; New Orleans Picayune for Aug. 3, 1850.

tender quality, while the coins that weighed less than 415 grains per dollar were specifically denied legal tender. None the less the people thought they were legal tender, and the belief had been confirmed by Treasury practice for a half-century. The fractional coins were commonly accepted at values of 50, 25, 12½, and 6¼ cents. In the cities, where the decimal system was making progress, the fractional re-mainders were often dropped, the real passing for 12 cents, the medio for 6. The great depreciation in weight of the foreign coins and the losses on recoinage were beginning to cause disturbance. The general public was not concerned so long as the coins could be passed on to any storekeeper. The merchant in turn could adjust his prices to the situation, and he could deposit the coins in his bank. But the banks could not ignore the deficiency in the coins, as they were not able to force them on customers who asked for United States coins. They had to take the old coins to the Treasury for recoinage. As early as 1832 banks in Philadelphia had protested the deposit of "large amounts of quarter-dollars by tale."

No settled policy was adopted until 1843, in which year the New York banks established a scale of values.[13] The double-real, real, and medio were not to be taken at values higher than 23, 10, and 5 cents, respectively. The post offices adopted the same valuations, despite public protests. Congress demanded an explanation from the Postmaster General, but took no further action. By 1848 the New York ratings had been adopted by banks and post offices the country over. The ratings permitted the banks to re-coin most of their foreign receipts without loss and en-

[13] The record of the Treasury and the banks in this connection can be traced only through scattered references in Hunt's Merchants Magazine, Vol. 24; Bankers Magazine, Vol. 5; Niles Register, Vol. 69; and House Executive Documents, 28th Cong., 1st sess. ,Vol. 4; 30th Cong., 2nd sess., Vol. 2; and 32nd Cong., 1st sess., Vol. 2.

abled the Treasury to carry out an extensive recoinage. But they also gave rise to a peculiar situation in which a general currency was received at one value in ordinary transactions and at another in dealings with the banks and post offices.

From 1830 onward there was a fairly steady increase in the coinage of copper cents, although it did not keep pace with the growth of population. The field of circulation of the copper coins expanded slowly. Many uses which modern life finds for a cent were non-existent. Cheap newspapers, post cards, "penny matches," small confections, and slot machines had not appeared. In most sections, especially in the South and the West, the medio and the half-dime were the smallest coins in circulation. In the Eastern cities diminishing margins of profit were making a small place for the cent piece. The half-cent was not widely used anywhere, and the coinage was negligible. Both the copper coins were of pure metal and turned black with use. Year after year the mint directors, in their annual reports, discussed the unpopularity of the copper coins and expressed the belief that they were at last coming into general use.

The circulation of two types of silver coins was beginning to cause annoyance in business, and the situation was aggravated by the adoption of the special ratings for Spanish coins by the Treasury and the banks. Price quotations of 5, 10, and 20 cents now predominated, but the Spanish coins were still the more widely used currency, and the smaller pieces were valued at 12½ and 6½ cents, or, as frequently, 12 and 6 cents. Making change was a matter of involved calculation, and the use of cents and half-cents was necessary.[14] It was probably this change use more than any

[14] In 1861 Nova Scotia created a ½ cent piece for the purpose of making change for the British six-pence, which was valued at 12½ cents in the Canadian decimal system. See McLachlan, 55.

other that kept copper coins in circulation. In the South and West the careless monetary habits of the people made the copper coins superfluous. The purchaser of a "half-bit's worth" of tobacco paid for it with a bit and should have received a half-bit, or 6¼ cents, in change, but he accepted the 5 cent half-dime when the storekeeper offered it. Throughout the South and the West the dime and half-dime¹ were commonly accepted as the change equivalents of the real and medio. In fact the dime was widely known as the "short bit." The storekeeper who paid out ten dimes when he should have given ten reals made a profit of 25 cents. The people were systematically victimized. The practice became so firmly intrenched that Congress was attempting to stop it as late as 1875.

CHAPTER IX

THE LAWS OF 1851 AND 1853

In 1844 the legal ratio turned the tide of silver movements against the country. From that year on the exports to England exceeded the imports from Mexico. In 1848 a new force was added to the steady pressure already exerted. The California mines began to pour a stream of gold into the world's currency, a volume so large that it was an influence in the world's markets in 1849 and a violent force in 1850. Early in 1851 the market ratio fell to 15.45 to 1. The silver in two half-dollars was worth $1.03½ in gold, and the profit on exportation became a decisive force. Further circulation of full-weight silver coins was impossible. In 1849 Congress had authorized the coinage of $1 gold pieces. To a limited extent these small coins could take the place of silver half-dollars and quarters and they went into circulation in great numbers, serving in small measure to help the currency situation, but also hastening the disappearance of silver.

While the gold production of California and Australia was inevitably leading to profound economic changes and critical currency conditions the world over, Congress was giving its attention to trivial proposals relating to the small

coins. In 1850 Senator Dickinson introduced a bill proposing two novel additions to the coinage. One was a cent
piece, to be made of one part silver to nine parts copper.
Its weight, 25 grains, would make the coin about half the
size of our present day cent. It was to have a hole in the
center, for stringing "on an upright stake or file." It was
to be coined on government account and sold to the public,
and its legal tender was limited to 10 cents. As Dickinson
expressed it, the cent could be made more popular "by increasing its intrinsic value and decreasing its size."

The other coin proposed was a silver 3 cent piece. It
was to have the weight, proportionate to its 3 cent value,
of 12⅜ grains, but the proportion of pure silver was to
be only ¾ instead of ⁹⁄₁₀. And it was to be a subsidiary
coin, with a legal tender limit of 20 cents.[1] The mint was
to coin the pieces from its own bullion and sell them to the
public, but only in exchange for foreign fractional silver
coins.

The proposed 1 cent piece represented a last effort to
have Congress adopt a "billion" coin. The committee
thought that the cent piece would be popular if it contained
silver. The proposed 3 cent piece had a different objective.
The rising value of silver had caused the withdrawal of all
coins not greatly reduced by wear, and the Treasury's recoinage operations were conducted at a loss, even with the low
valuations of 23, 10, and 5 cents given the double-real, real,
and medio. It was estimated that $6,000,000 in badly un-
derweight coins still circulated. If the government could
exchange for these pieces United States coins made at a
large profit recoinage would not show a loss. The committee did not foresee the approaching crisis in the silver
currency, and in proposing the 3 cent piece they did not
have in mind the problem of a retail currency. Still less

[1] The two coins are described in the Bankers Magazine, Vol. 5, 32.

did they realize that they were laying the foundations for a new monetary system. They had in mind only the withdrawal of worn Spanish coins without loss to the Treasury. The Spanish coins were to be accepted in exchange for the new coins at ratings of 25, 12½, and 6¼ cents instead of the inequitable values allowed at post offices and banks. The 3 cent denomination was selected because it fitted easily into the common 6 and 12 cent ratings of the medio and real, although it was ill adapted to the United States decimal system.

While the Senate was debating Dickinson's measure the House was considering a cruder proposal. The bill provided that after July 1, 1850, the valuations of the Spanish small coins should not be higher than 20, 10, and 5 cents, respectively. Evidently framed under the impression that these coins were still legal tender at their nominal ratings, the bill proposed to reduce these values without any recompense. To facilitate the withdrawal of the Spanish coins a standard 20 cent United States silver piece was provided for. The proposed measure would have been unfair to the public and injurious to the currency. The Spanish coins in their debased condition would stay in circulation in part, but every new United States coin substituted would disappear at once.[2] Both the bills failed of passage, and no other measures were proposed. With the silver currency of the country dwindling away, Congress did nothing.

In the next session a House committee brought in a bill reducing the letter postage rate from 5 cents to 3 cents. The committee thought that the unpopularity of the copper cent would lead to inconvenience in the purchase of the new stamps. They included in the bill a provision for Dickinson's fiduciary 3 cent piece, formulating the clause so care-

---

[2] For the two bills see Senate Bills and Resolutions, 31st Cong., 1st sess., no. 230; and House Bills and Resolutions, 31st Cong., 1st sess., no. 24.

lessly that essential details were omitted. It was provided only that the mint should coin a 3 cent piece of 12⅜ grains, the coin to contain 3 parts silver to 1 part copper, and to have a legal tender in payments to 30 cents. In the House debate it was brought out that the 3 cent denomination would have a tendency to perpetuate the English reckoning, while Dickinson, in the Senate, made a plea for the provisions of his earlier bill that were essential to make the law practicable.[3] All proposed amendments were voted down. The bill became a law March 3, 1851.

This almost forgotten statute is one of the most significant measures in American currency history. After resisting for sixty years every attempt to introduce any form of fiduciary silver coinage Congress adopted a subsidiary silver coin as an adjunct to the postal service, without realizing that the first step had been taken in the relegation of silver to the status of a subordinate monetary material. The new piece was the first silver coin in the history of the United States that was not legal tender for an unlimited amount. Subsidiary coinage had been established, but in a trivial way, by an unworkable law, and at a time when the entire silver currency was flowing out of the country. The law contained no provision for coinage on government account or sale to the public. A consideration of the debate in the two houses indicates that Congress actually intended to give the piece free coinage.

While the measure was going through Congress the fractional currency situation was becoming critical. The excess of silver exports over imports jumped from $2,000,000 in 1850 to $23,000,000 in 1851. In the two years the exports exceeded in amount the total volume of coinage of the twenty years preceding. Silver coinage had declined to small proportions. The coinage of half-dollars and quar-

[3] Congressional Globe, Vol. 23, 227, 672, and Vol. 24, 275.

ters in 1851 was no larger than that in 1804, when the mint was just beginning to function. Such coinage as there was resulted chiefly from the Treasury's recoinages. None of the new coins went into circulation.

Two coins were pouring into the gap in the currency. Gold dollars could in a limited way do the work of vanished half-dollars and quarters, and nearly 4,000,000 of these tiny gold pieces were coined in 1851, despite the efforts of the mint officials to discourage the production of small gold coins. The large number coined did not suffice, and before 1852 business houses were actually paying a premium of ½ to 1 per cent in larger gold coins.[4] The other coin was the new 3 cent piece. This auxiliary of the postal service suddenly emerged as the most important coin in the country. The Treasury officials, wisely ignoring the apparent meaning of the law, made the coinage subsidiary. They decided to coin the pieces from government bullion, to sell them in lots of 100 coins for any other United States coins of gold or silver, and to exchange them for Spanish fractions at the full public ratings of 25, 12½, and 6¼ cents. The mint was actually adopting, without any legal authority, the provisions of Dickinson's rejected bill. It would have been wiser to sell the coins for gold only, as withdrawal of any kind of silver coin was undesirable at the time.

There was a large demand for the 3 cent coin before the mint had prepared its machinery, and the Director thought it best to produce a stock of 500,000 pieces before public sale. Within six months more than 6,000,000 pieces had gone into circulation, and in 1852 more than 20,000,000 were coined, with a value much larger than that of all the other silver coinage The piece, with a weight about one quarter of the weight of our modern cent, is

[4] Hunt's Merchants Magazine, Vol. 29, 100.

the smallest coin that has ever circulated in the United States. It was non-decimal and had a limited legal tender. It flooded the channels of retail trade.

The piece was a genuine subsidiary silver coin. At the current gold price of silver a dollar's worth of the coins contained about 86 cents worth of silver. With the cost of copper and the expense of minting deducted there was still a profit to the Treasury of more than 10 per cent. This rate permitted the recoinage of much of the Spanish silver without loss. When they first appeared critics objected to the coins on the grounds that they were "debased." Hunt's Merchants Magazine defended them by attempting to prove that the costs of manufacture were so high that the Treasury made only a small profit. The coins were worth, of course, what the public paid for them, regardless of their costs at the mint. Any person could use 100 of them as the equivalent of 3 gold dollars. They lacked the quality of redeemability, but this could become important only if too many were issued.

Before the end of 1851 conditions in retail trade had become chaotic. Trade was being carried on with gold dollars, 3 cent pieces, underweight dimes and half-dimes, and badly worn Spanish reals and medios. The gold dollars were too small in size and too large in value. The dimes and half-dimes were the few survivors of a systematic culling out of good weight coins. The Spanish fractions were a motley collection of underweight coins. The adverse ratio had long since stopped the importation of Spanish coins of good condition, but badly worn pieces were still brought in. Sumner says that the whole world was ransacked for Spanish coins that had been discarded as unfit for circulation. Ordinary business was hampered and retarded by the state of the currency. No United States or Spanish silver coin could circulate unless it was reduced by wear as much as

3 per cent. The average depreciation was much larger, possibly as great as 15 per cent. Copper coins, if they had been in general circulation, might have been very useful, but they were very large, were unattractive in use, and had an uncertain legal status. The coinage of cent pieces showed a marked increase in 1851, but the total coinage from 1851 to 1853, inclusive, was only one piece for each person in the country. The total fractional coin currency of all kinds was quite inadequate. Railways, hotels, and stores, which required small change as a business necessity, were buying small coins at a premium, first gold dollars, then 3 cent pieces, and finally any sort of United States or foreign silver coins whatever. A customer who offered a gold dollar in payment for a small article would receive in exchange perhaps ten or fifteen 3 cent pieces and a half-dozen almost unrecognizable reals and medios. A Philadelphia paper refers derisively to shopkeepers scooping up 3 cent pieces with a ladle to make change for a $5 bank-note.[5]

The scarcity of currency was a concrete problem, but its solution involved all the theoretical perplexities of bimetallism and coinage ratios. Considered broadly, the problem could be met in three different ways. One way was to adopt the gold standard of the English system, closing the mints to silver and creating a subsidiary silver coinage. A second method was to adopt the single silver standard. The third alternative was to restore the double standard by changing the coinage ratio.

Of the three plans one was out of the question. The adoption of the silver standard was impossible, either as a defensible economic measure or as a practicable legislative proposal. The many public men who believed in the single

---

[5] The conditions are described in Hunt's Merchants Magazine, Vol. 28 and 29; Sumner, History of American Currency; and the Annual Reports on the Finances for 1851, 1852, and 1853.

silver standard in principle had been overwhelmed by the tide
of gold from California.   A proposal to close the mint to
this tremendous flow of wealth would not be entertained
in any circles.   Even on technical grounds the measure would
be defective, as closing the mints to gold would not immediately revive silver coinage unless the legal tender of the
current gold coins should be withdrawn.   Such a measure
was not to be considered.

The rejuvenation of the double standard by alteration
of the ratio was feasible politically, but it presented a difficult problem.   With gold production such as the world had
never known, a new coinage ratio, no matter how accurately
it was adjusted to the market value in London, might within
a few weeks show another discrepancy that would destroy the
silver coinage.   In 1850 the silver in four quarters was
worth $1.01⅘; in 1851 it was worth $1.03⅖.   The only
way to insure a silver coinage was to select a ratio unfavorable to gold, and such a measure would be equivalent to the
adoption of the single silver standard.

The third alternative, the adoption of the gold standard
with a subsidiary silver coinage, was a practical, efficient,
and immediate solution.   Such a plan had been in successful
operation in England for thirty-five years.   Congress had
been receiving proposals for fiduciary coinage of one type
or another for a half-century and had rejected formal plans
in 1800, 1816, 1819, 1832, and 1850.   It had only recently
adopted a 3 cent subsidiary piece, and the coin was going
into circulation at the rate of 350,000 pieces a week, yielding the government a profit and demonstrating the value of
subsidiary coinage.   The country was actually on the gold
standard, and adoption of a silver subsidiary system involved
no problem of demonetization, recoinage, legal tender contracts, or price level.

The one difficulty in the way of the subsidiary coinage

plan was the lack of knowledge of the principles of money. The people as a whole and members of Congress as a group were not sufficiently versed in currency matters to understand how silver currency could be maintained without a bimetallic standard. The aversion to "debased coin" and the deep-seated fear of private duplications of fiduciary coins were sufficient to defeat any thoroughgoing subsidiary coinage proposal. It should be added that there were many individuals who were sincerely opposed to the gold standard. There was a growing realization that bimetallism was impracticable—that it "wouldn't work"—but to a majority of Americans gold was still unfamiliar as a common medium. It was widely believed that gold was a less stable standard than silver. Only one country had adopted it as the sole standard.

With all three of the methods of currency reorganization blocked by technical or political obstacles Congress should have adopted a temporary measure. Early in 1850 free coinage of the quarter-dollar, dime, and half-dime should have been stopped. The three pieces should have been heavily reduced in weight, coined on government account, and sold to the public for gold. The scarcity of fractional currency would have been remedied at once. There would have been no change of standard. The actual standard was gold, the nominal standard bimetallic, and the two would have been retained. The immediate problem solved, Congress could have considered, entirely at its convenience, the questions of national interest involved in a fundamental reform.

In the end Congress adopted just this method, but only after two years of needless delay. Like the earlier laws of 1792 and 1834 and the later act of 1873, the law of 1853 became a part of the controversy over bimetallism. The motives of Congress in passing it have been misconstrued.

To make clear the actual facts it is necessary to follow in detail the course of the law from its inception in 1851 to its passage in 1853.

In January, 1851, the House rejected a proposal to consider the advisability of coining pieces "of mixed gold and silver," instructing a committee to consider instead the question of "reducing the weight of the silver coins." Apparently the committee made an effort to gather information, for Daniel Webster, Secretary of State, wrote to Ambassador Abbott Lawrence, asking him to give his opinion of the English system. In his reply Lawrence made a brief but acutely discerning analysis of the subsidiary system of England. He recommended that the United States make all silver coins subsidiary with a weight reduction of 10 or 12 per cent.

The Senate was more impressed with the possibilities of symmetallism than the House had been. On resolution of Senator Hunter his own Committee on Finance was directed to consider the coinage of pieces of "equal values of gold and silver at the existing legal ratio." [6] The committee was not in favor of this scheme. In February, 1851, it presented to the Senate an elaborate subsidiary coinage bill. With various modifications, this bill became the law of 1853. It abolished free coinage of the half-dollar, quarter, dime, and half-dime. These coins were specifically designated as the ones which should be made subsidiary. The committee definitely and deliberately left the silver dollar a standard coin at the ratio established in 1837.

Inasmuch as the bill in this original form did not become a law, it is unnecessary to discuss it in detail. It is sufficient to note its undoubted intent to leave the double standard untouched. It is worth while to note also one provision

[6] It is not widely known that Congress was for many years interested in this plan for a symmetallic coinage.

which illustrates the committee's conception of fiduciary coinage. The proposed reduction in the silver content of the half-dollar was about 7¾ per cent, while the reduction in the weight of the other three silver coins was only 7⅕ per cent. The committee evidently wished to reduce the coins just enough to make them fiduciary. They were reluctant to make any reduction beyond that which would prevent exportation. Having observed the tendency of larger coins to disappear more rapidly, they reduced the weight of the half-dollar a fraction more.

The bill passed its first and second readings in the Senate, but the session expired without further action. Meanwhile the House Ways and Means Committee had been making an extensive study of the situation. They asked Secretary Corwin to suggest a plan. In his annual report Corwin indorsed the Senate committee's bill, recommending that the reduction in the weight of the coins be such that all the new pieces would weigh 384 grains to the dollar. In March, 1852, Senator Hunter again introduced his bill, submitting with it a long report on the currency situation. The committee had made only one important change in the bill.[7] Corwin's weight recommendation was accepted, and the half-dollar, quarter, dime and half-dime were to contain 345.6 grains of pure silver per dollar, with a gross weight of 384 grains. The reduction from the standard weights of 371¼ and 412½ grains was a fraction more than 6.91 per cent.

The report, expressed in the florid and ambiguous phraseology of the time, was not always clear. There was no direct and decisive statement of the committee's attitude toward the silver dollar. There was, however, no question as to their intention to maintain the double standard. The mem-

---

[7] The original bill and the revised measure are in Senate Bills and Resolutions, 32nd Cong., 1st sess., Vol. 1. The report is no. 104, 32nd Cong., 1st sess.

bers of the committee favored bimetallism. With the market relations of gold to silver in a state of flux it was unwise to establish a new bimetallic ratio. They specifically recommended that a new ratio be established as soon as the market ratio showed "a reasonable degree of stability." In fact they agreed to "debase" the smaller silver coins very reluctantly, declaring that the new coinage was a temporary expedient made necessary by a crisis, to be tried out only until the time "when the relations between the two metals promise to be more permanent." They emphatically denied that they were adopting the English system, in which silver, "not a legal standard except for small debts, is used only for tokens."

The bill passed the Senate without adverse vote on March 20, 1852, and on May 3 the House referred it to the Ways and Means Committee. This committee was more exercised over an attempt to move the mint to New York, a scheme that had been before Congress for many years, and allowed the session to expire without reporting on the bill. Outside of Congress there was an unusual amount of public interest in the Senate bill. Sentiment was generally favorable, although many persons were opposed to any "debasement of the coinage." Hunt's Merchants Magazine editorially advanced twenty-one reasons for retaining the double standard. Ex-Secretary Ingham approved the bill and criticized the objections to subsidiary coinage presented by "the Secretary of the Treasury in 1830," who was none other than Ingham himself. The New York Herald suggested the coinage of $1.50 gold pieces, while the Philadelphia Ledger recommended the issue of 50 cent gold coins with a large hole in the center. There was nowhere any impression that the bill was intended to establish the gold standard.[8] The Director of the Mint wrote to the Senate

[8] For contemporary discussions of the bill see Hunt's Merchants Magazine, Vol. 27, 66, 175; Bankers Magazine, Vol. 5, 657.

requesting that the half-dollar as well as the dollar be omitted from the list of subsidiary coins, so that there would be two standard silver coins in circulation when the coinage ratio should again be in accord with the market ratio.

In January, 1853, Secretary Corwin and Director Snowden sent emphatic letters to Congress in reference to the currency crisis. Their solicitude was justified. Private deposits of silver had ceased. The only silver coinage was on government account, from recoinage of the Treasury's foreign coin receipts. Except insofar as the foreign coins were converted into 3 cent pieces, recoinage intensified the scarcity, since all new silver coins disappeared. When the Treasury paid out standard silver pieces in change, it was making a gift of 3 or 4 cents on each dollar and hastening the disappearance of fractional currency. The premium on small change had increased. A railway in New England was paying premiums of $75 or more every month to obtain change for its ticket offices. Fractional bank-notes, almost entirely driven out after 1840, had reappeared in many sections. It was charged that irresponsible banks were being organized in many places solely for the purpose of issuing fractional notes, and private "shinplasters" were beginning to circulate in states that forbade their issue. The New Jersey legislature memorialized Congress, declaring that it would soon be necessary to legalize fractional notes. In New England, where the banks generally refrained from issuing fractional notes, the old device of "odd sum" notes in such denominations as $1.25 and $1.75 was again being used. Private copper coins appeared only here and there. The scarcity was not in the 1 cent field, but in the 5, 10, and 25 cent denominations.[9]

[9] See Hunt's Merchants Magazine, Vol. 26, 461, and 28, 211; Numismatist, Vol. 26; New York Times for July 17, 1862; Senate Executive Documents, 32nd Cong., 2nd sess., no. 39.

In January, 1853, the Ways and Means Committee presented to the House the bill which had been held since the Senate passed it in March, 1852. It had been amended in various ways. Dunham, who was chairman of the committee, urged immediate passage. At the suggestion of Skelton, who preferred the Senate bill, the House voted down every amendment of Dunham's committee. The bill was debated on February 1, 2, and 3, passed on February 15 by a vote of 94 to 69, and signed by the President on February 21, 1853.

The silver dollar was not affected by the law. The United States was still on the double standard, with free coinage at the 1837 ratio of 15.988 to 1. Some of the silver coins had been denied free coinage, but the double standard was unimpaired. Congress had elected to leave the double standard as it was, adopting a fiduciary coinage of the smaller silver pieces. It has been shown above that the Senate committee which drafted the bill in 1851 exempted the dollar because they believed in bimetallism. A year later the committee again submitted the bill, this time with a report defending the double standard and explaining carefully that the measure did not establish the gold standard. The Senate passed the bill with this understanding. The House committee considered the bill for a year, going over every section and submitting many amendments but leaving the double standard untouched. The Director of the Mint had called attention to the plan to continue bimetallism by asking Congress to leave both the dollar and the half-dollar in the class of standard coins.

In the face of this incontrovertible evidence currency historians have uniformly declared that it was the intention of Congress to adopt the gold standard.[10] Professor Laughlin

---

[10] Laughlin, Bimetallism, 80; Hepburn, History of the Currency, 64; Watson, 107; White, Money and Banking, 35.

is primarily responsible for this view. To quote from his History of Bimetallism,

> The real demonetization of silver in the United States was accomplished in 1853. It was not the result of accident; it was a carefully considered plan, deliberately carried into legislation in 1853, twenty years before its nominal demonetization by the act of 1873.

The only evidence offered in support of this erroneous view is the record of the House debate on the bill at the time it was passed. It is worth while to examine this record. There were only three speakers, Dunham, who had introduced the Senate's bill, Skelton, who was interested in currency matters, and Johnson, who was afterward President of the United States. In all the annals of Congress it would be impossible to find a currency discussion which more completely befogged the issue.[11] Dunham, a man with a superior grasp of monetary principles, was at a loss to find words that would make the proposed bill clear to his colleagues. Skelton, apparently well-informed, made some absurd statements, one of them to the effect that making the subsidiary coins receivable for taxes would undermine the gold standard. Johnson, displaying a vast ignorance of monetary principles in general and the proposed system in particular, said at one time that the country needed no currency legislation and at another that he preferred Ambassador Lawrence's plan. Lawrence's plan proposed the gold standard which Johnson was condemning.

It is true that both Dunham and Skelton said in the course of discussion that the bill established the gold standard. These statements were contrary to fact, as both men made clear at later points in the debate, when Dunham explained that the gold standard was to be instituted only so

[11] The debate is in the Congressional Globe, Vol. 26 and 27.

far "as these coins are concerned" and Skelton said that it
was not the objective of the bill to change the monetary
standard but to provide small change. A remarkable feature of the debate is the fact that the silver dollar was not
once referred to. A simple statement by Dunham to the
effect that the silver dollar was still to be a standard coin
would have clarified the matter completely. Dunham and
Skelton evidently found it easier to defend the principle of
the gold standard than to explain the nature of the fiduciary
coinage system proposed in the bill. The attitude of the
one hundred and sixty members of the House who said no
word for or against the measure can only be surmised. Reform of the coinage was imperative, the ablest committees
in House and Senate had devised the bill, the Senate had
passed it without an adverse vote, and the majority of the
House members were ready to vote for it without attempting to delve into its technical mysteries. In this attitude
toward a currency measure they differed but little from members of Congress before and after their time. The point
of view of many who voted negatively was probably voiced
by the member who said he could not understand the bill
and would therefore vote against it.

It was not the intention of Congress to demonetize silver,
and the law did not effect this result.[12] Gold was the de facto
standard after the law was passed, as before. The silver
dollar was left in an anomalous position. If the market
ratio should reverse its trend and move back to 16 to 1 the

[12] Some writers have said that Congress wished to abolish bimetallism
but left the silver dollar in the system so that it would be available for export
to China and for the settlement of contracts specifically payable in silver
dollars. This notion is incorrect. The United States dollar was unpopular in
the Orient and but little used. In the United States the coin had never circulated generally and had been entirely unknown since 1806. There were
many contracts payable in Spanish silver dollars, but none payable in United
States silver.

coinage of the silver dollar would be revived. The Senate committee expected to take up the question of the coinage ratio at its leisure. They might well have taken action to suspend the coinage of the dollar at the time. Their failure to do so led to political turmoil a generation later.

Chapter X

THE SUBSIDIARY COINAGE SYSTEM IN OPERATION

DETAILS of the law of 1853—Scarcity of fractional coins relieved—Insufficient reduction in silver content of the coins—Misunderstanding of fiduciary coinage principles—Snowden's illegal administration of the law—Oversupply of silver coins—Results of the law of 1853.

The law of 1853 stopped the free coinage of the half-dollar, quarter, dime, and half-dime and reduced them to 384 grains per dollar in gross weight and 345.6 grains in fine weight. The alloy percentage, as in other coins, was 10 per cent. It was provided that the mint should buy silver bullion and manufacture the coins, selling them in lots of $100 for gold coin only. The legal tender of the coins was limited to $5. An odd provision directed the Secretary of the Treasury to regulate "the amount coined into quarter-dollars, dimes, and half-dimes." The omission of the half-dollar from this list obligated the Treasury to coin half-dollars without limit. Apparently the Senate committee were apprehensive lest the smaller coins should be produced in excessive numbers. The House committee's amendment to include the half-dollar was lost with the other amendments.

As the law was passed, it had no effective date of operation. The Senate bill, passed in 1852, set the date at June 1, 1852. The House committee in 1853 carelessly tacked on a clause saying "on the first day of June next" without removing the Senate's out-of-date provision. There was a defect of omission also. The law contained no reference

to the 3 cent piece, the piece which had become the chief
silver coin of the country. It was non-decimal, only three-
quarters fine, physically unsatisfactory, and legal tender to
30 cents. With an abundance of decimal coins in prospect,
the 3 cent piece should have been dropped It had served
little purpose in connection with the sale of 3 cent stamps.
But if it was to be retained its composition should have been
brought into conformity with that of the other silver coins.
Dunham twice urged the House to refuse to pass the bill
until provision for the 3 cent piece was included.

These two defects were remedied by an amendment of
March 3, 1853, passed ten days after the original measure.
The ineffective dates of the previous law were repealed, and
April 1, 1853, was designated as the time for the inauguration of the new system. The 3 cent piece was made 9/10
fine and given the weight proportionate to its value. But its
legal tender power was left at 30 cents. The $5 legal tender
for the other subsidiary coins made it possible for a debtor
to force 100 half-dimes on a creditor, and Congress, probably realizing that the 3 cent piece was a misfit at best, preferred to leave it with a discordant legal tender value.

The mint officials made plans for an extensive issue of
the new coins. The mint was closed to visitors and the coinage of copper was suspended. By the middle of April the
Director was able to offer coins for sale. For the first few
weeks quarters only were sold. This procedure bears wit-
ness to the state of the currency. The quarter-dollar was
the coin best adapted to bridge the gap between the 3 cent
piece and the gold dollar.

The objective of the law, a plentiful supply of fractional
currency, was fully accomplished. In a little more than six
months the coinage was about $9,000,000, and all the coins
went into circulation and stayed there. About $8,000,000
more was coined in 1854. During most of 1853 the mint

was unable to meet the demand, but early in 1854 a Philadelphia paper reported that the mint had "fully overcome
the complaint among the small dealers of a want of change.[1]
More than $1,000,000 in silver coins, it said, was stored in
the vaults awaiting purchasers. The demand for gold dollars and 3 cent pieces declined rapidly. In 1854 the number
of gold dollars coined was 800,000, whereas it had been
4,400,000 in 1853. The output of 3 cent pieces was only
3 per cent of the coinage of 1853. The new coins served
their purpose excellently. They were a life-giving force in
retail trade. For the first time since the beginning of the
nation the people had an adequate supply of fractional coins
of uniform quality and decimal denominations.

It was unfortunate that the success of this beneficent
economic measure should have been jeopardized from its
inception, but there were inherent dangers in the act and
serious evils in its administration. The law had reduced the
fine silver content of the coins from 371.25 to 345.6 grains,
with a gross weight of 384 grains per dollar. This reduction, amounting to 6.91 per cent, had been suggested by
Secretary Corwin at the urgent request of Director Snowden.
The weight of 384 grains is 4/5 of an ounce. The mint
usually bought its silver in ounce bars 9/10 fine. If the new
coins should weigh 384 grains, an ounce bar of standard
silver would produce exactly $1.25 in subsidiary pieces.
Snowden recommended the weight of 384 grains solely on
the grounds that it would be a convenient figure in mint calculations. No attention was given to the vitally important
considerations of silver values, the probable future ratio,
and the profit on coinage. At the time the bill was passed
the value of the silver in two half-dollars was about $1.04,
and a reduction of less than 7 per cent made the new coins

[1] See Daily Pennsylvanian for May 30 and June 6, 1853, and Hunt's Merchants Magazine, Vol. 30, 224, 610.

worth about 97 cents, with a scant 3 cents as a margin against disappearance.

The Senate committee had accepted Corwin's recommendation unwillingly. It will be recalled that their original bill made the reduction more than 7 per cent. In the year elapsing before they brought in their revised bill the value of silver had declined slightly. They were determined to have the reduction the very smallest that would make the new coins fiduciary. They could not visualize a coinage whose value depended on limitation of supply instead of bullion value, and they had a profound distrust of "debased coins" and a dread of "depreciation from debasement." They presented an involved calculation of bullion values and coinage costs, bringing in an imaginary factor which they called "the additional value given it by its character as a coin here," and arrived at the conclusion that a 5 per cent reduction would be sufficient to prevent exportation. Further than this they did not wish to go. They accepted the 6.91 per cent reduction as a Treasury recommendation, but took pains to place responsibility for "the greater debasement" on Secretary Corwin.

As a matter of fact the 6.91 per cent reduction was far too small, exposing the entire coinage to a continuous hazard of failure. If the committee's 5 per cent reduction had been adopted, the system would have broken down within two years and all the new coins would have disappeared. As a matter of history the system did not collapse as a result of the rising value of silver in terms of gold. The reduction of 6.91 per cent was sufficient, but the coinage was balanced perilously on the edge of disappearance from its first date of issue until the Civil War. In November of 1856 an ounce of standard silver sold for $1.24 in gold. A rise of 1 cent beyond this would have made four quarter-dollars the equivalent of $1 in gold. Throughout a considerable part of the year 1859 the value of a dollar in subsidiary coins hovered around 99 cents, sometimes going a half-cent above.[2]

This insistence of officials and legislators on a bullion value approximately equal to coinage value is one of the curious facts of our currency history. There is not in any one of the dozens of official documents of the time any hint of a perception of the elementary principle that the bullion value of fiduciary coins is almost a matter of indifference. In his annual report for 1853 Director Snowden said that the bullion value of the new coins was so high that a reduction would probably be necessary "at no distant day," but he did not question the wisdom of the original weight provision. On the contrary, he said that it was the duty of the government to reduce the coinage weights as often as the rising value of silver overtook the value of gold.

While the English system was now nearly forty years old, it was but little understood. No other nation had undertaken to establish a fiduciary silver coinage. None the less it is not sufficient to say that unfamiliarity with the practical operation of subsidiary coinage explains the attitude of the Treasury and Congress. The framers of the law were positively opposed to the principle. There was an almost universal belief that a coin legally rated at a value above its bullion value was a debased coin of doubtful honesty. In one statement after another the Senate committee's report made it clear that the members were doubtful of the integrity of the proposed coins and regarded their issue as a violation of sound coinage principles, justified only as a temporary measure to meet a serious emergency. They actually feared that the coins would be issued to excess and depreciate, despite the fact that their issue only for gold coin would narrowly limit the quantity in circulation. The one condition that justified their fear, the absence of a redemption pro-

[2] See Laughlin, Bimetallism, 258; also Appendix F.

vision, they did not appreciate. Such a provision would have made an excess impossible. Even the proposal to make the coins receivable for government dues was rejected. In all the reports, bills, and discussions of fiduciary coinage from 1790 to the Civil War there was not a suggestion of the desirability of redemption to prevent excess issues and to relieve the holders of worn-out coins from unmerited loss.

Besides this general misunderstanding of the nature of fiduciary coins there was also a widespread belief that subsidiary coins were exposed to a peculiar danger. It was thought that coins whose cost of production was materially less than their legal value as money would be manufactured and put into circulation by private coiners for the sake of the same seigniorage profit the government made. The theory was that these private pieces, exact duplicates of the mint's own product, could not be distinguished from legal coins. Nor could their producers be brought to book. In the minds of many this danger of private duplications was a conclusive argument against fiduciary silver coin. Ex-Secretary Ingham recommended that the reduction in weight be the very least percentage possible, since any material difference between bullion and coin values would bring forth a flood of private duplicates.

The idea that a seignorage on silver coins is a stimulus to private coinage rests on the two assumptions that it is impossible to distinguish the private coins and apprehend the makers and that production for the sake of the seigniorage will be profitable, despite the difficulties of small-scale production carried on in hidden places. As applied to our own time these two assumptions are wholly untenable. And yet we find modern economists of high standing obsessed with this notion of private duplications.[3] There was little danger

<hr />

[3] See, for example, Seager's Principles of Economics, 337, in which there is a warning against too great a reduction in bullion value, in the face of the

of duplications in 1853, although it was undoubtedly a more serious problem then than now. The law of 1806, the only anti-counterfeiting measure before 1853, did not prohibit private coinage of any kind, and thousands of gold coins were made by individuals in Georgia and California between 1830 and 1860. Some of these pieces were duplicates of United States coins. Director Snowden in his 1860 report referred with great indignation to the coinage of underweight $5 gold pieces by a Denver firm. The currency at all times included a large proportion of spurious coins, not duplications but counterfeits. Crude tin and zinc counterfeits of silver were common, while the counterfeiting of gold coins had developed into an art.[4] The prevalence of counterfeits however, was not an indication of the danger of private duplications of genuine coins. In fact there would be less likelihood of duplicates when cheap metal counterfeits could be easily circulated.

The reduction of only 6.91 per cent in the silver coin weights was a fundamental error. If the coins had been made redeemable, or even receivable for taxes, a reduction of 20 or 25 per cent would have been desirable. In the absence of such a provision it might have been well to limit the reduction to 15 per cent. Such a reduction would have eliminated the danger of disappearance. The seigniorage profit would have been, in the next ten years, from 10 to 12

---

fact that the bullion value of a dollar in our subsidiary coins was less than 50 cents in every year from 1896 to 1916 without the appearance of duplicates of private manufacture. This baseless fear arises from a confusion of imitations, or counterfeits, with duplications, which are not counterfeits but illegally made genuine coins.

[4] Counterfeiting was a major currency evil in the years before the Civil War, counterfeits constituting from 1 to 2 per cent of the coins in circulation. For an interesting discussion of the conditions see the Annual Report on the Finances for 1861.

per cent. This margin would not have encouraged duplicates. The 3 cent pieces had been giving a seigniorage profit of about 12 per cent, but no duplicates were reported, while counterfeits of various cheap metals were widely circulated. By good fortune the new silver coins escaped until the Civil War the danger created by the unwise reduction. At that time, as will be related in a later chapter, a disaster resulted from the high bullion value of the coins.

The absence of a redemption provision was another defect in the new coinage. There was no redemption clause and no clause providing that the government should receive the coins in payment of taxes. It was not clear from the wording of the law that the legal tender provision applied to debts to the government. In a later period the Treasury ruled that the legal tender law applied only to private debts. It was only a matter of time until the coins would become worn and the last holders would suffer loss. There was little likelihood that the impossibility of redemption would cause disturbance until the coins were badly worn. There was a crying need for small change and the country could absorb many millions. Under normal conditions there could be no oversupply for many years. The provision for their issue only in exchange for gold coin automatically adjusted the supply to the needs of business, and a redundancy could develop only through improper administration of the law.

This very thing the Treasury was guilty of from the first day of operation. The law explicitly directed that free coinage of the smaller silver coins be stopped, that the new coins be made from silver bullion bought by the mint officials, and that the coins be sold to the public only for gold coins. There was no ambiguity in the law. The provisions were specific, detailed, and emphatic. The procedure outlined was simple, and no departure from it was possible under the law. Instead of following this simple procedure Director Snowden adopted a policy so peculiar that it defies explanation.[5] On March 31 Snowden advertised that he would buy all silver bullion presented, the price being fixed at $1.21 per standard ounce. The bullion would be paid for "in gold coins or in silver coin of new emission, at the option of the seller." He declared further that in the issue of the new coins preference would be given to those who offered silver bullion. Inasmuch as the law prohibited the issue of the new coins except in exchange for gold coins and provided for the purchase of bullion with gold from the bullion fund, his procedure was a violation of the statute. The Director, anxious to attract silver bullion to the mint, apparently decided that an offer of the much wanted subsidiary coins would stimulate the supply of bullion. His action was illegal and unnecessary, but not of such character as to cause serious trouble.

In August the practice was modified. The Director, unable at first to coin the bullion as fast as it was presented, adopted the practice of paying bullion owners either with gold coins or with Treasury drafts payable in silver coins after the bullion was minted. On August 15 a new method of payment was instituted. All bullion owners were paid immediately in gold coins, but they received a bill of sale which authorized them to return after the bullion was coined and receive silver coins for gold to an amount equal to three-quarters of the value of the bullion originally sold. It is possible to suggest a motive for this singular arrangement. Snowden was still under the impression that the best method of attracting bullion was to offer subsidiary coins. But mercantile interests in great need of small change were clamor-

[5] The story of this practice of the mint, hardly mentioned by currency historians, must be pieced out from scattered references in Hunt's Merchants Magazine, Vols. 28, 29, and 30; Bankers Magazine, Vols. 6, 7, and 8; Senate Executive Documents, no. 62, 33rd Cong., 2nd sess., and no. 1, 35th Cong. 1st sess.; and the annual reports on the Finances from 1853 to 1873.

ing for silver coins in exchange for gold. By paying bullion
owners with gold in the first instance and then giving them
the privilege of exchanging the gold for silver coins, Snowden was exchanging coins for bullion and at the same time
nominally obeying the provisions of the law as to the purchase of bullion and the issue of silver coins. The limitation
to three-quarters was doubtless a result of the pressure of
business men to obtain silver by the legal method of direct
purchase for gold coin.

Before the end of 1853 the mint was able to offer subsidiary coins to all who asked for them. The purchases of
bullion were so large that bullion owners were no longer
pressing for payment in silver, and the one-quarter proportion reserved for the general public was ample to meet all
demands. At this point the last excuse for the irregular
procedure was gone, and adherence to the law was a self-
evident necessity. Instead of adopting this policy Snowden
dropped all pretense of obeying the law. He publicly announced that he would buy all silver bullion offered, payment
to be in gold coin or silver coin at the option of the seller.

At first glance it is difficult to see how this clumsy, roundabout operation differed from the legal procedure. The
essential difference lies in the offer to buy all silver bullion
offered. Purchases were made without reference to the
needs for silver coins. The situation was made worse by
the setting of a fixed price for bullion. Silver fluctuated in
value and at times the Director's fixed price was much above
the market rate. At such times all the metal in the market
went to the mint. The bullion was converted into subsidiary
coins as fast as it was received. Even then there would have
been no public injury if the coins had remained in the vaults.
There would have been an irregular and unnecessary coinage
of silver, but no other serious consequences. But the bullion
fund was not adequate to stand the strain of indefinite out-

lay for bullion. The excess coinage had to be put in circulation. While the bullion owner was nominally permitted to sell his silver for gold, the mint offered him subsidiary coins, and it is clear from the records that pressure was brought by the mint to force this form of payment.

The price of silver rose sharply in 1854. Snowden raised his fixed price to $1.22½ per ounce and maintained it at this level after the market value had fallen. The purchases of bullion and the coinage of subsidiary pieces became extraordinarily large. When the accumulation of coins became inconvenient Snowden took the final step in this chapter of errors. He gave notice, in July, that he would continue to buy all bullion offered, at a price of $1.21½ per ounce, but that he would pay for it only with subsidiary coin. This virtually established free coinage of silver, with a ratio, so far as bullion owners were concerned, approximately that of the market ratio of silver to gold. Whenever the fixed price offered by the Director was higher than the current market value the volume of silver coinage was limited only by the amount of bullion in the market. An oversupply of subsidiary coins was inevitable. Inasmuch as there was no provision for redemption, no opportunity to force the coins on the government in tax payments, and no possibility of exporting them, redundancy was inevitable and incurable.

No explanation of Snowden's practice was ever made. It was not questioned in any official document until 1870. Knox, an experienced official, with the records of the Treasury for twenty years before him, was unable to give any adequate explanation. It is evident that the first steps were taken in an effort to attract silver bullion. The acute shortage of small change explains the initial moves, although it does not justify them. The only plausible interpretation of the continuance of the practice is to be found in the general misunderstanding of subsidiary coinage. It has already been pointed out that the committee which framed the law and the Congress which passed it failed to understand its nature. Director Snowden apparently thought of subsidiary coinage as a new form of free coinage of silver. Starting with this misconception, he finally arrived at a policy which actually achieved the free coinage of silver. The most striking feature of the matter was the failure of six secretaries of the Treasury and two Directors of the Mint who succeeded Guthrie and Snowden to question the procedure, although it was the most arbitrary and unintelligent practice in the history of the mint.[6] The most casual reading of the law of 1853 by any of these officials would have disclosed the illegal character of the procedure.

The inevitable redundancy came quickly. Within a month after Snowden's announcement of July, 1854, it was evident that there were too many new silver pieces in circulation. When the accumulated coins became a problem Snowden stimulated their issue by shipping large amounts to the various Treasury offices for distribution in government operations. He offered them in exchange for Spanish fractions, paid them out for silver bullion, and sold the remainder for gold coins to the general public. The Treasury was buying all silver bullion presented and issuing the resulting coinage through every possible channel, without regard for the law or for the public need for change. In the cities silver coins became a nuisance. Retail stores refused silver except in small payments, and banks even declined to accept deposits in silver coins. Creditors refused payments above the $5 amount required by law.[7] The situation was so serious that

[6] Snowden himself was the first individual to point out the impropriety of the practice, explaining it to Knox in 1869, years after he had retired as Director. See Chapter XVI.

[7] See Hunt's Merchants Magazine, Vol. 43, 75; Senate Miscellaneous Document no. 132, 41st Cong., 2nd sess.; Phila. Public Ledger for March 19, 1863; Annual Report on the Finances for 1861, 63.

Secretary Guthrie temporarily suspended the coinage of half-dollars and quarters. He did not look into the mint practice that was responsible.

In his annual report for 1855 Snowden said that there was an oversupply of silver "in several of the Atlantic cities." He asked Congress to raise the legal tender of subsidiary silver to $50 or $100. He also asked that Congress outlaw bank-notes of a denomination less than $10. In two subsequent reports he emphatically urged these measures. His successor, Pollock, was as late as 1861 urging Congress to raise the legal tender limit on subsidiary silver to $100, saying that the $5 limitation "unnecessarily discredits the currency and is productive of much inconvenience." In 1858 a bill to raise the legal tender limit to $25 would have passed Congress had not Secretary Corwin, Snowden's superior, asked that the measure be killed.[8] This effort of Snowden to make a place for the excess silver coins showed his complete failure to understand his own practice. Increasing the legal tender of subsidiary coins to $100 would have made intolerable a situation already bad.

The redundancy prevailed from 1854 to the Civil War. In January, 1862, the New York Herald commented that "for two or three years the supply of silver currency has been in excess of the wants of trade." Business houses that received large amounts were obliged to sell their surplus coins to brokers at a discount. There was never a time, however, when all the coins in circulation sold at a fixed rate of discount. The greatest excess, naturally, was in the cities. The legal tender quality made it possible to pass them on, and they could be sent back to the Treasury in some degree through the post offices. But they were a source of widespread annoyance in banking operations and retail trade.

---

[8] Annual Report on the Finances for 1858, 66; Senate Bills and Resolutions, 35th Cong., 1st sess., no. 44.

The redundancy was intensified by the panic of 1857, which reduced the general volume of trade. It is a curious fact that the coins could not go to a large discount, regardless of the volume issued. It has already been pointed out that the very small difference between their bullion values and their currency values kept the new coins close to the melting point from 1853 to 1862. If the excessive issues in this period had caused a high rate of discount, the currency value would have dropped below the bullion value and the coins would have been melted in sufficient numbers to reduce the excess and lower the discount.

With the wide distribution of the new silver coins the need for one dollar gold pieces was practically eliminated. The extraordinary number that the silver shortage had called into circulation before 1853 became excessive after the appearance of the subsidiary quarters and half-dollars. Its small size made the coin unsatisfactory for large transactions as well as small. In his annual report for 1859 Snowden explained, incorrectly, that the coin was very unpopular because of the competition of $1 and $5 bank notes. The devices on the coin had been changed in 1853 in order to make the piece wider, and Snowden asked Congress to authorize the recoinage of all the "old thick pieces" into larger denominations. Eventually the unpopularity of the coins caused millions of them to pile up in the sub-Treasuries. Snowden thereupon took the law into his own hands and recoined all the thick pieces.[9] This action eliminated some $8,000,000 in one dollar pieces, increasing the circulation field of the silver coins and thereby reducing the oversupply of fractional silver.

Despite its defects the law of 1853 was a beneficial measure. Despite its mal-administration it solved the problem of fractional coinage in the United States. After the country

[9] Annual Report on the Finances for 1860, 52.

had endured a wretched currency for sixty years fiduciary coinage had been forced upon a reluctant Congress as the last expedient in an emergency. Although the United States was nearly forty years behind England in establishing subsidiary coinage, it was none the less the second nation to adopt it. In light of the fact that the English law of 1816 actually created a bimetallic system with a fiduciary silver coinage grafted on and became a genuine subsidiary coinage measure only through extra-legal treasury policy which was not confirmed until 1870, it is proper to say that the United States was the first nation to pass a subsidiary coinage law. The 3 cent law of 1851 and the general law of 1853 were the first of their kind. Switzerland followed in 1860, France in 1864, and many others later, all driven to it by the same conditions that forced it on the United States in 1853. The high ratio of 16 to 1 in this country exposed silver to the immediate influence of the flood of gold from California. The European ratio of 15½ to 1 was upset a few year later.

It has been shown that the subsidiary coinage law of 1853 did not establish the gold standard and was not intended to establish it. Notwithstanding this fact, the law demonstrated the possibility of maintaining an efficient silver currency without a double standard. It paved the way to the gold standard. In all the literature of money there is hardly a reference to this relation between fractional silver and the gold standard. It is assumed that the gold standard, with silver reduced to a subsidiary function, was adopted after careful consideration of its merits, when in fact it was the fortuitous result of the action of inexpert legislators desperately seeking a remedy for an acute shortage in small change. This was the case in England and in the United States. So confused were the legislative bodies and the administrators that in England the law of 1816 creating subsidiary coinage was a double standard measure which was converted into a gold standard practice by unauthorized action of the Treasury, while in the United States the law of 1853 was a genuine subsidiary coinage measure which was by illegal action of the Mint Director administered as if the subsidiary pieces had free coinage.   A few years later the disappearance of fractional silver coins in Europe brought about the formation of a gold standard Latin Monetary Union.   The substitution of the gold standard for the double standard throughout the world was primarily due to the impelling need for a stable and convenient small change currency.

CHAPTER XI

THE LAW OF 1857

With the appearance of the subsidiary coins in 1853 foreign silver coins ceased to circulate in the cities. The Treasury recoined all its foreign silver receipts, and the mint exchanged the new subsidiary coins for all Spanish and Mexican silver pieces presented. In 1857 Snowden estimated the total silver coin in the country at $25,000,000, of which $20,000,000 was in subsidiary coins, $2,000,000 in "old silver," and $3,000,000 in Spanish and Mexican fractions.[1] The old silver was that part of the standard silver coinage before 1853 that had because of its worn condition escaped melting or exportation.

In its exchange of subsidiary coins for Spanish fractions the mint did not adjust its payment to the bullion value of the foreign coins. Fixed prices of 23½ cents, 10%10 cents, and 5⅕ cents were paid for double-reals, reals, and medios. These values were somewhat higher than the regular ratings of 23, 10, and 5 cents allowed in payments to the government. The higher rates at the mint were evidently designed to hasten the withdrawal of the foreign coins. Inasmuch as the payment of subsidiary coins for foreign silver was en-

[1] House Executive Document no. 42, 34th Cong., 3rd session.

tirely without authority of law, the Director could arbitrarily set whatever rates seemed best adapted to his purpose, and this purpose was to eliminate Spanish coins.

Long after the foreign coins ceased to circulate in the cities they continued to be used in the sparsely settled regions, in some sections at the old valuations of 25, 12, and 6 cents. The benefits of the coinage law of 1853 could not be completely realized until every foreign coin was driven out. There had been no reform of the copper coinage. The two pieces were still unpopular, unattractive, expensive to produce, and uncertain in legal status, as they had been for sixty years. After the redundancy of subsidiary coins developed in 1853 there was an excess of copper coins in the cities. Outside the cities cents and half-cents hardly circulated at all. The cost of making and distributing the copper coins had risen, and Snowden reported that they "barely paid expenses."

In 1856 Senator Hunter's committee introduced a bill which was intended to improve the copper coinage and eliminate Spanish silver. The provisions of the bill, which was evidently drafted by Director Snowden, are interesting. The authority of the President to change the weight of the copper coins, granted in 1795, was enlarged to include the power to change the materials. Since the President would necessarily be guided by the Director of the Mint in exercising such authority, this provision was intended to put into the hands of the Director the control of the weight and materials of the minor coins. Other provisions abolished the half-cent and gave the cent a legal tender power to 10 cents. It was further provided that the mint might exchange copper cents, of the new type to be created by the President, for Spanish double-reals, reals, and medios at the fixed rates of 25, 12½, and 6¼ cents, although these pieces should be legal tender, for two years, at rates of only 20, 10, and 5 cents. The high rates offered were expected to cause a rapid flow of foreign silver to the mint, while the losses on the bullion value of the coins would be offset by the seigniorage profit on the new copper cents.

A House committee presented a rival bill, in which it was proposed to abolish the half-cent and to create a new cent piece of 96 grains, of which not more than 5 per cent could be in "some metal other than copper." [2] The committee evidently wished to restrict the Director's authority to determine the composition of minor coins. The new copper pieces could be exchanged for Spanish fractions, but only at the ratings of 20, 10, and 5 cents. This bill was ungenerous in spirit. Inasmuch as the seigniorage on the new copper cents would be large, the government could well afford to offer better rates for coins that had in many parts of the country been circulating for sixty years at valuations of 25, 12½, and 6¼ cents.

A conference finally evolved a measure that was satisfactory to both houses. It became the law of February 21, 1857. The half-cent was abolished. Neither the Senate provision giving the President power to determine the materials of the cent piece nor the House provision permitting the mint to use a limited amount of "some metal other than copper" appeared in the measure. The materials of the new piece were definitely specified in the law. The cent was to weigh 72 grains, 88 per cent in copper, 12 per cent in nickel. The new coins were to be issued to the general public in exchange for gold coins, silver coins, or the current pure copper coins. And they were to be given in exchange for Spanish or Mexican double-reals, reals, and medios at the ratings of 25, 12½, and 6¼ cents, regardless of the state of wear of the foreign silver. This offer was to hold

[2] For the two bills see Senate Bills and Resolutions, 34th Cong., 1st sess., no. 190, and 3rd sess., no. 190.

good for two years only. No foreign coins of any kind should be legal tender, and foreign fractions should be received in payments at all government offices only at the ratings of 20, 10, and 5 cents. There was no reference in the law to the legal tender status of the new copper pieces.

This law of 1857 has an important place in our currency annals. In refusing to accept Snowden's proposal to extend the President's powers Congress clearly indicated its intention to prevent the control of currency from shifting to the executive branch. The old law of 1795 giving the President authority to change the weight of the copper coins was not repealed. In fact it never was repealed. But the law of 1857 was evidently intended to deny the authority.

A more important feature of the law was its authorization of a coin of nickel alloy. It marked the beginning of a political struggle over nickel coinage that was not finally settled until 1873. Nickel was an unfamiliar coinage material at this time. Joseph Wharton declared in one of his monographs on nickel coinage that some pattern pieces of nickel alloy had been presented to the government in 1837. He said further that by virtue of the law of 1857 the United States was the first nation to adopt nickel as a material of coinage. This latter statement is erroneous. In 1850 Switzerland adopted "billon" coins containing a mixture of copper, zinc, silver, and nickel.[3]

---

[3] The rise of nickel as an industrial and coinage material is one of the romances of modern economic history. For more than 2,000 years the Chinese have been making a copper-nickel alloy called in modern times "white copper." There are in the British Museum "white copper" coins which were made in Bactria more than 200 years before the time of Christ. European workers in metals were unable to overcome the peculiarly stubborn qualities of nickel until the 19th century. Less than 100 years ago European metallurgists developed the 75–25 copper-nickel alloy which has been adopted for coinage all over the world. The Bactrian coins had almost identically the same composition. See Barton, Nickel Coinage; also Wharton, Small Money and Project for Reorganizing the Small Coinage.

The new coin was much more attractive than the bulky 168 grain copper piece. The mint officials had chosen 72 grains, which is 3/20 of an ounce, as a convenient weight. The alloy proportions of 88 per cent copper and 12 per cent nickel were decided upon, after experiment, as desirable from the standpoint of cost, appearance, wearing qualities, and "coinability." This latter quality was at that time a matter of vital importance. The extraordinary hardness and intractability of pure nickel and of alloys with high nickel percentages presented serious problems in coinage. In his report for 1863 Director Pollock, who was bitterly opposed to nickel as a coinage material, said that the adoption of the composition in 1857 was due to the erroneous belief that it was necessary to add a more precious metal if the copper content of the cent piece was to be materially reduced. In other words, Pollock thought that nickel was introduced in an attempt to make a new type of "billon" coins. It is probably true that the desire to maintain a high bullion value in the reduced coin was one of the factors in the choice of a nickel alloy. The Swiss coins of 1850 were avowedly adopted as billon coins. Pollock was the first official in the history of this country to recognize the truth that the bullion value of fiduciary coin is of no practical consequence.

But Snowden was undoubtedly moved by practical considerations as well. The mint officials had long recognized the unpleasant physical properties of the current copper coins. The nickel alloy adopted was much superior to pure copper. The color, which was a light yellow, was new in coinage. The alloy would not tarnish easily, it was very durable, and it could be imitated only with great difficulty. It is probable that Snowden was also inclined to encourage a new mining industry in his home state of Pennsylvania. Nickel had been discovered in the ores of a copper mine at Lancaster Gap, and an effort was being made to develop nickel commercially.[4]

From the currency standpoint the most important feature of the law was the provision for exchanging the new copper-nickel cents for the current Spanish fractions. The high valuations offered to those who would accept cent pieces were designed to bring all the foreign coins to the mint, and this was a highly commendable objective. The limitation of the offer to a period of two years would hasten the process. The least sophisticated classes were still accepting the coins at the old ratings, and it was a matter of fair dealing to recall the coins without forcing these classes to accept the valuations of 20, 10, and 5 cents.

But the procedure adopted under the law was of doubtful wisdom. The high ratings were to be given only when the cent pieces were accepted in payment. The provision had two objectives, to introduce the new copper coins in the face of popular prejudice and to offset the loss on the bullion value of the worn Spanish fractions with the seigniorage profit on the copper coins. The seigniorage return on subsidiary silver, hardly more than 1 per cent, was so small that exchanging them for the Spanish coins would involve a loss as great as 15 or 20 per cent. Payment with copper coins was the only alternative to a large deficit in mint operations. Snowden's estimate of the Spanish fractions still in circulation was $3,000,000. This estimate was undoubtedly too low, and supplies were still coming across the border. The changes in market values accruing from the California

---

[4] Snowden had been Treasurer of the state of Pennsylvania. He was throughout his official career interested in promoting nickel coinage. He had drafted the rejected bill which virtually put in his own hands the power to alter the materials of the minor coins as well as the bill which, as the law of 1857, created nickel coinage. Apparently he was a man of great force of character, ignorant of monetary principles and but little hampered by any regard for laws that did not accord with his views.

gold discoveries had stopped the importation of full-weight
Mexican coins, but badly worn pieces still came in. Snowden's law of 1857 proposed to issue copper cents to the
value of $3,000,000 or more, an amount far beyond the
maximum the country could absorb. And these 300,000,000
copper coins were to go into a circulation that already contained a burdensome excess of small silver coins, especially
in the 3 and 5 cent denominations.

The impracticability of the measure should have been
obvious. It is a question whether it was not wrong in principle. Forcing an unpopular currency on the public in order
to save a few dollars was false economy. The copper coins
should have been left to make their way on their merits.
The subsidiary silver coins should have been reduced in
silver content to the point where they could be exchanged
for the foreign silver without loss, and issue of subsidiary
silver should have been temporarily suspended, except in exchange for the Spanish coins, until the foreign pieces were
eliminated and the redundancy of small change relieved.
The unwise copper coin exchange provision of the law of
1857 was one more consequence of the error in the silver
weights of the subsidiary coins of 1853.

One other feature of the law is worth attention. There
was no provision regarding legal tender for the new cent
piece. The Senate bill had made the coin legal tender in
payments to 10 cents. The House bill contained no legal
tender clause, and the conference bill finally passed eliminated the Senate's provision. After more than sixty years
of agitation for the settlement of this minor matter Congress refused to determine the status of the copper cent,
although it was passing a measure providing for the issue
of 300,000,000 pieces. In his 1859 report Snowden offered
an explanation of the attitude of Congress. He suggested
that Congress construed the Constitutional provision pro-

hibiting a state from making anything except gold and silver a legal tender as an implication that base metals are unfit to have a legal tender quality. The explanation is unsatisfactory. The real reason lay in the failure of Congress to understand fiduciary money. They could not bring themselves to see that a coin could have a value independent of its metallic value, and they regarded copper coins not as money but as token substitutes.

As a measure for withdrawing the Spanish coins the law of 1857 was a success. The foreign silver pieces flowed into the mint in a steady stream. It is related that when the mint in Philadelphia began distribution of the copper-nickel cents people stood in line with bags and boxes of worn Spanish coins, while brokers met those leaving the building and offered small premiums for the first issues of the new coins.[5] There was a decided advantage in exchanging foreign coins for cent pieces, but it seems probable that the benefits of the measure accrued to banks and bullion dealers rather than the general public. The banks could accept the coins for deposit at the established valuations of 20, 10, and 5 cents and exchange them for cents at a profit of 25 per cent. Brokers could make a profit by purchasing the coins at a slight premium over the government and bank ratings. That the dealers actively competed with the banks is evident from the number of advertisements of Wall Street brokers that appeared in the New York papers, with offers as high as 23 cents for double-reals and 11 cents for reals. Individuals could take advantage of the government's offer only if they were near the mint or a sub-Treasury office.

In the last half of 1857 nearly 18,000,000 copper-nickel cents were issued, as contrasted with 3,000,000 copper cents in 1856, and in 1858 the issue was 24,000,000 pieces. Early in 1859 the two year limit on the exchange provision expired.

[5] See Bankers Magazine, Vol. 8, 341.

In the period of its operation great numbers of Spanish coins had been withdrawn, but at least half of them were still outstanding. Inasmuch as their legal tender quality had been revoked, they would gradually disappear through sales to banks and government as mere bullion. Snowden was anxious to eliminate them more rapidly, even if it required the issue of a large excess of irredeemable copper coins. At his instance there was tacked onto the general appropriation bill of 1859 a short clause renewing for two more years the exchange of cents for Spanish silver coins. The bill was passed on March 3, 1859, without any discussion of this provision.[6]

In the year following the passage of the renewal clause nearly 40,000,000 copper nickel cents were issued. Long before the year was up the cent pieces had become a public annoyance and Snowden was obliged to have his renewal law repealed. Like the original measure, it was inserted in an omnibus measure and passed without comment. The date was June 25, 1860. From the passage of the law of 1857 to the repeal of the renewal clause in 1860 the issue of cents reached a total of 95,000,000. In the same period the mint had recoined almost $2,000,000 in Spanish fractions. Less than half the foreign coins had been exchanged for cent pieces. More than half the total had been bought as bullion at prices much below the exchange values, and many pieces had come in through the post offices.[7] This failure to take advantage of the high rates offered in cent pieces was due in part to the limited opportunities for exchange provided by the mint and scattered sub-Treasuries. It was simpler to take a loss in the purchase of stamps than to ship the

[6] This measure is not mentioned in any currency history. It does not appear in the Treasury Department's pamphlet copy of all the laws of coinage. See Appendix G.

[7] The figures on copper coin redemptions and new issues are given in the annual reports of the Director of the Mint for 1859, 1860, and 1861.

coins to the Treasury.   But the more important reason was
the redundancy of copper coins.   The banks accepted foreign fractions at the ratings of 20, 10, and 5 cents and could
sell them as bullion without loss.   They actually preferred,
apparently, to dispose of them in this manner and to forego
the large profit they would realize if they would burden
themselves with the copper coins they could obtain in exchange.

It was fortunate that less than half the holders of Spanish
coins presented them in exchange for cent pieces.   Cents
to the number of 200,000,000 would have been an intoler-
able nuisance.   The 95,000,000 issued was much beyond
the saturation point.   They were redundant from 1859 to
the middle of 1862.   Director Pollock said that it was "part
of the hourly finesse of buyers and sellers to get rid of
them."   Business establishments that received large numbers
actually suffered loss, as they were obliged to sell them to
brokers at discounts as high as 3 per cent.   In Philadelphia
the prevailing rates of discount were 4 to 5 per cent.[8]   This
condition of an actual discount on a metallic currency issued
in exchange for other metallic money is a rare phenomenon.
When it is realized that the coins were not forced upon
creditors by a legal tender provision, the case becomes unique.

The excess was most burdensome in the Eastern cities.
The South and West did not absorb any great number.   In
his annual report for 1860 Snowden frankly admitted that
there were far too many cent pieces in circulation, but did
not attribute the situation to the law of 1857 or the renewal
measure of 1859, both of which he had sponsored.   And
he avoided reference to the repeal of the renewal clause.
After the repeal Snowden issued the cent pieces only in exchange for the old copper cents.   He even went so far as

[8] Philadelphia Public Ledger for July 10, 1862, and Philadelphia North
American for July 3, 1862.

to refuse to sell them for gold coins, a policy which was clearly beneficial under the circumstances but also in violation of the law.

The law of 1857 was inherently unsound, and the renewal provision of 1859 was a blunder. And yet the measure made two material contributions to currency progress. One of these was the withdrawal of the Spanish coins. In 1859 the Philadelphia Board of Trade requested all storekeepers to discontinue price quotations in eighths and sixteenths of a dollar, since there were no longer any corresponding coins in circulation. In 1859 Snowden reported that Spanish fractions had ceased to circulate except in remote districts. He predicted correctly that in a short time the antiquated terminology and reckoning of the past two hundred years would be displaced. The British reckoning which Hamilton thought he could drive out in three years survived until the law of 1857. The decimal system became popular as well as official after that date. The terminology which had developed in colonial days was gradually given up. Only one term, "bit," has survived, although the inaccurate term "penny" is still occasionally heard and the word "shilling" is still understood in certain rural sections in the East.

A second result of the law of 1857 was a greatly enlarged sphere of usefulness for the cent piece. The very large issues forced the coins into channels in which they had not gone before. Their physical superiority to the old copper coins gradually won popular favor. The coin had the diameter of our present day cent, although it was considerably thicker, and a piece of these dimensions was a novelty to a people accustomed to the unwieldy copper coins of earlier days. The 1857 coin had an attractive design in the form of a flying eagle This was changed in 1859 to the Indian head device which has come down to our time. In

the South and West, where copper coins had never been received, the new cent made little progress, but in the Eastern
states the coin became a useful instrument of retail trade,
and this development was an economic benefit. The idea
of Jefferson and Hamilton that the currency of money of
small value benefits society is, within definite limits, sound
doctrine. The wide use of a one cent coin encourages competition in price quotations and leads producers to attempt
the manufacture of articles that can be marketed at a one
cent price. The refusal of the South and West to accept the
one cent piece was evidence of the fact that the Industrial
Revolution was not an accomplished fact in those regions.

In this period before the Civil War the silver dollar
occupied an anomalous position. Legally it was a standard
coin in a bimetallic system. But it was worth anywhere
from 2 cents to 5 cents more than a gold dollar, and it did
not appear in circulation. The coin remained as it had been
from the beginning, an unknown element in our currency
system. A small number were coined annually, but most of
them were exported at once to South America or the Orient.
The reports indicate that they were coined from bullion
brought from Mexico.[9] In the years from 1857 to 1863 the
mint directors, Snowden and Pollock, repeatedly urged Congress to drop it from the statutes or, failing this, to reduce
its weight and make it a subsidiary coin.

Two minor incidents revealed by the records illustrate
the uncertain status of the dollar. The San Francisco branch
mint was set up in 1854 without any machinery for coining
silver dollars. In 1859 local merchants presented bullion
for coinage into dollars for export. When Director Snowden refused the superintendent's request for dies, that official
insisted, saying that there was a great excess of subidiary
silver in California which might possibly be relieved by the

[9] Annual Report on the Finances for 1860, 69, 88.

coinage of silver dollars. Snowden yielded to this absurd suggestion.[10] The excess of subsidiary silver was due to the illegal method of issue, and coining dollars would not relieve it. Neither official realized that the silver dollar was a standard free coinage unit of the United States whose coinage was a fundamental obligation of the government. The other incident is equally illuminating. In his 1861 report Pollock commented that it was his practice to sell silver dollars in small lots "at the even price of 108 cents." This extraordinary statement meant that the Director was buying silver with the bullion fund, coining it into dollars, and selling the coins to collectors and others who wanted a dollar or so for souvenir or specimen purposes. The price he charged was about 4 cents above the bullion value. He was making silver dollars as subsidiary coins on his own responsibility.

The laws of 1853 and 1857 were belated measures that should have been instituted many years earlier. Both had serious defects that endangered the currency and brought wholly unnecessary complications. There were omissions in connection with legal tender and redemption that left the currency system incomplete. They were badly administered, in ways that violated the law. Despite these faults the country had developed after seventy years' experience an adequate currency for both large and small transactions. There was an ample supply of standard gold coins, a more than ample supply of silver subsidiary coins, and a satisfactory type of minor coin. Foreign coins had at last been driven out, and the country was for the first time in its history enjoying a reasonably efficient coinage of its own minting. This situation, finally achieved in 1860, was to endure just one year, after which the Civil War was to bring about conditions even worse than those that had existed at any time after 1792.

[10] Bankers Magazine, Vol. 8, 932.

CHAPTER XII

THE CIVIL WAR PERIOD: PRIVATE ISSUES OF FRACTIONAL PAPER MONEY

COIN HOLDINGS at the outbreak of war—Pollock's error in silver coin estimates—Fiat money régime—Disappearance points of metallic currencies—
Complete disappearance of silver—Proposed remedies—Chaos in retail
trade—Emergency currencies—Paper notes—City issues—Character of
paper notes—Volume of emergency currencies.

Hostilities between the Northern and Southern states
began in April, 1861. In his annual report for that year
Secretary Chase said that he accepted Director Pollock's
estimate of the amount of metallic money in the Union
states. Pollock had in October, 1861, estimated the total
amount of specie in the whole country at $275,000,000 to
$300,000,000, of which all but $20,000,000 in gold was in
the North. A year later, in his 1862 report, Secretary
Chase said that the total amount of "coin" in the North in
1861 was not less than $210,000,000.

At first glance this statement appears to conflict with
Pollock's estimate. As a matter of fact it is merely a con-
firmation of the earlier estimate. In his 1862 report Pollock estimated that the Northern states held $45,000,000 in
subsidiary silver in 1861. When in his 1861 report he said
that the country had not less than $275,000,000 in "specie"
he was undoubtedly including this $45,000,000 in subsidiary
silver. By subtracting from the total of $275,000,000 the
country's $45,000,000 in silver coin and the $20,000,000 in
gold which Pollock thought was held in the South Chase

arrived at the figure $210,000,000 for the total gold hold-
ings in the North.[1]   When he used the term "coin" Chase
referred to gold, which was the basis of all his financial operations.   There is thus no discrepancy between the estimates
of Chase and Pollock.   In fact Chase had no figures except
those furnished by Pollock.

There was, however, a major error in Pollock's figures
on the silver outstanding.   He overlooked the fact that a
large part of this subsidiary coin was held by the Southern
states.   One contemporary estimate places the amount in
the South at $18,000,000.[2]   Possibly the total reached $20,-
000,000.   Pollock's estimate of $45,000,000 as the amount
in the whole country is probably accurate.   The total coinage of subsidiary silver from the law of 1851 to the end
of 1861 was about $48,000,000, this figure including the
3 cent pieces coined before the law of 1853.   Under ordinary conditions this entire volume should have been in circulation in 1861.   The coins were new, and none had been
worn below the circulation point.   None had been redeemed
by the government.   Their bullion value had been perilously
close to the melting point throughout their history, but none
had been melted.   Only a few had been lost.   But an unusual
situation had caused their exportation.   Canada had adopted
the decimal system in 1858, with a dollar unit like that of
the United States.   The British government had forwarded
only a small quantity of the decimal coins, and United States
fractional silver had come into wide use.[3]   In the West Indies
and other Latin-American areas United States silver coins
were in common use.   There had been for some years before

---

[1] See Annual Report on the Finances for 1861, 25, and for 1862, 13; Annual
Report of the Director of the Mint for 1861, 8, and for 1862, 9.

[2] Hunt's Merchants Magazine, Vol. 47, 155.

[3] McLachlan, 65; Annual Report on the Finances for 1859.   Details of
Canadian currency history not otherwise available have been given the writer
by officials of the Royal Mint of Canada.

the Civil War a steady exportation of subsidiary silver to Canada and to Latin-America. If the losses from this source were as great as $3,000,000, as they may have been, $45,-000,000 may be accepted as a fair estimate of the silver circulation of the country. If $18,000,000 of this total was in the South, the North's silver holdings were approximately $27,000,000.

The number of copper coins in circulation was more than 100,000,000, with a value greater than $1,000,000. They consisted chiefly of the copper-nickel cents of 1857. A small number of the old copper cents and half-cents were also in circulation. Only a small proportion of these coins were in the South, where payments in copper coins were still unfashionable. It appears, therefore, that the Union states held about $210,000,000 in gold coin, about $27,000,000 in subsidiary silver, and nearly $1,000,000 in copper coins. While these figures are merely estimates they are probably approximately accurate. Pollock's careless error in his estimate of the subsidiary silver in the North caused the Treasury to make mistakes in its fractional currency administration.[4]

Approximately $200,000,000 in state bank-notes were in circulation in the North at the beginning of the war, and in the later months of 1861 more than $30,000,000 in Treasury demand-notes were current. Before the end of the year the Treasury's efforts to finance the war by loans had failed and at the beginning of 1862 gold payments were suspended, except on the Pacific Coast, in private and government transactions. Silver and copper coins remained in circulation.

[4] Pollock's mistake and the apparent difference in the statements of total coin by Pollock and Chase have led no less an authority than Professor Wesley C. Mitchell to make rather questionable estimates of the monetary resources of the North. His figures, the accepted estimates, are apparently too high for the gold holdings by $35,000,000 and for the silver coins by about $15,000,000. See Mitchell, History of the Greenbacks, 178–180.

The country shifted to a paper money régime with little confusion. State bank-notes and Treasury demand notes went to a discount in terms of gold. The subsidiary and minor coins were fiduciary money, circulating at values above their values as metal. They did not disappear, but remained in circulation as fractional parts of a dollar in bank-notes or demand-notes. But the silver and copper coins had a bullion value, which the paper money did not possess. If the paper money continued to depreciate, dragging the subsidiary and minor coins with it, the fractional coins would eventually be worth less as money than their bullion value as raw metal. The holders of fractional silver could melt the coins and exchange the bullion for more in paper money than the fractional coins were worth as currency.

The point at which the silver coins would disappear was a matter of the weight of the coins. The average ratio of silver to gold for the year 1862 was 15.35 to 1, and the monthly averages were close to this figure.[5] At this ratio the 345.6 grains of silver in a dollar in subsidiary coins were worth almost exactly 97 cents in gold. When the value of a paper dollar should fall below 97 cents, a dollar in silver coins would be worth as currency less than 97 cents in gold, and holders of the silver coins could make a profit by exchanging two half-dollars for 97 cents in gold and selling the gold for more than a dollar in paper. The disappearance point of the 3 cent pieces of 1851 was much lower. A dollar in these small coins contained 309⅜ grains of silver, and they would remain in circulation until paper money fell below 87 cents in gold. The disappearance point of the copper-nickel cents will be discussed in a later chapter.

In practice, of course, the expenses of collection and melting were a factor, and brokers collecting coins for export required an additional margin to cover the risks of a change

<hr>

[5] See Laughlin, Bimetallism, 258.

in the value of silver. But exportation is only one of the phenomena of disappearance under the conditions of 1862. One of the early developments is hoarding, not only by speculators but also by business concerns that anticipate a scarcity which will embarrass their operations. There are indications that hoarding began early in 1862.

In the second week in January, 1862, months before greenbacks were issued, $100 in bank-notes or demand-notes were worth less than $97 in gold. On the 10th the rate was $95.24, and on that day the New York Herald reported that brokers were offering a premium of 1 per cent in paper for subsidiary coins. The depreciation of the paper money was not great enough to cause a general disappearance of the silver coins, but it was sufficient to induce hoarding, and it was much more than sufficient to cause exportation to Canada. This movement of silver coins to Canada was governed by special conditions. It has been explained that United States silver had been drifting across the border for some years prior to the war. Conditions were such that the appearance of even a slight premium on gold would stimulate this movement. Canada was on a gold basis, and United States silver coins were accepted as equivalent to gold. With paper money at a discount it was possible to exchange paper for silver coins, ship the silver to Canada, exchange it for gold, and sell the gold in the United States for paper at the premium rate. The operation became profitable as soon as the gold discount on paper exceeded the costs of collecting silver, shipping it, and bringing back the gold. The transaction was free from risk and attractive to bankers who would not have considered melting coins or speculating in bullion. United States silver was pouring into Canada long before paper money fell to the point where it was profitable to melt coins or export them as bullion.[6]

[6] See American Annual Cyclopedia for 1862, 462. Professor Mitchell, in

The high premium on gold which appeared early in January receded to low levels, and silver remained in circulation, slowly declining in volume with the steady flow to Canada. It was now bearing a double burden. There had been many $1 gold pieces in circulation in 1861. The silver coins were insufficient to fill the gap left by the withdrawal of the small gold coins. There would have been a serious scarcity of small change even if there had been no general disappearance of silver.

The first issues of greenbacks, authorized by the law of February 25, 1862, appeared in April. By the end of June about $100,000,000 were in circulation. This volume of fiat money was immediately reflected in the premium on gold. On May 5 paper money was again below 97 cents.[7] It dropped to 95 cents on June 13 and to 92 cents on June 30. In the last week in June and the first week in July more than $25,000,000 in subsidiary silver vanished from the circulation of the Northern states. With the further depreciation of paper money the 3 cent pieces of 1851 also disappeared. The remote states of the Pacific coast alone retained their silver coins.

It was a headlong disappearance. In 1852 the withdrawal had been gradual, the better weight coins preceding the worn pieces. In 1862 the silver coins were new, none of them more than eleven years old. It is a curious fact that the newspapers took notice of the situation only after the shortage had become acute. Offers of large premiums by brokers indicate a scarcity already well developed. There was a premium of 5 per cent in Boston on July 1, while the

his summary of the coinage history of this period, fails to take account of the situation in Canada, assuming that silver did not go across the border until the paper money depreciated by more than 4 per cent. See History of the Greenbacks, 157.

[7] The quotations of greenback depreciation in this chapter are taken from Mitchell's Gold, Prices, and Wages under the Greenback Standard.

Philadelphia North American reported on July 2 that the premium in that city was 6 per cent. On the 3rd the Public Ledger reported that copper cents were "about the only specie in circulation" in Philadelphia. The first reference to the situation in New York appeared in the form of a despatch to the Philadelphia Public Ledger from its New York financial correspondent, dated June 28. It read as follows:

> The retail dealers are making much complaint about the growing scarcity of silver, the premium upon which has materially advanced within the past day or two. The railroads and the restaurants appear to suffer the most inconvenience.

A later dispatch reported that on July 1 the premium in New York was 5½ per cent. On July 9 the New York Tribune said that silver coins were not being given in change except by a few large stores and ferry companies and then only at a premium charge to customers of 5 or 6 per cent. On the same day the New York Herald said the prevailing premium was 7 to 8 per cent. In the West the first reference, apparently, was in the St. Louis Republican of July 10, and the report in that paper indicated that the scarcity had been noticeable for a number of days. The Chicago Tribune of the 11th referred to a general scarcity and in its issue of the 15th said the ruling premium was 13 per cent.

The rates quoted in the dispatches were approximately equal to the entire difference between the bullion value and the currency value of silver coins. They left scant margins of profit in bullion operations. The Herald's quotation of 8 per cent on July 9 meant that brokers were giving $108 in greenbacks for $100 in silver coins. On that day the metal in $100 in silver coins was worth just about $97 in gold, and this sum in gold would purchase about $108 in greenbacks. The Herald's financial writer noted this phenomenon and commented that he could not see how a profit could accrue to the brokers.   The explanation lies in the fact that business houses in dire straits for change were forcing the brokers to pay the highest premiums bullion operations would permit.   There were undoubtedly many brokers who did not offer the "ruling premium."   The Springfield Republican said that the "prevailing" premium in Boston was 5 per cent, but brokers exporting the coins to England were offering 2½ per cent.

When the scarcity of change became acute in the first week in July, it was a matter of discussion everywhere. Newspapers devoted columns to it. Contributors joined with editors in proposing remedies.   As the New York Times editorially expressed it, the disappearance of the currency had "puzzled the wits of the whole community and driven it almost to distraction." Apparently no one in or out of the government service suggested the one plan that was efficient and practicable.   That plan was to reduce the proportion of silver to copper in all the subsidiary coins, without any other change whatever.   The machinery of the mint was now idle, and the entire equipment could have been devoted to turning out millions of new coins identical with the ordinary pieces except in the matter of the proportions of silver and copper. This was the only plan that could be instantly adopted.   All other practicable measures would require a period of preparation.

The government did not in the first two weeks after the disappearance of the silver coins adopt this measure or any other, and the solution of a currency crisis that was paralyzing business was left to the general public.   Nearly all the proposals in the public press contemplated one of three measures, a reduction in the size of the subsidiary coins, the issue of fractional notes by banks, or the issue of notes or metallic tokens by city governments.   The New York Herald suggested the coin-reduction plan, fractional bank-notes, or an embargo on silver exports. The New York Times urged the issue of 10-cent notes by the city.

No one of these plans was adequate. An embargo on exports, even if successfully enforced, would not have prevented hoarding or melting.[8] An uncontrolled issue of notes by city councils throughout the country was undesirable. In most states it was constitutionally impossible. The coin-reduction plan was impracticable, as it would have taken the mint many days to prepare dies and machinery for coins of new dimensions.

Of many odd emergency solutions proposed only one was worth considering. In the New York Tribune of July 12 Horace Greeley suggested the adoption of a general agreement throughout the country to accept silver coins at increased values in greenbacks. The 5 cent piece would be accepted as 6 cents, the dime as 12 cents, the quarter as 30 cents, and the half-dollar as 60 cents. This plan, reminiscent of the colonial attempts to rate up foreign coins, was not the fantastic scheme it appears to be at first thought. If it had been adopted as a government measure, by a law making the coins legal tender at Greeley's ratings and redeemable in greenbacks at the same values, the plan would have been, as a temporary measure, a perfect solution of the problem. No one would have been injured by the rating-up of silver coins. They had formerly been equal in value to gold, and they were now disappearing because they were by law equal in currency value only to a depreciating fiat money. Rating them up to the values suggested would have kept them in circulation until the value of greenbacks fell to approximately 80 cents. On the 14th the editor of the

---

[8] Under different conditions an embargo on exports was partly successful in the Philippines in 1905. See Kemmerer, Modern Currency Reforms, 354.

Times savagely ridiculed Greeley's proposal, and nothing more was heard of it.

There were millions of 1 cent pieces in circulation, but they were quite inadequate to fill the void created by the disappearance of approximately $27,000,000 in silver coins. There were in circulation a small number of $1 and $2 state bank-notes. In 1855 Secretary Guthrie had estimated the volume of small notes at $50,000,000, but the proportion of $1 and $2 denominations in this total was small and in the intervening years the states had made unceasing war on such issues.[9] The demand notes and greenbacks in circulation were not issued in denominations less than $5. The $1 and $2 bank-notes were insufficient to take the place of the vanished gold coins and as substitutes for fractional silver coins they were almost worthless.

Thus the country found itself, in the midst of a war boom, virtually without a currency between the 1 cent piece and the $5 note. It is not possible to visualize all the disorder and demoralization in business and social life such a situation entails. The somewhat similar conditions developed in Europe in our own time were much less disastrous because of the smaller standard units of the fiat money issues. Among the less obvious and visible results in 1862 was a heavy decline in the volume of retail trade, especially in the case of business establishments that sold for cash, such as groceries, confectioneries, saloons, barber shops, street car and bus services, and ferries.

An early development was the refusal of retail establishments to give change. In the first few days of the shortage some retail stores attempted to attract trade by advertising that they were making change without premium charges. In Philadelphia a store advertised that it would give the prevailing premium to all customers who presented

---

[9] See Annual Report on the Finances for 1855; Dewey, State Banking.

silver change. This was virtually an effort to put into effect
Greeley's rating-up proposal. Many enterprises made fran-
tic efforts to maintain business by extending credit on small
purchases and by purchasing silver coins wherever they could
find them, paying a premium and charging the customers the
same premium when change was given. A few concerns, with
no very fine sense of commercial ethics, made a profit from
the public distress. The Tribune reported on the 14th that
the ferry companies, which took in more silver coins than
any other New York enterprise, had for weeks been insist-
ing that their customers present silver, refusing to make
change in return, and selling their receipts to brokers. Some
of the companies were making a profit of $100 per day from
this source.

Early in July all retail establishments gave up the
attempt to do business with silver coins, and customers were
told to increase their purchases to the amount of the paper
notes they had or go without. In innumerable cases they
went without. The Tribune of July 14 reported as follows:

> In this city thousands and tens of thousands of persons dur-
> ing the past week have been compelled to walk to and from
> their places of business.

In another issue it said that in every line of retail business
there had been a heavy "loss of custom and profit." The
Herald of the 14th said that the conditions were "intol-
erable."

This condition of public inconvenience and business loss
could not continue. The people had to find substitutes for
silver coins, and find them they did, in every imaginable device. Among the earliest to be adopted was the United
States postage stamp. A wretched currency physically, it
had the advantage of stability of value. Stamps came into
use immediately, but they did not become a general circu-

lating medium until Secretary Chase in the latter half of July made his extraordinary decision to have them adopted as a legal currency. Another substitute was Spanish silver. These coins, only recently driven from circulation by the law of 1857, re-appeared in large numbers almost overnight, and as suddenly disappeared. Only worn pieces were brought in, but the depreciation of the greenbacks proceeded with such pace that even the old Spanish coins became more valuable as bullion than as money.

In some localities $1 and $2 bank-notes were cut into fractional parts, after the fashion of 1837 and 1853. A bank in Hartford, Connecticut, advertised that it would redeem any fragments of its notes that the public had been using as small change. But the volume of these crude substitutes was not large. Still another device was the fractional bank-note. In most of the states such issues were illegal. In a few states the laws were ambiguous, not specifying the minimum denominations permissible. There was no method of controlling the circulation in one state of notes issued in another. Pennsylvania had repealed her small note law in April, 1861, and fractional bank notes were widely issued in that state. Many were issued in New Jersey. In some states the very old colonial device of notes with fractional remainders was again resorted to, a few banks issuing notes for $1.25, $1.50, and $1.75.[10]

The total volume of fractional bank-notes was relatively small. In view of the urgency of the situation a tremendous issue might have been expected. Quite apart from the matter of their illegal status fractional bank-notes in volume sufficient to replace the missing silver coins could not be issued, for the notes were a source of loss instead of profit. They wore out so rapidly that the expenses of issue and re-

[10] For references to various substitutes see Bankers Magazine, Vol. 17, 161, 366, 404, 766, 821; New York Herald for Aug. 28, 1862.

printing were greater than the interest returns to the issuing bank. A 10 cent note cost more to issue than the 1 cent interest earned in a year. Fractional notes cost more than they earned unless a considerable proportion failed to return for redemption. Hence we find that the issues by banks in the large cities were almost negligible. The issuers were usually banks in out-of-the-way places or small institutions in suburban districts surrounding the metropolitan centers.

Regardless of the question of legality, fractional bank-notes were efficient emergency instruments. If the legal and economic circumstances had been favorable to a large issue, much business distress would have been avoided. As it was, the issues were such as to be of little help in the large cities, where they were most needed. It is significant of the character of the notes that certain banks continued to issue them long after the government had supplied a subsitute for the missing coins and had made fractional bank-notes illegal by Federal statute. Two banks in Jersey City and one in Hoboken issued notes in December, 1862. There are a few specimens in collections that bear the date 1863.

Following the precedent of earlier periods, many cities undertook to issue fractional notes. The best known issues were those of Newark, Jersey City, Albany, and Wilmington. The Albany city council passed its first issuing ordinance on July 17, 1862, which happened to be the date on which Congress provided for a far less efficient currency. The Albany ordinance authorized a total issue of $50,000, but in September another $50,000 was issued, and in November, months after the Treasury had undertaken to supply small change, still another $20,000 was authorized. These figures indicate that the notes were accepted not only in Albany but elsewhere and that they were considered a success by the city officials. Of the total authorized, $117,000 in

5, 10, 25, and 50 cent notes went into circulation. The proportion redeemed was extraordinarily large. Nearly $115,000 had been redeemed before 1864 and less than $2,000 are outstanding at the present day.

The Wilmington issues were also successful. Although the population of the city was only 25,000, the total volume of notes put out amounted to approximately $150,000.[11] The first issue was authorized on July 24, 1862, in the sum of $50,000. The proceeds from the sale of the notes to the general public were invested in United States certificates of indebtedness. The notes enjoyed such wide popularity in the Middle Atlantic States that additional issues were being authorized as late as January, 1863, and there were no redemptions before March of that year. By the end of 1864 about $125,000 had been redeemed, leaving outstanding a larger proportion than the Albany issues showed.

It can not now be determined how many municipalities issued fractional notes. Apparently none of the largest cities made any issues, although a number considered the project. Cincinnati abandoned its plans when it was ruled that its charter did not permit such issues, and on similar constitutional grounds Philadelphia gave up plans for a very large issue. New York City went farther. On December 9, 1862, the city council voted to issue the sum of $3,000,000 in fractional notes, and only the Mayor's veto prevented the carrying out of this extraordinary proposal.[12] Smaller cities were not deterred by fear of legal complications, and many towns issued notes of various kinds. In some states, Pennsylvania especially, other government units such as counties and tax districts undertook to supply fractional currency.

[11] For the histories of these two city issues the writer is indebted to L. J. Ehrhardt, Comptroller of Albany, and to E. B. Griffenberg, formerly connected with the Wilmington city government.

[12] See New York Herald for Dec. 10 and 23, 1862.

Lycoming County, Pennsylvania, for example, made an issue of 5 cent notes in January, 1863. It would appear from an inspection of notes now held in collections that some of these local governments, as well as many private enterprises, entered into an arrangement with local banks to deceive the public. Notes were printed in such a form that they gave every appearance of being fractional bank-notes, but the wording was such that they were legally checks on the banks. Such notes were technically exempt from attack either as bank-notes or as local government notes, although clearly intended to serve as money.

The notes issued by the city councils and other local government bodies were the best of all the emergency currencies. The primary purpose of their issue was to supply a desperately needed currency and in so doing to protect the public from the results of indiscriminate issue by dishonest or irresponsible private parties. It seems probable, as Mitchell implies, that the city councils were also aware of the profit accruing from the issue of non-interest bearing notes, some of which would not be returned for redemption. But the notes had definite advantages. They were of responsible origin, freely redeemable, and limited in volume. They were popular everywhere. In Philadelphia the Wilmington notes, as well as those issued by Newark and Jersey City, were widely used, despite the strong prejudice of the local papers against them. Municipal notes competed on equal terms with the fractional currency finally put out by the United States Treasury, and they were the last of the emergency currencies to disappear in 1863.[13]

[13] Every type of fractional note, except these notes of local governments, was illegal by federal law. Despite the fact that the notes of cities were not prohibited by federal statute, publications of the time, notably the Bankers Magazine and the Philadelphia Public Ledger, opposed all such notes as illegal and urged their suppression.

The total of all these paper currencies—fractional bank-notes, scraps of notes of larger denominations, and notes of local governments—was inadequate to meet a deficiency of more than $25,000,000. Transportation companies, hotels, saloons, and retail stores that could not carry on business without change proceeded to manufacture their own currency. A vast quantity of notes, tickets, and due-bills poured into circulation. They bore the promise of the issuer, explicit or implied, to redeem them in money or in goods. Customers offering bills in payment at a store received in change a handful of the proprietor's own notes or due-bills. They had to accept these paper promises or forego their purchases. Patrons of saloons and barber shops had to accept such items as change and pass them on as best they could. Notes of hotels were especially common. The derisive term "shinplaster," whose origin dates back at least to the Revolution, was applied to the whole mass of city, bank, and private issues.

The notes of honest and solvent concerns served a useful purpose. The customer who received the notes of a reputable store could usually pass them on to others. If not, he could use them for later purchases at the issuing establishment. Used in this latter way, the notes were not money. They were due-bills for merchandise, but they took the place of money. The best of the shinplasters were unsatisfactory substitutes for silver coins, but they met the emergency after a fashion.

A large proportion of the notes, however, were issued by irresponsible and unscrupulous persons. A saloon or restaurant of doubtful character could exchange large amounts of its own notes for greenbacks and close up shop with a profit. All reports refer to the promiscuous character of the issuing concerns. As the Tribune expressed it, "the saloon-keeper, the cigar-dealer, and the barber have turned banker." Notes issued by this type of enterprise were frequently not redeemable at the place of issue. In distant localities they sooner or later became unacceptable. As always, the losses fell on the poor and the ignorant.

An inherent cause of loss was the flimsy character of the private notes. Some were made by the well-equipped bank-note companies of New York and Boston, but most of them were made in local printing shops on the cheapest grades of paper. They were of the greatest diversity of size, shape, and design, some of them representing curious whims of the issuers. All of them became "filthy rags" after a short period of circulation. When they would no longer be accepted as currency, they had to be redeemed by the last holders. In thousands of cases redemption was impossible.[14]

The legal status of these shinplaster notes was dubious and confused. In many states they were clearly illegal. In some states, such as Pennsylvania, the statute was not clear. In New York private notes were prohibited by statute and when the shinplasters first appeared the New York papers emphatically pointed out this fact. The Herald on the 11th quoted the state law in full and three days latei commented as follows:

> At least one hundred retailers in various lines of business in this city have issued shinplasters, very many of which are in direct contravention of the law.

The United States postage currency law of July 17, 1862, to be explained in the next chapter, contained a provision making it criminal for any person, company or banking association to issue notes of a denomination less than one dollar.

[14] Philadelphia Public Ledger for March 12, 1863: Springfield Republican for Jan. 29, 1863. The Ledger says: "A very few weeks showed a depreciation of these illegal issues and most of them sank out of sight, many of them a dead loss in the hands of persons least able to bear it."

This sweeping prohibition, which outlawed all fractional
notes except those issued by cities, had little effect. Business could not go on without small change, and the law was
ignored. Both in New York and in Washington City the
prosecuting officers publicly announced that after July 31
they would prosecute all issuers of shinplasters under both
the Federal and the local laws. When cases came to trial
in New York the supreme court of the state declared the
Federal law of July 17 to be unconstitutional. Apparently
all efforts to suppress shinplasters through Federal authority were thereafter abandoned, although futile efforts to
apply the state statutes were made at intervals. In November, 1862, the state's attorney of New York announced his
intention to prosecute issuers after November 30, and seventeen persons were indicted in Illinois in December.[15]

The emergency currencies created or sanctioned by the
Federal government in the summer of 1862, which will be
described later, were quite inadequate to meet the needs for
small change, and for the remainder of 1862 and the first
months of 1863 the country depended chiefly on a conglom-
erate mass of torn notes, fractional bank-notes, municipal
notes, and shinplaster notes of private issuers. These notes
bore a double burden in 1862. They served as substitutes
not only for fractional silver but also for the $1 gold coins.
The greenbacks were issued under the delusion that they
would serve briefly as a currency for large transactions before going back to the Treasury in exchange for bonds.
Hence they were issued in denominations of $5 and upwards.
The $1 issues provided for by the law of July 11, 1862, did
not appear until later in the year.

Any attempt to estimate the volume of shinplaster issues
would be speculative. If it is considered that the vanished

---

[15] See New York Herald for Aug. 28, 1862; New York Tribune for Nov.
18, 1862; Bankers Magazine, Vol. 17, 567.

silver amounted to more than $25,000,000 and that the shinplasters probably represented much more than half of all the emergency currencies, it seems fair to assume that the issues reached a sum greater than $15,000,000. It is doubtful whether half of this total returned to the original issuers for redemption. The amount lost, destroyed in use, or held as souvenirs must have exceeded $5,000,000. The figure represents only a small part of the social and financial losses entailed by a complete collapse of the retail currency such as that which occurred in 1862. The losses from destruction of notes and irredeemable issues were minor matters when contrasted with the demoralization of retail trade and the general annoyance and disturbance the country had to endure.

CHAPTER XIII

THE CIVIL WAR PERIOD: POSTAGE CURRENCY AND FRACTIONAL CURRENCY

PROPOSALS of Secretary Chase—The postage stamp proposal—The law of 1862—Run on the post offices—Controversy between Chase and Blair—Redemption of stamps—Character of the postage currency—Disappearance of emergency currencies—Law of 1863—Character of the fractional currency—Amendment of 1864—Retirement of postage currency—The fractional note régime.

On July 14, 1862, Secretary Chase wrote to Congress requesting action to meet the fractional currency emergency. Professor Mitchell, with too lenient judgment, refers to this action as a prompt step to relieve the situation. The letter was written five months after the danger of silver disappearance became obvious and imminent, five weeks after the price of greenbacks had brought silver coins to the melting point, and almost two weeks after the entire small change currency of the country had disappeared. Chase asked Congress to consider two plans, submitting for each a law already prepared. Both bills contained a sweeping prohibition of private issues of notes.

One of the plans called for a reduction in the size of the silver coins. Regarding this measure the Secretary said:

> Should Congress see fit to adopt this expedient, a return to the existing basis, on the termination of the insurrection, will be practicable and easy.

This proposal was sound enough, but it was not practical. Reducing the size of the coins would call for new designs, new dies, and new machinery, and the loss of time involved made the proposal impracticable. The other plan called for the legalization of the use of ordinary postage stamps as money. His preference for this plan was obvious from his comment:

> The same object may be accomplished, and perhaps with less incidental evil consequence, by a similar prohibition, accompanied by a provision for the receiving of postage and other stamps in payment of the fractional parts of a dollar.

It is at first glance difficult to believe that a responsible finance minister would propose the circulation of tiny squares of glue-coated paper as a national currency. Sheer panic is the only explanation of such a grotesque plan. The "other stamps" referred to were internal revenue stamps even less adapted to currency use. Postage stamps had long been the customary means of making small payments by mail. In the New York Tribune of the 9th Greeley urged the use of stamps, suggesting that they be pasted on half the surface of a sheet of paper, with the other half folded over to protect them. On the 14th a Wall Street firm was selling sheets of stamps on "light vellum paper" folded over after Greeley's suggested method. Various containers for stamps were selling widely before Chase wrote to Congress. The Chicago Tribune of the 15th advocated stamps in preference to shinplasters.

It seems probable that credit for the proposal to legalize stamps belongs to F. E. Spinner, Treasurer of the United States. When the work of the Treasury became demoralized by the scarcity of change Spinner conceived the idea of pasting postage stamps, which were issued in varying sizes, on slips of paper of uniform size. These he paid out in government business. He had carried this to the point of arranging with the Post Office Department for the exchange of pieces that had become soiled. In later years Spinner maintained that the government had adopted his plan. On the other hand, the coin-reduction plan appears to have been urged upon Chase by Director of the Mint Pollock. In the absence of any clearly defined ideas of his own Secretary Chase presented both plans to Congress, implying rather vaguely that he preferred the postage stamp plan.[1]

Congress accepted the postage stamp measure and adopted the bill presented by Chase. Not a member of Congress questioned the wisdom of the plan, although a number of members of the House voted against it on the grounds that it was unconstitutional to prohibit shinplasters.[2] The Senate approved it unanimously, and President Lincoln signed the law on July 17, 1862. The measure provided that the Secretary should furnish "to the Assistant Treasurers, in such sums as he may deem expedient, the postage and other stamps of the United States, to be exchanged by them, on application, for United States notes." After August 1 the stamps were to be receivable for government dues in amounts less than $5 and redeemable in greenbacks at all Treasury offices. A second section prohibited the issue of shinplasters. There was no provision in the law for legal tender or limitation of issue and none for manufacture or purchase of stamps by the Treasury.

The immediate effect of the law was a run on the post offices of the country. The statute directed that the Treasury sell the stamps to the public, but the Treasury had no stamps and at the moment had no plans for getting them. Naturally the people turned to the post offices when the gov-

---

[1] For Spinner's participation see Valentine, Fractional Currency, 8. Chase's letter is in the Congressional Globe, 37th Cong., 2nd sess., 3405. The Globe did not print a copy of the coin-reduction bill. An exhaustive search by the writer has failed to find a copy in the government records.

[2] Congressional Globe, 37th Cong., 2nd sess., 3402, 3406.

ernment's sanction of stamps as currency became publicly known. In New York, for example, where the normal daily sales were around $3,000 in volume, $10,000 worth of stamps were bought on the 18th after the law's passage was announced, $16,000 on the 19th, and $24,000 on the 22nd. The post offices everywhere refused to accept shinplasters, forcing buyers to purchase $5 worth of stamps at a time, but purchasers were not discouraged.[3] Here and there resistance to the use of stamps appeared. The Herald warned the public that anyone refusing them would "run a strong chance of going unpaid," and the Tribune suggested that unwilling bus conductors be turned over to a policeman.

Out of the rush for stamps a curious episode developed. Chase had proposed his postage stamp bill without any plan for its operation. A despatch from Washington, in the Herald of the 22nd, discloses the situation:

> Much difficulty is experienced in carrying out the law authorizing the issue of postage stamps for currency. The act appears to have been hastily drawn, without consultation with the Postmaster General. It inaugurates a conflict of authority between the Post office and the Treasury departments. . . . The details in reference to the issue of stamps have not yet been arranged.

The run on the post offices had exhausted the supply of stamps and demoralized the postal service. Postmaster General Blair, undoubtedly incensed by the Treasury's procedure, refused to permit the further sale of stamps for currency use. The postmaster of New York, telegraphing to Washington for more stamps, received the following reply:

> Restrict sales of postage stamps to former customary amount per diem, as this department is not to furnish postage stamps for currency.

[3] See New York Herald for July 20, 1862; New York Tribune for July 24, 1862; Report of the Postmaster General for 1862, 131.

The next day's despatch disclosed that the Treasury had put the matter in the hands of Commissioner of Internal Revenue Boutwell for arbitration and that Boutwell had made what the Herald called "five propositions to the Postmaster General." The sum of these was that Blair provide the Treasury with postage stamps bearing special distinguishing marks, that redemption of such stamps be through the Treasury, that the post offices accept them for postage uses, and that either party be free to withdraw from the agreement. Blair accepted this treaty and made arrangements for the manufacture of the stamps.[4]

Meanwhile Blair was resolutely attempting to divorce his postal service from the unnatural use which the ill-considered law of July 17 had brought about. The public was given notice that post offices were not to sell stamps under the act of July 17 and that stamps "soiled and unfit" because of currency use would not be redeemed at the post offices or accepted as postage payment. All offices required purchasers to declare that they were not buying the stamps for currency use. But the general public continued to storm the offices. In 29 of the largest cities the sales in July, August, and September were above normal by $800,000. The New York papers reported instances of business houses actually paying premiums for postage stamps.

Many millions of stamps went into circulation, although their unfitness for such use was immediately evident. Physically these glue-coated bits of paper were the worst form of currency ever used by a civilized people. Many devices were employed to make their circulation possible. A favorite practice was to inclose them in small mica cases. Stationers sold these everywhere, and enterprising retailers presented

---

[4] The record of this episode must be pieced out from references in the New York Herald for July 21, 22, 24, and 25, 1862, and the annual reports of Secretary Chase and Postmaster General Blair for 1862.

them to their patrons. The government granted a patent to an inventor of one of the cases. An express company devised a flap envelope with spaces for the different denominations, which were an odd adaptation to the Spanish and the United States fractional currency, 1, 3, 5, 10, 12, 24, 30, and 90 cents. Sometimes the stamps were attached to cards or ordinary paper sheets, and millions were circulated without any protective device, soon becoming dirty, sticky and shapeless.[5]

In the later months of 1862, as other currencies came into use, the question of redeeming the stamps became acute. Blair refused to consider redemption of a mass of soiled stamps that had been used as currency over his protest. There was no law requiring post offices to redeem uncancelled postage stamps. Secretary Chase likewise refused redemption, instructing the Treasury offices to deny all requests. Technically a case could be made for this ruling. The law of July 17 required the Treasury to redeem all postage stamps that had been sold to the public by the Treasury, but no stamps had been so sold. Actually the refusal of the Treasury to redeem was a breach of faith, since it was responsible for both the situation and the law. But the Treasury could not redeem more than a million dollars worth of stamps unless it was in turn reimbursed by the Post Office.

Blair, who was blameless throughout the affair, had to surrender. A contemporary writer says:

> This inflicted a grievous wrong upon the people, who held millions of the worn and dilapidated stamps. The popular will ultimately compelled the Postmaster to issue notice that they would be redeemed under certain regulations.

[5] See New York Tribune for Aug. 19 and 30, 1862; Drowne, United States Postage Stamps.

Redemption began on December 15. Again the post offices were besieged, this time by crowds bringing masses of crumpled, sticky stamps. The postmasters reported that it was impossible to determine whether the stamps had been used on letters. Frauds were perpetrated by thousands.[6] The New York city post office alone redeemed $300,000 worth of stamps. In his annual report for 1862 Blair avoided direct criticism of Chase, but he pointedly referred to the "misconception" which confused postage stamps sold by the post offices with the currency provided for by the law of July 17.

The agreement between Commissioner Boutwell and Blair called for the manufacture of ordinary postage stamps which would be accepted for postage payments. They were to bear special marks and to be sold by the Treasury, but they were to be postage stamps none the less, as the law of July 17 contemplated. Before they were arranged for some one had the good judgment to prevent this final blunder. It was decided to issue the bits of paper without glue. Printed in this form, they were not stamps but promissory notes of the Federal government. They bore the statement that they were issued under authority of the law of July 17, 1862. This was not true. The law of July 17 referred to postage stamps, and these new notes were issued without any legal authorization whatever. Chase had persuaded Congress to adopt an absurd measure whose character had been disclosed by the clash with Blair. Confronted by an impossible situation under the law, he had arranged for the issue of notes that were virtually fractional greenbacks. The action was a breach of his constitutional authority. In his annual report for 1862 Chase made the following statement:

[6] American Annual Cyclopedia for 1862, 463; New York Herald for Jan. 5, 1863; New York Tribune for Dec. 19, 1862, and Jan. 21, 1863.

An arrangement was made with the Postmaster General for a supply of postage stamps to be distributed for use in such payments. It was soon discovered, however, that stamps prepared for postage uses were not adapted to the purposes of currency. Small notes were therefore substituted.

This statement is ingenuously inaccurate. No arrangement was made with Blair for a supply of postage stamps, and no postage stamps were ever sold by the Treasury.

There was delay in the issue of the new currency. On August 18, more than a month after the enactment of July 17, the papers announced that the concern printing the notes would soon be able to deliver stamps at the rate of $27,000 worth per day. The Herald commented that at this rate the shortage would not be relieved for more than three years. On August 21 the Treasury distributed a small lot to army paymasters, and some two weeks later sales were made to the general public. Thus the law of July 17, calling for immediate sales of postage stamps to relieve an emergency, resulted in the issue of unauthorized fractional paper money in September.[7]

The new "postage currency," as it was inaccurately called, was distributed very slowly, and the supply was inadequate. For many days after sales began long lines of people stood before the sub-Treasuries in New York and other cities.[8] Less than $800,000 was outstanding on October 1, and only $7,000,000 was issued during the year. Secretary Chase reported that with every energy exerted only

---

[7] Historians have been confused as to the facts about "postage currency." Faulkner, for example, in his American Economic History, 494, gives an inaccurate account of this currency. See also Dewey, Financial History of the United States, 309.

[8] See New York Herald, Times, or Tribune for Sept., 1862; Philadelphia Public Ledger for Sept. 11, 1862. The Assistant Treasurer in the New York sub-treasury regularly used a printed sign begging the public to refrain from asking for postage currency until additional supplies arrived.

a fraction of the demand had been met. At the beginning of 1863 the daily issue was raised to $100,000 per day, and it was subsequently increased to more than $130,000.

The first issues were printed in sheets, with perforated edges on the notes similar to those on postage stamps. The paper was tough, and so many notes were mutilated in detaching that the Treasury announced that torn notes would not be redeemed. The designs on the small paper rectangles were taken from those on the postage stamps. They were printed in yellow and in white, the 50 cent notes with the portrait of Washington repeated five times, the 25 cent note with five copies of the likeness of Jefferson. The denominations were 5, 10, 25, and 50 cents, entirely satisfactory divisions which, like the notes themselves, were not authorized by the law of July 17. In later issues the perforated edges were abandoned and the notes, printed in large sheets, were cut off with scissors. The need for $1 bills was so great that the sheets were frequently cut into blocks of $1 total value and circulated in that form.

With the beginning of 1863 the postage currency began to fill the void, and the heterogeneous currencies slowly became obsolete. Late in January the New York Herald announced that it would no longer receive subscriptions in shinplasters. On January 29 the Springfield Republican said that there was a general agreement in Boston to drop shinplasters, the notes of the Parker House alone being acceptable. The Philadelphia Ledger reported on March 4 that the city was "tolerably well supplied" with postage currency, although the rival city of New York was still burdened with "an immense circulation of all sorts of trash." In the spring of 1863 the makeshifts of 1862 generally disappeared, rapidly in the cities, more slowly in the rural sections. Even the notes that had formerly enjoyed the highest credit, such of those of Wilmington and Newark, fell to a discount. The revenue law of March 3, 1863, contained a section providing for a tax of 10 per cent on fractional notes issued by any individual, corporation, or bank. This little clause not only repealed the futile prohibition of July 17, 1862, but gave Federal sanction to the issue of shinplasters. There is no indication in the records that any taxes were ever collected from this source. The fever of private issues had run its course. The postage currency became the small change everywhere in the Northern states except on the Pacific coast. Issues were steadily increased until they reached a total of $20,215,635 on May 27, 1863.[9]

There were no further issues after this date. The small change shortage had been relieved. This maximum of $20,-000,000 was considerably less than the total silver coinage that had disappeared and less than half the total of postage currency that Secretary Chase had expected to issue. In his 1862 report, as explained in the previous chapter, Chase had accepted the careless estimate of Pollock that the Union states held about $45,000,000 in silver coins. He had counted upon, as part of his Treasury resources, a total revenue of more than $40,000,000 in greenbacks from the sale of postage currency. The cessation of issues before the total reached the volume of silver formerly circulating, something over $25,000,000, was due to special factors. The rapid rise of greenback prices had greatly reduced the number of exchanges involving sums less than one dollar. The Treasury had begun to issue $1 greenbacks, and 33,000,000 of these notes were in circulation in June, 1863, while copper-nickel coins had attained a use unknown before the war. Finally, it seems probable that the postage currency rate of circulation was high, whereas many of the larger silver coins had been held in reserves of various kinds.

In his report for 1862 Secretary Chase said that he had

[9] See Knox, United States Notes, 104.

as an experiment undertaken to print small notes "substantially like the small notes now substituted for postage stamps." The cost of greenbacks and postage stamps as made by the bank-note companies was high, and the second legal tender act of July 11, 1862, had authorized the Treasury to undertake government printing.[10] The Secretary hoped, he said, that Congress would approve his experimental operations and authorize the printing of such "revenue stamps" by the Treasury. This was virtually a request for approval of the unauthorized substitution of "postage currency" for the stamp currency actually provided for and a plea for government printing of fractional notes. The law of March 3, 1863, generally known as the third legal tender act, contained a section which embodied both recommendations.

A House committee presented originally a section which provided for "fractional notes" to be issued in exchange for postage and revenue stamps. This queer proposal to tie up the fractional currency with postage stamps was probably suggested by the Treasury as a solution of the problem of redeeming the postage stamps, which at the time Postmaster General Blair was refusing to redeem. Fortunately the Senate rejected this proposal.[11] As finally passed, March 3, 1863, the law provided that "in lieu of postage and revenue stamps for fractional currency and of fractional notes, commonly called postage currency," the Secretary of the Treasury might issue "fractional notes of

[10] It would appear from the records that two bank-note companies, under a common control, obtained a virtual monopoly of the manufacture of government currency and charged unreasonably high prices. See Valentine, 11–15. A Treasury official named Clark had his portrait engraved on one of the new fractional notes. This so incensed Congress that by a law of April 7, 1866, it was provided that portraits of living persons should not appear on any securities or currency of the United States.

[11] Congressional Globe, 37th Cong., 3rd sess., 485, 927, 1039.

like amounts." The notes were to be sold for greenbacks and were to be receivable for postage and revenue stamps, redeemable under such conditions as the Secretary might prescribe, and receivable in sums less than $5 for all dues to the government except import duties. The Treasury was authorized to print the notes. The total issues, "including postage and revenue stamps issued as currency," were to be limited to $50,000,000. Inasmuch as there had never been any postage or revenue stamps "issued as currency," this clause was inaccurately worded, but its intent was obviously to restrict to $50,000,000 the combined issues of the outstanding postage currency and the proposed "fractional currency."

The effect of the law was to sanction the postage currency outstanding, to authorize government manufacture, and to commit the government to a policy of fractional paper money. There were no essential differences between the new fractional currency and the postage currency in circulation. The Treasury continued to issue postage currency after the law was passed and made no effort to rush the manufacture of the new notes. There was a minor difference between the two. The postage currency was receivable for all government dues in amounts less than $5, the new notes for all such dues except import duties. After the law was passed Secretary Chase suspended the issue of 25 and 50 cent postage currency notes. When importers continued to pay duties with postage currency the Secretary issued orders to refuse to accept such payments.[12] Legally this action was indefensible, even if, as Chase said, the postage currency notes had been "inadvertently" made equivalent to gold for customs payments. The law of March 3 did not alter the status of the postage currency, and forcing importers to find uncurrent silver coins was neither legal nor fair.

[12] New York Herald for March 6 and 7, 1863.

On October 10, 1863, seven months after the passage of the law, the Treasury began the issue of the new fractional notes. The designs were more attractive than those of the postage currency, the paper was stronger and less easy to counterfeit, and the colors were different. The denominations, as provided in the law, were 5, 10, 25, and 50 cents. The notes of the two lower values were somewhat smaller, an unsatisfactory feature probably adopted on the theory that identification would be easier.

At the time the new notes appeared the postage currency notes in circulation amounted to less than $18,000,000, having declined from the maximum of about $20,000,000 in the preceding June. Thus the new notes were not to be additional currency, but merely substitutes for the postage currency that had accidentally emerged from the confusion of 1862. The Treasury adopted the policy of withdrawing all postage currency that reached the Treasury from any source. The process was unexpectedly slow. By the end of June, 1864, only $5,000,000 in postage currency had been withdrawn, although the Register of the Treasury reported that he had during the preceding year destroyed 31,000,000 pieces of fractional paper money. The $5,000,000 withdrawn had been replaced by an equal amount of fractional currency notes, and $3,000,000 additional of the new currency had been issued.[13] The total circulation of both types stood nominally at $23,000,000. Actually it was much less, as the number of postage currency notes that had been lost or destroyed in use was large.

In the Treasury bill which became the law of June 30, 1864, there was a section which amended the fractional currency act of March 3, 1863. The new law was chiefly a more intelligible restatement of the earlier measure. The provision making fractional notes acceptable in payments

---

[13] See Annual Reports on the Finances for 1863 and 1864.

for postage stamps was for some reason dropped. It was hardly a necessary provision, but it was harmless. The only important change was in a provision authorizing the Secretary to determine the form of the notes, the methods of manufacture, and the terms of redemption. The provision permitted the Secretary to exercise his discretion in various particulars, more especially in the matter of denominations.

Chase availed himself of this privilege to issue a 3 cent note, apparently with the idea that such a denomination would be useful in the purchase of stamps. The ordinary letter rate was 3 cents. Purchasers had to buy as many as 5 stamps at a time or find copper cents, which had, for reasons to be explained later, become extremely scarce. But this possible service of a 3 cent note was not sufficient to justify its issue. The denomination was never popular, and it was withdrawn after about a year. In 1869 Secretary McCulloch, under the authority of this provision, added a 15 cent note to the paper currency. Like the 3 cent note, it was unnecessary and never enjoyed wide circulation.

The process of retiring the postage currency, begun in October, 1863, with the issue of the fractional currency notes, was continuous thereafter. The following table shows the rate of progress:

	Postage Currency Outstanding	Fractional Currency Outstanding	Combined Currencies Outstanding
Sept. 30, 1862	$ 787,000	. . . .	$ 787,000
June 30, 1863	20,192,000	. . . .	20,192,000
Sept. 30, 1863	17,766,000	. . . .	17,766,000
June 30, 1864	15,167,000	$ 7,727,000	22,894,000
June 30, 1865	9,915,000	15,090,000	25,005,000

Less than $8,000,000 in postage currency notes had been redeemed by the end of the war, although every note reaching the Treasury was cancelled. The figure of $10,000,000 for postage currency outstanding at the time represented in the main the amount that had been lost in circulation, and the major portion of the issues of fractional currency notes in 1864 represented replacements of this lost postage currency. In fact no figures for total notes outstanding from 1863 until the end of the paper money régime accurately portray the actual circulation. From the beginning such figures included an uncertain but large and growing sum representing notes lost or destroyed. Ordinary wear and tear accounted for many, while conflagrations and ordinary accidents of business and travel added to the totals.

With the relief of the scarcity in the summer of 1863 the question of small change ceased to be a national problem. The people learned to use the small pieces of paper, and silver coins were all but forgotten. The paper currency was one of the results of war, and there was little complaint despite the fact that the notes were never satisfactory substitutes for silver coins. Knox, in his history of the greenbacks, says of them:

> The little notes were stuffed into the trouser pocket of the soldier, with the jack-knife, the cartridge, the plug of tobacco, and other handy articles, and soon became unfit for circulation. They wore out rapidly and became ragged and filthy, and were frequently returned for redemption.

The story of the fractional currency in the years from 1861 to 1865 is a dismal chapter in our financial annals. Responsibility rests officially on Secretary Chase. Historians have not included his administration of the fractional currency in the list of his mistakes in policy, but his failure to foresee the inevitable crisis, his delay after the crisis had arrived, and his blundering measures of relief constitute together one of the most serious errors in his conduct of the finances of the war. It was certainly the least defensible. There was no occasion for the loss of the country's silver currency in 1862 or the paralysis in business which followed. A less immediate responsibility rests on the Congress that accepted Chase's recommendations.

CHAPTER XIV

THE CIVIL WAR PERIOD: MINOR COINS

COPPER AND NICKEL cents at outbreak of war—Extraordinary demand for cents—Causes of the premium on cents—Cost of production of cents—Private copper coins—Their legal status—Pollock's opposition to nickel coinage—Efforts of Wharton to promote nickel—Law of 1864 creating new bronze 1 and 2 cent pieces—Law of 1865 creating 3 cent nickel coin—Law of 1866 creating 5 cent nickel coin—Redemption provided for—Metric weight of the new coin—Problem of redeeming 1, 2 and 3 cent pieces—Attempts to increase nickel coinage—Redemption of all minor coins by law of 1871—The motto "In God We Trust."

The number of copper-nickel cents in the country at the outbreak of the war was not far from 100,000,000.[1] As already explained, these coins had been forced into circulation by exchange for Spanish silver coins, as well as by sales for gold and silver coins of the United States, until they flooded the channels of retail trade, became a public nuisance, and sold at a discount in the cities. The repeal of the law authorizing the exchange for Spanish fractions had greatly reduced their coinage, and in 1861 only enough were produced to replace the old copper coins returned for redemption.

The majority of the coins were in the Northern states, especially in the East. There were none in circulation in the Pacific region, and the Southern states had very few, possibly not more than fifteen or twenty millions. These copper-nickel coins, worth as bullion about half as much as their

---

[1] The actual coinage from 1857 to the end of June, 1861, was 104,566,000. See Appendix E; also Annual Report of the Director of the Mint for 1863.

money value, did not disappear when the silver coins vanished in July, 1862. They continued to circulate and for a short while, before the vast outpouring of shinplasters, they constituted the only small change in the Northern states. Tied up in bundles of 25, 50, or 100 pieces, they were widely used in retail trade. Bus companies, theatres, and restaurants accepted these rolls everywhere. A retail store in New York received so many that the floor of the room in which they were stored collapsed.

The cent pieces, offering as they did the only means of making change, immediately acquired a scarcity value. The premium appeared first in Philadelphia, where the coins should have been most plentiful. The parent mint in Philadelphia was the only one in which copper pieces were coined. In its issue of July 4, 1862, the Public Ledger reported as follows:

> Cents being about the only specie in circulation, are in anxious demand, and we have heard of two per cent in some instances being paid for them.

The New York Commercial Advertiser of July 10 said the premium in New York was 4 per cent, while the Springfield Republican of the 15th reported a like premium in Massachusetts.[2]

In a vain effort to satisfy the demand the mint forced itself to a rate of production even higher than that of 1858. By the end of July the weekly issue amounted to 1,200,000 pieces. One-third of this total was reserved for Philadelphia, the remainder going to the other large cities. No applicant anywhere received more than $5 worth. The coinage jumped from 12,000,000 pieces in the year ending June 30, 1862, to 47,800,000 in the following year. Even

---

[2] See also Blake, United States Paper Money.

this extraordinary value in cents, $478,000, was a small sum when contrasted with the $25,000,000 or more in silver coin that had disappeared. The demand for the cent pieces was never satisfied. The conditions in Philadelphia, which were duplicated in other cities, were described in the Public Ledger of July 18th:

> The difficulty among small shopkeepers, provision dealers in the markets and the city generally, in making change, has caused an extraordinary demand for cents, and all that can be commanded at the Mint are eagerly bought. . . . Though many of those who desired cents stood in line for hours, waiting an opportunity to get into the Mint, they had to go home without them, as the supply on hand was exhausted before half the applicants were accommodated.

The existence of a premium on the cent pieces in July and the later months of 1862 is easily explained. For a time the copper-nickel coins provided the only small change. After the appearance of the shinplasters the cent pieces were the only United States coins in circulation in the midst of a nondescript lot of dubious and inconvenient paper notes. In its issue of July 24 the Philadelphia North American asks the question:

> What causes this premium on nickels? They are not exported. They are of use only at home. And yet the panic-mongers have driven them up to three or four per cent premium.[3]

The answer lay in the fact that in July the possession of a few copper cents meant that the owner could ride rather than walk. And for months after it meant that he could buy

---

[3] Note the use of the word "nickels." This was the popular name for the 1 cent piece of 1857. The term was later transferred to our present day 5 cent piece.

a postage stamp without an altercation with the clerk or a cigar without receiving in change a handful of the dealer's own manufactured currency.

But the continuance of the premium after the general scarcity of small change had been relieved is another matter. By the end of March, 1863, the postage currency had driven out the shinplasters and completely filled the void in the fractional currency, but copper-nickel cents still sold at a premium throughout the country. On March 9, 1863, the Philadelphia Public Ledger reported that cents were "so scarce as to command a premium of 20 per cent." Ten days later it said that the cent pieces were "universally hoarded." In his annual report for the year ending June 30, 1863, Director Pollock said that cents had commanded a premium during the past two years and were still "scarcely to be had." He described the situation as follows:

> The coinage and issue of the nickel cent during the year has been very large—almost unprecedented. The demand still continues, and every effort has been made to meet it. This coin has been distributed to every part of the country, and orders for large amounts are daily received. It is not easy to offer a conjecture as to the amount of cents that will be required to meet the public demand.

It is thus evident that the copper coins were much sought after, generally scarce, and worth more than their face value long after there was an ample supply of fractional paper notes. The newspapers made little mention of fractional currency of any kind after the summer of 1863 and apparently made no references to copper cent pieces, but it is clear that the 1 cent pieces commanded a premium until the middle of 1864. Pollock in his report for the year 1864 again referred to the matter:

> Large quantities are hoarded, and thus kept from circulation. They have also been bought and sold by small brokers

at a premium; this has induced individuals to collect them for
the purpose of sale, thus producing a scarcity and inconvenience
to the public that ought not to exist.

Professor Mitchell, who has made an excellent summary
of some of the fractional currency developments of the war
years, has concluded that the premium on cents in 1862 and
1863 was due to the general scarcity of change, but that in
the end the continued depreciation of the greenbacks made
the copper-nickel coins more valuable as bullion than as
money and drove them to the melting pot.[4]   It is desirable
to examine this point at length.   After 1862 copper coins
as well as copper and nickel bullion were bought and sold
in greenbacks.   Copper cents would be melted or exported
only when the copper and nickel in 100 pieces were worth
more than $1 in greenbacks.   This condition was never
reached, or even approximated.   The greenbacks went to
low levels in 1864 in terms of gold, but this could not affect
the cent pieces so long as they were worth less than greenbacks.

There is official testimony in this connection.   In each
of his annual reports for the three fiscal years from June
30, 1861, to June 30, 1864, Director Pollock stated specifically that the cost of production of the copper-nickel coins
was well below their value as money.   In the 1863 report
he said that the cent contained "a half-cent's worth of metal
more or less, according to market fluctuations."   In the
earlier report he says that "the cent we issue costs the government scarcely half a cent."   Ten years later the annual
report of the Mint Director for the year 1873 presented a
study of the costs of copper-nickel coinage.   This report
gives the actual costs of coinage in each of the war years.   In
the first half of 1863 about 40,000,000 pieces were coined

[4] History of the Greenbacks, 167–171, 180.

at a total cost for materials and manufacture of $250,000, approximately ⅝ of a cent per coin. In the fiscal year ending June 30, 1864, the mint produced about 36,000,000 copper-nickel cents and many millions more of the new bronze 1 and 2 cent pieces authorized in that year. The cost of the metal in all three of the issues was $220,000. Even if the entire sum were charged to the copper-nickel cents alone, the cost was only ⅗ of a cent.

The matter is equally clear from the standpoint of bullion dealings. The copper-nickel cent weighed 72 grains, of which 88 per cent was copper and 12 per cent nickel. To obtain one pound of nickel and about seven pounds of copper it was necessary to collect and melt more than 800 cent pieces. The price of nickel fluctuated widely in the war period, averaging about $2.00 per pound in 1862 and $3.00 in 1864. In this latter year a peak price of $3.20 was reached.[5] The average price of copper in 1864 was about 50 cents per pound, and the top price attained at any time in the war period was 55 cents. The melting of 800 cent pieces would thus have yielded, at the peak prices for the metals, $3.20 worth of nickel and $3.85 worth of copper. During most of 1864 the bullion value of $8.00 in cents was less than $6.50. This takes no account of the heavy expenses involved when 100,000 pieces had to be gathered, counted, packed, and shipped to make a $1,000 turnover. As for melting, nickel alloys were a terror to the most efficient metallurgists of that day.

As a matter of historical fact, therefore, the copper-

[5] Professor Mitchell bases his calculations on one contemporary quotation of the price of nickel and an assumption that Pollock's estimated costs were gold costs. The elaborate survey in the 1873 Mint report gives the actual greenback costs. For the necessary data on nickel costs and coinage costs see United States Senate Reports, 52nd Cong., 2nd sess., no. 1394, parts 1 and 2; Stanley, Nickel Past and Present, Appendix; and Annual Report of the Director of the Mint for 1873.

nickel cents did not reach a bullion value that would drive them to the melting pot or force their exportation. The papers make no reference to exports or to melting in all their comments on scarcity and premium values. The Public Ledger went so far as to recommend that Congress declare the coins acceptable only at their bullion values so that dealers would be unable to charge a premium.[6] These coins were the only metallic currency, except that on the Pacific Coast, which remained in circulation during the Civil War period. They were insufficient in number, widely hoarded, and worth a premium over all other currencies.

The premium on the coins furnishes a rare illustration of an important principle of monetary science, the principle that a currency may for a long time command a premium over other forms of money when its only advantage is a physical quality which makes it popular. A premium on metallic currencies is a commonplace of economic history, but such premiums are usually matters of bimetallic ratios or credit standing. Here we have a premium on fiduciary coins that could not be melted or exported and were not even redeemable in the standard greenbacks over which they enjoyed a premium. The explanation lies in the physical qualities of the cent pieces. They were metallic currency in a period when the people were forced to accept flimsy and inconvenient bits of paper. Secretary Chase's 3 cent fractional notes did not appear until late in 1864, and the copper-nickel cents were the only currency of a lower denomination than 5 cents. They were very useful in the purchase of stamps, bus tickets, newspapers and other articles of small value. The mint, though devoting itself almost entirely to the coinage of cents, was quite unable to meet the extraordinary demand.

---

[6] Philadelphia Public Ledger for July 9, 1863. Mitchell quotes the statement of an Illinois senator to the effect that in his travels he seldom saw cent pieces. Cents had never been in wide use in Illinois.

In the history of the United States this phenomenon has appeared four times, first in the payment of a premium for fractional silver and $1 gold pieces in the 1853 scarcity period, again in the premium paid for postage stamps and $1 greenbacks in the summer of 1862, a third time in the premium on copper-nickel cents, and finally in a premium on fractional notes which developed in 1876.

One result of the scarcity of cent pieces was the circulation of private copper coins. They appeared almost as suddenly as the shinplasters, but their greatest vogue was in 1863, long after the general scarcity of small change had been relieved. Their wide circulation was made possible by the scarcity of copper-nickel cents. As in the case of the 1837 private coins, they appeared in the two general forms of tradesmen's coins and anonymously issued imitations of the legal cent pieces. The first type, usually issued to provide change and advertise the dealer's wares, bore an implied or an explicit promise of redemption in goods or money. The second type were simply unauthorized substitutes for government coins, produced at a profit by private manufacturers and put into general circulation through various agencies.

They were of great variety in composition and design.[7] The majority were more or less faithful imitations of the copper-nickel cent, some of them actual counterfeits. A few of this type have the word "not" in very small letters above the "one cent" engraving of the legitimate coin. Many pieces, especially of the tradesmen token type, were individual in color, devices, and size, representing any caprice of design or slogan that appealed to the maker. The most widely circulated of all the coins bore the portrait of the New York saloonist who issued them. Some were political

[7] Falkner's Private Issue of Token Coins gives the best description of these private coins.

or patriotic in character, carrying the likeness of some military leader such as McClellan or bearing such inscriptions as "millions for contractors, not one cent for the widows."

The volume of these issues will never be known. Their ubiquitous appearance and doubtful character precluded official records. Falkner, after a careful study, hazarded the estimate of a total issue of 50,000,000 pieces, quoting, however, a manufacturer of the coins who placed the amount at 25,000,000. One collection gathered many years ago contains 5,000 distinct types, of which four-fifths give some indication of the identity of the issuers. In the Lehigh University collection about half are anonymous. The coins appear to have been issued in every part of the North, and there are many specimens from states such as Ohio and Michigan that had made little use of copper coins before the war period. The greater difficulties in obtaining cents from the mint and the less general resort to shinplasters in the West may partly account for the relatively large issues in these states.

The legal status of these coins was uncertain. Director Pollock thought they were illegal, and in his report for 1863 has the following to say:

> . . . illegal cent tokens of the size of the legal cent were made and freely passed, although they contained no nickel, weighed on the average about 51 grains, and were worth not more than one-fifth of a cent. Not less than 300 varieties of these false and illegal tokens or cents were issued, and until suppressed were freely used as coins by the public. They were in direct violation of the laws of the United States; and the prosecution of certain parties issuing them has deterred others and will soon drive them altogether from circulation.

There was no law prohibiting the issue of tradesmen's tokens or of private coins not in imitation of United States coins,

whether of gold, silver, or copper. The old anti-counterfeiting law of 1806 referred only to fraudulent imitations
of gold or silver coin. There had never been any law prohibiting duplicates or imitations of copper coins. Pollock
probably referred to efforts to prosecute private coiners under the law of 1792, which had been a dead letter from its
passage.[8] Falkner could find no record of any prosecutions,
but he found cases where manufacturers had ceased issuing
because of threats of Federal action. Congress evidently
believed that there was no existing remedy, for a law was
passed on April 22, 1864, prohibiting the issue of any 1 or
2 cent coins, tokens, or devices for use as money, and on
June 8 another law which abolished private coinage of every
kind. Even before this date private copper coins were disappearing from circulation, leaving behind them the inevitable record of losses to innocent holders. They came into
existence only because of the scarcity of government coins,
and they disappeared as soon as the bronze coins of 1864
met the public demands for small copper change. It has
been pointed out that the margin of profit in shinplasters
was very small and that real gain accrued only to issuers who
could evade redemption. This was even truer in the case of
private cent pieces. Pollock was referring to their bullion
values when he said they were worth only $\frac{1}{5}$ of a cent. The
costs of manufacture were such that few issuers could produce them for as low a cost as three-fourths of a cent. The
many millions in circulation represented a total loss to the
final holders in 1864 unless these holders happened to be the
original issuers.

In his report for 1863, written in October, Pollock urged
that nickel be dropped as a material of coinage. In an earlier
chapter it has been noted that Pollock thought nickel was
originally adopted in 1857 because of the mistaken notion

[8] See Chapter VI; also Appendix G.

that every coin should have a bullion value approximating its money value. In his report he said:

> . . . To this end, and for other reasons, an alloying metal was sought which should command a comparatively high price in the market, without being properly a *precious metal*. The change was well intended, but the experience of other countries, and indeed of our own, has taught us that it was an unnecessary liberality; and that all the nickel we have thus used, has been so much money wasted. . . . We have given it away under the mistaken notion that value was essential to secure the circulation of our inferior coinage and to prevent its being counterfeited.

This statement revealed a clear understanding of the nature of fiduciary coinage. The use of nickel could be defended only on the grounds that it made an attractive alloy. On this score Pollock was strongly opposed to nickel, maintaining that it destroyed his mint machinery. He said that it was the most obstinate and intractable of metals, "requiring the fiercest fire," and that it was "very destructive to dies and all the contiguous parts of the coining machinery." After a discussion of the possibilities of the "lately discovered metal" aluminum, he recommended the abolition of the copper-nickel cent and the substitution of coins of a "mixture called bronze," 95 per cent copper and 5 per cent tin and zinc, which the French nation had recently adopted for its smallest coins. Secretary Chase submitted these recommendations to Congress without comment, and Congress ignored them.

The demand for cent pieces continued to tax the powers of the mint. Furthermore, difficulty in obtaining nickel, which had to be imported from England in the midst of war, threatened to stop the coinage. The situation was so serious that Pollock, on March 2, 1864, sent an urgent letter to Chase, in the course of which he said that the United States

Assay Commission had officially indorsed the French alloy. With the letter he inclosed a bill providing for 1 cent and 2 cent coins of this material. Chase submitted Pollock's letter and draft to Congress on March 5, with the recommendation that the bill be passed at once.

The reasons presented by Pollock were sound, and his conclusions, supported by Chase and the Assay Commission, should have been decisive with Congress. But the proposals, as Mitchell says, encountered the opposition of the friends of Joseph Wharton. The nickel mines at Lancaster Gap, Pennsylvania, which had been counted upon as a source of nickel when the coins were adopted in 1857, had not been successful, and nickel for the coinage had been imported for a number of years. In 1863 Wharton acquired the Lancaster Gap mines as well as a refinery in Camden, New Jersey, which had been struggling with the problem of reducing nickel ores. In the 1863 report in which Pollock first recommended the abolition of nickel coinage he referred to this development, as follows:

> An effort is now making to re-establish in our country the manufacture of nickel from native ores. If successful, as present appearances indicate it will be, the Mint may be supplied from this source, to the entire exclusion of the foreign article.

On March 19, two weeks after Chase submitted the original bill, Pollock again wrote the Secretary. The situation was critical. The mint's supply of nickel was exhausted, and there were no supplies available from abroad. He goes on:

> We are thus shut up to the home supply, from the works of Mr. Wharton; but if we could receive all made at his establishment the amount would be wholly insufficient, would be from five hundred to eight hundred pounds per week, not more than one-half the amount required under ordinary circumstances.

. . . The wants of the public could be fully met by substituting bronze for the nickel alloy. But private interests have induced opposition to this proposition. Can these private interests be reconciled, and at the same time the public interest and convenience be promoted? I think they can, by reducing the weight of the nickel cent from seventy-two to forty-eight grains and continuing the coinage of the nickel alloy at this reduced rate, making a more convenient and desirable coin, and at the same time authorizing the coinage of a two cent bronze piece. This will meet the wants of the people and Government and be satisfactory to Mr. Wharton and his friends.

In other words, it was not possible to institute a necessary reform at a critical time because a private citizen insisted that his prospective profits should not be reduced. Chase submitted the letter and Pollock's amended bill to Congress with the comment that nickel coinage ought to be discontinued entirely, but that Pollock believed private interests would defeat the original proposal.

But Congress declined to compromise with the nickel interests. A Senate committee introduced the original bill and passed it without debate. In the House its opponents managed to delay its passage for a month. Thaddeus Stevens, one of the most influential men in the House, fought it bitterly, admitting, however, that he objected to it only because it adversely affected Wharton's interests. It was finally forced to a vote by members of the Committee on Coinage and became the law of April 22, 1864.[9] The meas-

---

[9] For the letters of Chase and Pollock and the legislative history of the bill see Congressional Globe, 38th Cong., 1st sess., 1207, 1227, 1763, 1772. See also Bankers Magazine, Vol. 18, 980. Snowden, no longer Director, was active in urging the retention of the nickel coins. All the parties to the controversy over nickel except Chase were from Pennsylvania. Stevens represented the district in which the mine was located. Wharton was a resident of Philadelphia. Pollock had been governor of the state, as well as a member of Congress. Wharton had made marked improvements in the methods

ure abolished the 1857 nickel cent and provided for a 1 cent piece of 48 grains and a 2 cent piece of 96 grains, each of them to be made of Pollock's "French bronze," the alloy of 95 per cent copper, 5 per cent tin and zinc. The coins were to be sold by the Treasury for "the lawful currency of the United States (except cents or half-cents issued under former acts of Congress)." The 1 cent piece was to be legal tender in payments to 10 cents, the 2 cent piece in payments to 20 cents.

This measure was, of course, the work of Pollock rather than of Congress, which had not discussed a single feature other than the effect on the market value of nickel. Certain provisions were notable. At last the copper coins had a legal status. A provision which had been opposed by every Congress and every Mint Director from 1792 to 1860 was adopted without a comment. The quaint feature of a double legal tender power for the 2 cent piece as against the 1 cent coin was probably due to a notion of Pollock that the number of coins rather than their value was the best basis for limitation. The provision which prevented the exchange of the new coins for the outstanding pure copper and copper-nickel coins is not easily explained. Acceptance of the outstanding coins would for a long time prevent the earning of large seigniorage profits, and Pollock was counting on an annual mint profit of $200,000. Probably he was moved less by this consideration than by the fact that exchange of the coins would not result in an increased supply of the badly wanted copper coins, but only in the substitution of new coins for old. In any event the effect of the provision was to keep the old coins in circulation, giving the country a minor coin currency of pure copper cents and half-cents, copper-nickel cents, and bronze 1 cent and 2 cent pieces,

of handling nickel alloys. He said in his "Project" that he had revived the Lancaster Gap mines at the instance of Pollock.

five different coins of very small denomination, of five different sizes and three materials, three of them without legal tender quality.

The 1 cent piece of this law is the familiar 1 cent coin we use today. From 1864 to the present it has been changed only in the devices on the coin and in legal tender power. The coinage of a 2 cent piece was unnecessary. While it was popular at first because of the great public demand for metallic small change, it was a superfluous denomination, and its circulation waned rapidly after the 5 cent nickel coin was introduced. Pollock was probably led to recommend it by technical considerations. For two years the mint had been unable to cope with the demand for copper coins. The establishment could produce in a given time as many 2 cent pieces as 1 cent coins, and the creation of the larger coin would lessen the strain on mint facilities.

From the first the bronze coinage was a success. In his 1864 report, written in October, Pollock said that the demand for the 1 and 2 cent pieces had been "unprecedented" and that every effort had been made to increase the output. In the fiscal year ending June 30, 1865, the coinage of the new cent amounted to 54,000,000 pieces, a record figure. Nearly 27,000,000 of the 2 cent pieces were produced. Pollock said that it was "a most convenient and popular coin." This outpouring of bronze coins completely satisfied all demands, and there was not again any deficiency of copper currency until our day. The seigniorage returns were even greater than Pollock had expected. The profits on copper coinage amounted to $146,000 in the fiscal year ending June 30, 1864, and in the next year reached the high figure of $558,000.[10]

In his 1864 report Pollock ignored the subject of nickel,

[10] The profits from minor coinage in the war years are summarized in the Annual Report of the Director of the Mint for 1873.

although he again referred to his experiments with aluminum alloys. He was not, he said, seeking another alloy
for his 1 and 2 cent coins, which were a proved success,
but for 5 and 10 cent coins to take the place of fractional
notes pending the revival of silver coinage. It is clear
enough that he did not want to use nickel for any purpose.
The private interests concerned with that metal had apparently been badly worsted, but their defeat was temporary.
In April, 1864, the month in which nickel coinage was abolished, Wharton published his "Project for Reorganizing
the Small Coinage," in which he proposed an alloy of 75
per cent copper and 25 per cent nickel for all minor coins.
This alloy, since become the most widely used minor coinage material in the world, had been experimentally adopted
by Belgium in a coinage law of 1860. Wharton argued
that this composition was harder than the 88-12 alloy of
the 1857 cent and therefore less easily counterfeited, ignoring the fact that the 1857 alloy had been condemned by
the Director as too hard for coinage.

Wharton proposed the coinage of 1, 2, 3, 5, and 10
cent pieces of the 75-25 alloy, but the success of the 1 and
2 cent bronze pieces made it inexpedient to war on these
two denominations. Secretary Chase had begun the issue
of 3 cent notes at the time when the bronze coinage was
filling the circulation with 1 and 2 cent coins. The note
was unnecessary and unpopular, and the nickel interests
seized upon it as the point of attack. There was an all-
night session of Congress on March 3, 1865, on the eve
of the President's inauguration the following day. In this
session the chairman of the House committee on coinage,
Kasson, who had led the fight to stop nickel coinage the
year before, introduced a bill providing for a 3 cent nickel
coin. There was no report and no explanation. The bill
was passed without comment and sent over to the Senate,

where it was passed in the early hours of the morning, again without comment. The influences that brought about the passage of the measure in this fashion were never revealed. it was signed by the President as of March 3, 1865.[11]

The law provided for a new 3 cent coin of the 75–25 copper-nickel composition, weighing 30 grains. It was to be legal tender in payments to 60 cents, and was to be sold to the public for lawful currency. No fractional note of a denomination less than 5 cents was to be issued, and the 3 cent notes outstanding were to be cancelled as they came into the Treasury. And finally it was provided that the legal tender of the 1 cent and 2 cent bronze coins should be reduced from 10 cents and 20 cents, respectively, to 4 cents.

The alloy of 75 per cent copper and 25 per cent nickel was unfamiliar in Europe and entirely new in America. Nickel has in high degree the power to dominate the color of its alloys, and the new material was almost as light as silver, whereas the 1857 copper-nickel cent was yellow. Apparently the composition was the first white alloy used for minor coins in modern history. It has great wearing qualities and does not tarnish easily. The mint officials finally acquired a technique that conquered the stubborn qualities of the metal, and the new alloy, later adopted for our 5 cent piece, became a permanent part of our coinage system.

But the institution of a 3 cent piece at this time, in the face of the protests of the Mint Director, was solely for the benefit of private interests. There were in circulation five varieties of copper coins of ½, 1, or 2 cent denomination. The coinage law already provided for a 3 cent silver coin, not then in circulation, it is true, but likely to return within a few years. There was no place for the 3 cent nickel coin. The law tacitly recognized this not only in

11 Congressional Globe, 38th Cong., 2nd sess., 1372, 1390, 1430.

the provision for withdrawal of the 3 cent note but also in the provision reducing the legal tender of the 1 and 2 cent coins to 4 cents. This petty attempt to limit the circulation of the bronze coins lacked even the merit of being efficient. Legal tender provisions for minor coins, though useful for certain purposes, have little influence on circulation. The new piece, weighing only 30 grains, was very small, and it had the further disadvantage of resembling in size and color the 3 cent silver coin of 1851 and the 5 cent silver piece of 1853, both of which were legal coins even if not in circulation.

The effect of the issue of the 3 cent nickel coins was to reduce the output of 1 and 2 cent pieces. In the calendar year 1864 about 53,000,000 of the 1 cent pieces had been issued and almost 20,000,000 of the 2 cent coins. The respective figures for 1865 were 35,000,000 and 14,000,000. About 11,000,000 of the new coins were also issued in this year. This large volume of minor coins, added to the millions already outstanding, brought the circulation almost to the saturation point. In 1866 the country could absorb a total of only 18,000,000 coins of all three denominations.

In his report for the fiscal year 1865 Pollock only indirectly referred to the superfluous character of the 3 cent coin, and he made no further objection to the use of nickel. Referring to the new coin he said:

> If, in addition to the already prohibited issue of three-cent notes, the five-cent notes of the fractional paper currency were withdrawn or the circulation limited and gradually reduced, the demand for this new coin would be much increased.

Later on in the report, he recommended the coinage of a 5 cent piece of the copper-nickel alloy. This proposal seems strange in view of the fact that Pollock undoubtedly realized that the country already had all the minor coins it could absorb. But he had been strongly opposed to paper fractions from their first appearance and had been anxiously awaiting the time when the resumption of silver coinage would be undertaken. He realized, apparently, that the nickel interests would support a proposal to extend the use of nickel and thought a 5 cent piece of that material would serve as a temporary metal substitute until silver coinage should be revived. "Tokens, or coins of inferior alloy," he said, "should not be permitted to take the place permanently of silver in the coinage of pieces above the denomination of three cents."

But most important of all his recommendations was the following:

> If the nickel alloy coin of five cents shall be adopted, temporarily or otherwise, provision should be made for its redemption in currency, in sums not less than one hundred dollars, and in a manner to suit the convenience of the government, and prevent its becoming troublesome by capricious use. At the proper time similar provision should be made for the redemption of the three-cent piece, in sums not less than sixty dollars. This would secure confidence and circulation for this coin.

Pollock, who had been the first Treasury official to understand the nature of fiduciary coins, was likewise the first to recognize the necessity of redeeming them when they were redundant or too worn for further circulation. His failure to suggest redemption of the bronze coins and his hesitation in the case of the 3 cent nickel coins show that he did not clearly understand the principle involved. Possibly he hesitated to recommend a measure that would reduce the seigniorage returns on the smaller coins. In the year preceding his report the profits had reached the figure of $650,-000. The total profits from minor coinage in the five years preceding June 30, 1866, had enabled the mint to pay all

expenses and then turn in to the Treasury a profit of
$1,000,000.[12]

Congress accepted Pollock's recommendations and embodied them in the law of May 16, 1866. The measure
provided for a 5 cent copper-nickel coin, with a weight of
77.16 grains and a legal tender limit of $1. The alloy
was to contain not more than 25 per cent of nickel. The
5 cent notes were to be withdrawn and cancelled. The new
coins were to be redeemable in lawful money when presented
in lots of $100. This brief measure has an important place
in our currency history. It created the 5 cent piece we use
today, and it was the first law in our history to provide for
the redemption of a current coin. The 1857 law providing
for the exchange of copper-nickel cents for the old copper
pieces was not a redemption measure but a withdrawal act,
aimed at the elimination of a discontinued currency.

Certain features of the law are worth noting. Redemption was provided for only in the case of the new 5 cent
piece. The vast volume of copper half-cents, copper cents,
bronze 1 and 2 cent pieces, and copper-nickel 3 cent pieces
had no such privilege. The abnormal demand for these
coins had been due in considerable measure to the unpopularity of the 3 and 5 cent paper notes. The issue of a 5
cent metal piece would reduce the demand for the smaller
coins and make millions of them redundant. A provision
making the new coin redeemable and leaving the current
coins outside the privilege was ill-adapted to the conditions.

The fractional weight of the new piece, 77.16 grains,
calls for explanation. The original bill, probably drawn up
by Pollock, made the weight 60 grains, and the House
passed the bill in this form. In the Senate the Finance
Committee amended the bill, Senator Sherman reporting

[12] For the annual coinages, profits, and expenses see annual Reports of the
Director for the years from 1863 to 1866; also Appendix E.

that the committee, after conference with Pollock, Secretary McCulloch, and the House committee, had decided to change the weight to 77.16 grains. The Senate accepted this incomplete explanation and the House concurred.[13] The purpose of the amendment was to give the coin a metric weight. Since the time of Jefferson there had been an intermittent interest in the matter of a universal system of coins and measures. Senator Sherman was a leader in the movement. The Senate committee wished to give the new coin a weight of 5 grams, but could not bring themselves to use the metric term. They adopted, therefore, the awkward fractional figure of 77.16 grains, which is approximately the equivalent. Inasmuch as there was not anywhere else in Treasury or mint operations any use of the metric system the provision was an empty gesture. It has never been changed, and our present day 5 cent piece still has a metric weight.

There was a large demand for the new coin. The mint used the maximum nickel proportion of 25 per cent already used in the 3 cent piece, and the light-colored coins were popular. They did not fill any vacancy in the fractional currency. They merely displaced a large number of 5 cent notes and a still larger number of 1, 2, and 3 cent coins that were being used for 5 and 10 cent purchases because the 5 cent notes were unsatisfactory. The inevitable effect of the issue of the 5 cent coins was to make the smaller pieces redundant. Given a choice, the general public had chosen small copper coins in preference to paper notes, and there was now an opportunity to choose a 5 cent piece in preference to 2 and 3 cent coins. But the fractional notes were redeemable in greenbacks, while the discarded small coins could not be redeemed.

Pollock was succeeded as Director in 1867 by H. R.

---

[13] Congressional Globe, 39th Cong., 1st sess., 1452, 1875, 2520.

Linderman. In his first annual report Linderman discussed the situation:

> A provision was incorporated in the act of May 16, 1866, Section 5, to redeem in national currency the five cent nickel-copper coins. . . . It is easy to see that one effect of this enactment is to restrict the issue of such coins and prevent them from flooding the community; a most wise and just provision it is; and it is greatly to be deplored that it does not as yet extend to the pieces of one, two, and three cents.

Linderman continues with an interesting discussion of the causes of redundancy in copper coins, in which he brings out the fact that banks and business concerns, anxious to give customers fresh coins, will continue to purchase new issues from the mint long after the coins in general circulation have become so redundant as to go to a discount. While this is generally true, such practices can not long continue in a well-ordered system. The excess coins flow back to banks and stores in such volume that new issues are automatically stopped. An extended period of redundancy can only be due to inadequate laws or mal-administration. The small minor coins were now becoming redundant because the Treasury was displacing them with new coins without providing any outlet for the discarded pieces. In the same way the subsidiary coins of 1853 had become redundant because the law providing for their sale only for gold coin had been violated and the copper cents of 1857 had become excessive because Snowden had forced their issue in exchange for Spanish silver coins.

In his report for the following year, 1868, Linderman again urged the redemption of the smaller coins. He reported that he had been buying the copper-nickel cents of 1857 with new 3 and 5 cent coins, some 13,000,000 pieces having been retired in this way. The exchange served an excellent purpose, even if it was a violation of two specific prohibitions in the laws of 1865 and 1866. His request for redemption received support from United States Treasurer Spinner, who was, it will be remembered, chiefly responsible for the postage currency fiasco of 1862. In 1868 Spinner, through whose office fractional money of all kinds was redeemed, made a statement so clearly outlining the vexed currency conditions that its quotation at length is justified. Referring to the fractional paper currency, he says:

> This convenient small change, that was in various ways receivable for public dues, and at the same time convertible into lawful money of the United States, has been replaced, under the specious plea of a "speedy return to specie payments" by an almost worthless irredeemable, poisonous, and stinking copper and nickel token currency. The five cent tokens are made a legal tender for $1, and are redeemable in sums of not less than $100. All the others, including the one cent, the two cent, and the three cent tokens, and whether made of copper alone or of copper and nickel, are entirely irredeemable, and, as irredeemable currency, have already become a nuisance by their great accumulations in the hands of small dealers.
>
> Officers engaged in government collections, especially those connected with the Post Office Department, suffer in consequence. Postmasters are by law compelled to receive these government tokens in payment for postage stamps, and are then immediately liable to the government for the amount of such sales in good money. But the government that sold these tokens at par for their face value, or paid them as money to its creditors, now turns round and refuses to receive them back in payments from its own officers, who were by law compelled to receive them on account of the government.
>
> Postmasters who were so obliged to receive these tokens have offered them by the bagful in payment of their post office receipts at the counter of the Treasury, and have been compelled to carry them home again, because the Treasurer cannot receive over 60 cents in three-cent pieces, nor over four cents in one or two-cent pieces in one payment. Was there ever an act of the government of a respectable people, that, for meanness, can

compare with this? An individual that would practice such a confidence game would be branded as a two-penny thief, and would soon be consigned to a house of correction. A government that practices such frauds upon the people cannot hope long to retain the respect of anybody. It has been intimated, and there are those uncharitable enough to believe the story, that the ownership of an unprofitable nickel mine had something to do in influencing the passage of these "speedy-return-to-specie-payment" laws.[14]

Spinner's statement that he could not as Treasurer accept minor coins in sums beyond their legal tender limits reveals a curious conception of legal tender. The attitude of the Treasury was, as Spinner said, unfair. It was also incorrect. The law did not provide for redemption of the 1, 2, and 3 cent pieces, and it limited the tender of the bronze coins to 4 cents and that of the 3 cent piece to 60 cents, but construing these statutes to mean that the Treasury could not receive the coins in larger amounts from another division of the government was absurd.

Linderman's proposals were supported by Secretary McCulloch as well as by Spinner. In 1866 the Treasury had sent J. J. Knox on a special mission to the branch mint in San Francisco. In his report on the condition of the mint Knox pointed out that the general coinage law, passed in 1837, was antiquated. He referred especially to the many acts relating to minor coins, which were, he said, "entirely disconnected and incongruous."[15] The ultimate result of his report was a general revision of the coinage laws in 1873. A more immediate result was the submission to Congress by Linderman of a proposed law completely reorganizing the minor coinage.

The bill, which was introduced in March, 1868, by Rep-

[14] For these statements of Linderman and Spinner see Annual Reports on the Finances for 1867, 327, and 1868, 255, 428.

[15] See Annual Report on the Finances for 1866, 267.

resentative Kelley of Pennsylvania, never became a law, but
its history is part of the record of our fractional currency.
After the House committee on coinage had made minor
amendments the bill was again presented by Kelley in the
following February. The measure provided for the discontinuance of paper notes of less denomination than 25
cents, of the 3 and 5 cent silver coins legally established but
not in circulation, and of all the minor coins created under
existing law. The place of all these currencies was to be
taken by three coins, a 1 cent piece of 1½ grams, a 3 cent
piece of 3 grams, and a 5 cent piece of 5 grams. All three
were to be composed of copper and nickel, with the nickel
proportion not less than 25 per cent nor more than 33 per
cent. Legal tender and unlimited redemption for all three
coins were provided for.

The bill had three main objectives. The first was to
extend the use of nickel. The measure permitted a large
increase in the nickel content of the 5 cent piece, an increase in both the size and the nickel proportion of the 3
cent piece, and the substitution of a nickel cent for the bronze
1 and 2 cent pieces. As Kelley said, Linderman had discovered the possibility of coining pieces containing as much
as 33 per cent of nickel. Inasmuch as there were no silver
coins in circulation, the entire currency below the 25 cent
note would be made up of nickel coins. A second objective
was to adopt metric weights for all the minor coins, as
a first step, Kelley said, in the establishment of a universal
coinage. The third objective was uniform legal tender and
redeemability for minor coins.

The bill aroused a discussion that was sordid in tone and
redolent of the spoils system. The nickel interests of Missouri insisted upon an amendment prohibiting the purchase
of nickel from foreign producers and finally obtained a provision which allowed purchase from abroad only when the

domestic price was 20 per cent higher. In this form the bill passed the House. The Senate ignored it. Kelley again presented the bill in the next session, and this time the Missouri representatives demanded an amendment providing for the purchase of nickel by open bidding. Despite Kelley's opposition the House inserted the amendment before it passed the bill. For the second time the Senate rejected the measure.[16]

Meanwhile, in 1869, Pollock had been restored to his position as Director. He was opposed to the provisions that Linderman had recommended. In his first annual report he severely criticized the proposal to substitute for his bronze coinage a 1 cent nickel piece of 1½ grams, less than half the size of the cent piece. And he was still averse to redemption of the bronze coins, as he had been in 1865. "No consideration," he said, "of public interest or private convenience demands the redemption of the bronze one and two cent pieces." He said that whatever redundancy there was had been "gradually diminished" by the exchange of 3 and 5 cent nickel coins for the bronze pieces. In his report for the fiscal year ending June 30, 1870, Pollock repeated his arguments against redemption.

Pollock's aversion to redemption of the bronze coins when he had been responsible for the law providing for redemption of the 5 cent piece is inexplicable. In any event he was wholly wrong. The country was overrun with minor coins. In the two fiscal years ending in June, 1869, more than $360,000 in 1 and 2 cent pieces had been bought by the mint with 3 and 5 cent coins, but even this large redemption, entirely without authority of law, had failed to relieve the situation. Millions of the coins had accumulated in the hands of postmasters, newsdealers, bus companies, and

---

[16] The legislative history of the bill is in the Congressional Globe, 40th Cong., 2nd sess., and 41st Cong., 1st and 2nd sess.

other concerns which could dispose of them only with difficulty. Treasury officials and members of Congress were bombarded with petitions for relief.[17]

In the annual Treasury report for 1870 with which he submitted Pollock's arguments against redemption Secretary Boutwell asked Congress to pass a redemption measure at once. In January, 1871, the Senate Committee on Finance approved a bill providing for the redemption of the "copper and other token coins." Both Senate and House passed the bill after brief discussion, and it became the law of March 3, 1871. It provided for the redemption in lawful currency of all the minor coins when presented in lots of $20 and authorized the Secretary to suspend the issue of the coins when the volume of redemptions indicated redundancy. Within three months of the passage of the law 11,000,000 minor coins were redeemed with greenbacks, and in the next fiscal year nearly 26,000,000 coins, with a value of $475,-000, were withdrawn.[18]

The law of March 3, 1865, which authorized the 3 cent nickel coin contained a provision of general character. It provided that it would be lawful to inscribe the motto "In God We Trust" on all coins of the United States. This was the outcome of a letter in 1861 from a clergyman to Chase, suggesting that the national faith be recognized by an inscription on the coins. Chase directed Pollock to devise a suitable motto, and Pollock suggested "God Our Trust." Chase amended this slightly, selecting the familiar inscription still used on our coins.[19] The law of 1864 providing for the bronze coins left the devices to the discretion of the Treasury, and Pollock put the inscription on his first

---

[17] See House Executive Document no. 307, 41st Cong., 2nd session.

[18] See Annual Report on the Finances for 1871, 429, and 1872, 420.

[19] Watson, Chapter VIII; Annual Report of the Director of the Mint for 1896, 106.

issue of the 2 cent piece.   The law of 1865 officially sanctioned its use on all coins.

The end of the war found the South without currency
of any kind, and the people welcomed the new bronze and
nickel coins.   Pollock noted this as early as 1865, saying
in his report for that year that the new bronze coins had
been "distributed to almost every part of the United States,
and many into states, west and south, that heretofore refused to use such coins as currency."   A year later he reported that they had been sent "to all parts of the United
States, but principally to the western and southern states."
The ancient prejudice that had come down from colonial
times was breaking down.

The story of the minor coinage in the Civil War era is
a record of hand-to-mouth legislation, always after the emergency, always planless, always fortuitous, and sometimes
tainted with improper influence.   And yet marked progress
had been made.   Out of this war period came the 1 cent
and the 5 cent coins we use today.   Without any fixed policy
whatever, the Treasury and Congress had in the end instituted limited legal tender for all the minor coins and provided for their unlimited redemption, given up the conception of bullion value close to money value, and put an end
to counterfeits and duplicates of all kinds.   Pollock had been
instrumental in effecting all these results, although he had
unwisely opposed them in part.   He is one of the neglected
figures in American currency history.

CHAPTER XV

THE CIVIL WAR PERIOD: SILVER COINS

DISAPPEARANCE of silver in 1862 a result of error in law of 1853—Continuance of coinage after disappearance of silver—Snowden's irregular coinage continued by Pollock and Linderman—Export of silver coins to Canada and Latin-America—Profits of dealers—Special conditions on the Pacific Coast.

In Chapter X extended reference was made to the serious error in the provision of the law of 1853 which established a weight for the new subsidiary coins only 6.91 per cent below the standard coin weight of 412½ grains to the dollar. As a result of this mistake the new coins were worth as bullion in the period from 1853 to 1862 from 97 to 99½ cents per dollar in the standard gold coin and were in danger of disappearance during the entire period. The small reduction was fundamentally a mistake, even if the coins did not pass the disappearance point. A much larger reduction would have been safe, as well as as profitable.

In a later chapter it was shown that the silver coins disappeared entirely, and with extraordinary rapidity, as soon as the gold value of greenbacks fell below the gold value of the silver in the subsidiary coins. This gold value of silver was, throughout most of 1862, about 97 cents per dollar, and the greenbacks fell below that figure in June and remained below it for many years thereafter. The crisis in the fractional currency which developed in June, 1862, was thus due to the failure of Congress to understand the nature of fiduciary coinage in 1853. If the reduction, by the law of 1853, had been as much as 25 per cent, the coins would not have disappeared until the greenbacks fell to a gold value of 78 cents. They did not reach this point until October 10, 1862. With a 20 per cent reduction the disappearing point would have come with a greenback value of 83 cents, which was attained on September 25. With a reduction of 20 or 25 per cent the Treasury would have had the entire summer of 1862 in which to prepare for the disappearance of silver coins, and it seems reasonable to believe that even a dilatory and careless administration would have made ample provision for the inevitable and thus prevented the collapse of the fractional currency, the unfortunate experience with postage stamps, and the flood of shinplasters.

Under the ordinary conditions of subsidiary coinage the general public purchases the subsidiary pieces with gold coins, dollar for dollar, and the subsidiary coins are worth their nominal values in standard money. If a paper money régime is established and the paper falls to a discount in gold, the government may adopt one of a number of policies. It may continue to offer the subsidiary pieces only in return for gold. In such case the public will lose the amount of the paper discount on its purchases of silver coins, and purchases will be continued only by business concerns so greatly in need of change that they will suffer the loss rather than go without. But when the paper discount reaches the point where the silver coins disappear as soon as they go into circulation, all purchases stop. The government may, on the other hand, undertake to preserve the fiction that the paper money is equal to gold by offering to accept paper in payment for subsidiary silver. In such case it is the treasury that suffers the loss from the gold discount on paper. It can stand this loss because of the seigniorage offset until the bullion value of the silver coins is greater than the value of the depreciated paper. Beyond that point the government will be making the coins at a net loss on cost of production, bankrupting itself to produce coins that go to the melting pot as soon as they are issued. No government can do this for any extended period.

It is thus evident that in any ordinary circumstances subsidiary silver coinage must stop, regardless of the terms of issue, when the value of the paper falls below the bullion value of the coins. It ceased in every country involved in the World War when the paper money reached that point. By all normal standards it should have stopped in this country in the Civil War period. But it did not, and its continuance is one of the strange developments in our currency history. It will be recalled that Director Snowden, for reasons that cannot now be fathomed, administered the law of 1853 in irregular fashion, exchanging the coins for silver bullion instead of selling them for gold coins in the manner required by the law. By the time Snowden retired from office in 1861 the practice of setting a fixed price for bullion and buying all that was offered, with payment in subsidiary silver, had become a fixed routine of subsidiary coinage. It would appear that the price was deliberately set at a point somewhat above the current market price, so that the seigniorage on the subsidiary silver was divided between the government and the bullion owner. Thus the amount of silver coinage was not regulated by the public need for small change, but by the amount of bullion that came into the market. The only force limiting the coinage was the difficulty the bullion owner encountered in disposing of subsidiary coins that had become seriously redundant and were selling at a discount. For two years before the Civil War the fixed price was $1.21 per standard ounce. Since an ounce produced $1.25 in subsidiary coins the government's profit was the difference between these two figures, less the costs of alloy and coinage.

When Pollock succeeded Snowden he continued the practice. He found nothing irregular or abnormal in the procedure, although the most cursory inspection of the coinage law would have shown that it was illegal, while the redundancy of silver coins in circulation, now become a public nuisance, was positive evidence of a serious defect in the system. The market price of silver rose in 1861 and Pollock increased the mint price in January, 1862, to $1.22½ per ounce. In his annual report for 1862 he referred to this increase in his "mint price of silver" and in connection with certain proposals in regard to the revival of silver circulation he said that a high mint price would encourage the bringing of

> . . . silver bullion from the Washoe mines and other sources, by holders desirous of realizing a premium and of accommodating their own business; so much of the gain as would be necessary to draw the material should go in that direction: the remainder would pay expenses of coinage and transportation.

This statement meant that Pollock, like Snowden, did not understand the coinage law he was administering. Silver coinage was a sort of free coinage, at a ratio to be determined arbitrarily by the Mint Director.

At the time Pollock wrote this report, in October, 1862, no silver coins were in circulation in the United States, except in the Pacific regions. They had not circulated for months. There was no avoidance of the fact that the mint was still coining and issuing millions of subsidiary pieces that completely vanished as soon as they left the mint. Pollock must have faced the problem of the propriety of further coinage. Why it did not lead him to the discovery that the method of coinage was illegal is beyond explanation.

Just as Snowden continued this coinage practice for years in the face of a nation-wide excess of silver coins, so Pollock continued the coinage through the Civil War era.

Pollock must also have known what became of the coins after they left his hands. For a time, in July, 1862, they were sold by the bullion owners to brokers or to business houses. Bullion owners could send their silver to foreign markets or they could take it to the mint and exchange it for silver coins that could be sold at a greenback premium. The profit on coinage under these conditions was not high, and it could not continue after silver coins ceased to circulate. What, then, was the motive for coinage after this point was reached in July, 1862, and what disposition was made of the small but steady output of subsidiary coins produced throughout the fractional paper period? The answer is found in fugitive references in the reports and news records of the period. The coins were going to various foreign countries, in which they served as a fractional silver currency on the same fiduciary basis as in the United States. It has already been pointed out that Canada accepted United States coins at their nominal values in exchange for gold. From 1858 to 1862 a steady stream of subsidiary silver went across the border. After the greenbacks fell to a discount in 1862 the profit on export to Canada became large, and in a short while Canada was over-run with United States silver. When the saturation point was reached in the fall of 1862, the Canadian market was wiped out.[1]

An even larger field for export, however, was available. The countries of Latin-America had currency systems based on the Spanish dollar. Their half-peso and two-real pieces

[1] Before the end of 1862 United States silver was at a discount of 3 per cent in Canadian gold. The Detroit Advertiser said that the City Treasurer of Toronto had half a ton of U. S. silver coins that he could not dispose of. In this country a greenback dollar would buy about 80 cents in subsidiary coin. Across the line a Canadian paper dollar would buy $1.03 in the same coin.

were almost identical with our half-dollars and quarters in weights and gold values. Coinage facilities were meagre, even in the countries that had long had mints. Many had no mints whatever and depended on foreign coins. In nearly all of them our subsidiary silver coins were accepted as equivalent to their own. In some cases they bore a premium. As early as 1854 the Merchants Magazine reported that United States silver was accepted in the West Indies at a premium of 12½ per cent over local coins. There was a profit in taking silver to the mint, having it coined into subsidiary pieces, and shipping the coins to Central America, South America, or the West Indies. There the coins were exchanged for gold or for foreign silver coins containing more metal. Dealers had discovered the possibility of this trade soon after the passage of the law of 1853 and had exported part of the large excess of silver in circulation before the Civil War.

It has long been thought that the subsidiary coins which suddenly disappeared in 1862 were melted or sent to Europe and sold as bullion. As a matter of fact only a small proportion were disposed of in this way. The great majority went to countries where they had values as coins above their bullion values, some to Canada but most to Latin-America. Their dramatic reappearance many years later is described in a subsequent chapter. The capacity of Latin-America to absorb United States silver was obviously limited, but there was some place for new coins even after the wholesale exportation of 1862, and in later years the mints continued to coin silver for bullion dealers who shipped the coins to Latin-America and brought back gold or foreign silver coins. After June, 1862, the United States mints were, so far as silver was concerned, merely establishments conducted for the benefit of New York and San Francisco bullion dealers.

In 1872 one of the dealers testified before a House Committee that the operation was highly profitable, not only because of the gain from the exchange of the coins in Latin-America but also because of the high rate offered by the mint in exchanging coins for bullion. He said that in some years his business amounted to $2,000,000 and his profits to $100,000. The situation was not unlike that of the West Indies silver dollar "endless chain" to which Jefferson put a stop in 1806. In the fiscal year ending June 30, 1863, the coinage of subsidiary silver amounted to $1,109,000. More than $800,000 of this was coined at the San Francisco mint. Since silver coins remained in circulation in the Pacific states, it is probable that a small part of this coinage stayed in California, although long before this time there was a burdensome redundancy of silver coins. But the bulk of it was exported. All of the $300,000 produced at the Philadelphia mint left the country. One of the reports of the time states that in only nine months of 1866 more than $500,000 in "treasure (chiefly silver)" was shipped from San Francisco to Panama and Chili, and much additional to Central America.[2]

Linderman, when he succeeded Pollock in 1867, continued the irregular coinage of silver. He maintained the current rate of $1.22½ per ounce for standard silver, although this rate was by his own testimony at a later date somewhat above the value of silver on a market basis and more than sufficient to give bullion dealers the necessary profit on export of the coins.

There was no general movement to restore silver coinage to circulation after the Treasury adopted a paper fractional currency in 1862. Pollock was opposed to the circulation of paper fractions and in his reports from 1862 to 1867 frequently referred to the advisability of reviving

[2] Annual Report on the Finances for 1866, 263.

the silver currency. In the 1862 report he recommended that the silver coins be reduced 25 per cent. At that time coins so reduced would have remained in circulation only a few weeks, as they would have reached the disappearance point a little later with the further depreciation of the greenbacks. By the end of the war the people had come to accept fractional notes as an established currency, even if they were physically unsatisfactory.

In the states on the Pacific slope the situation was quite different. These states, with their own gold and silver supplies, a branch mint, and a mountain barrier to block off the paper currency of the Eastern states, remained on a coin basis in all transactions. They resolutely refused greenbacks, declined to use fractional notes, and rejected the bank-notes created by the national bank act of 1863. The mint in San Francisco coined subsidiary silver throughout the war period, not only for export but also for domestic use, and the coinage was much larger than that at the Philadelphia mint, all of whose product left the country. Half-dollars preponderated in the San Francisco coinage, as this denomination was most desirable for export. But there were many quarters and dimes in circulation. No silver 3 cent pieces or half-dimes were coined before 1868, and no copper, bronze, or nickel coins for many years after that date. As elsewhere in the country, the silver coins became redundant in the Pacific states as a result of the irregular method of coinage adopted in 1853. The sparse population, the large supplies of silver bullion, and the presence of a mint combined to make the excess extreme in California, and subsidiary coins were selling at a discount before 1860. Since paper money was not admitted into the currency, the war made no change in the situation. Silver coins were legal tender at par with gold coins and could not be melted at a profit. If the demand in Latin-

America failed to take away the surplus, the coins remained in circulation and went to a discount in gold. When in 1862 the East was wholly without any coins for retail trade and business was in chaotic condition, silver coins were a drug on the market in California. They sold at a discount continuously from 1860 to 1873.[3]

[3] See Snowden, Ancient and Modern Coins, 128; Coin Collectors Journal, vol. 6, 116.

Chapter XVI

THE LAW OF 1873

CURRENCY SITUATION at end of war—Paper notes unsatisfactory—Problem of restoring silver coinage—Knox undertakes general revision of coinage laws—Knox's bill of 1869—The irregular coinage of silver—Legislative history of the bill—The law of 1873—Details of the law—The silver dollar and the trade dollar—No improvement in subsidiary coinage provisions—Irregular coinage legalized—Metric weights for subsidiarv coins—Minor coin provisions.

The year 1869 may be taken as the time when the temporary expedients and experimental currencies of the war period reached their most confused condition. The standard currency was the greenback. The fractional currency was a disorderly collection of notes and coins. The conditions can best be shown by a table of the fractional money actually in use, as outlined on page 224.

A number of these notes and coins had been officially discontinued. The postage currency had been displaced in 1863, the copper coins in 1857, the nickel cent in 1864, the 3 cent note in 1865, and the 5 cent note in 1866. The public did not discriminate between current and uncurrent money, accepting all forms without question. No legal provision had been made for the redemption of the discontinued nickel cent piece and millions were in circulation. The law provided for the cancellation of postage currency as it came into the Treasury. The post offices were the chief agencies through which withdrawal was accomplished, and postmasters had been instructed to return all postage currency as well as mutilated or badly worn fractional notes. But these officials had become entangled in the regulations, which permitted them to forward unregistered packages under their franking privilege but forced them to pay for registration out of their own pockets.   Unregistered pack-

FRACTIONAL CURRENCY IN USE IN 1869

Type	Denominations	Legal Tender	Redemption
Fractional notes	50 cents	none	in greenbacks
	25 cents	none	in greenbacks
	15 cents	none	in greenbacks
	10 cents	none	in greenbacks
	5 cents	none	in greenbacks
	3 cents	none	in greenbacks
Postage currency	50 cents	none	in greenbacks
	25 cents	none	in greenbacks
	10 cents	none	in greenbacks
	5 cents	none	in greenbacks
Copper-nickel coins	5 cents	to $1.00	in greenbacks
	3 cents	to 60 cents	not redeemable
	1 cent	none	not redeemable
Bronze coins	2 cents	to 4 cents	not redeemable
	1 cent	to 4 cents	not redeemable
Copper coins	1 cent	none	not redeemable
	$\frac{1}{2}$ cent	none	not redeemable

ages were frequently stolen.   The postmasters solved the problem by ignoring the order to return old and mutilated notes.   Congress permitted this condition to exist from 1865 to 1870.[1]

The continued circulation of this bewildering assortment of fractional currencies was undesirable.   There was an

[1] Annual Reports on the Finances for 1869, 270, and 1872, 261.

embarrassing excess of nickel and bronze coins in circulation. The total volume, estimated at $8,000,000 to $10,-000,000 in 1, 2, 3, and 5 cent pieces, was much greater than the country could use. The redemption law of 1871, described in the previous chapter, was still three years away. The war was over, but greenbacks were still much below par and a restoration of the old subsidiary silver coinage was not a possibility. Retail business was now carried on chiefly with fractional paper notes, and there was little public complaint that they were unsatisfactory. There were officially outstanding a total of $33,000,000 in postage currency and fractional notes, although an unknown proportion had been destroyed or permanently lost. The government would have to redeem the entire amount actually in circulation if silver coins were restored.

On the other hand, the paper notes were coming to be a fiscal problem. They wore out very quickly, and almost the entire mass was returned annually for sorting, counting, destruction, and replacement. The process was expensive. Even so, the methods of redemption and reissue were not efficient, and the notes in circulation were in bad condition.[2] With the gradual recovery of trade and industry after the war the demand for fractional notes was steadily increasing, and the wisdom of establishing a definite fractional money policy was increasingly evident. In 1870 Pollock again recommended a reduction in the size of the silver coins, proposing that the weight be reduced from 384 to 280 grains per dollar. He said that distinguished financiers and "leading commercial newspapers" had indorsed his plan. In April, 1870, Representative Mercur introduced in the House a bill providing for Pollock's proposed coinage, but nothing came of it.[3]

[2] Annual Report on the Finances for 1868, 254.
[3] Congressional Globe, 41st Cong., 2nd sess., 2961, and 42nd Cong., 2nd

Meanwhile Secretary Boutwell had directed Knox, now Deputy Comptroller of the Currency, to undertake a complete revision of the coinage laws such as Knox had recommended in his 1866 report, referred to in the preceding chapter. Knox was assisted by Linderman, who had completed a two-year term as Director of the Mint. Knox first went over the existing statutes line by line. He then segregated those that needed to be retained, added many new provisions, and codified the entire group into a unified statute. This completed draft was submitted to officials and experts in currency and coinage, including former mint directors and officials. Many of the suggestions of these critics were accepted and incorporated in the measure. The final draft was sent to the Senate Finance Committee in 1870 by Boutwell. The House asked for and obtained copies of all the papers and letters that had been used by Knox in connection with the bill.[4]

The bill which Knox prepared became the law of 1873, but in the three years before its passage the measure was altered and revised in almost every section. Some reference, however, to Knox's original proposals and to the considerations which led him to recommend them is essential to an understanding of the measure finally adopted by Congress. Knox's bill dropped the many antiquated and superseded laws that had not been formally repealed and reworded those that were to be retained. The important provisions were those concerned with mint administration, the seigniorage on gold, the silver dollar, and the minor coins.

---

sess., 308, 395. See also Moring, Suggestions to Congress, a pamphlet outlining a project of the New York Chamber of Commerce for the coinage of 10 and 25 cent pieces of mixed copper, nickel, and silver.

[4] All the documentary records of the bill are brought together in Senate Miscellaneous Document no. 132, and House Executive Document no. 307, both of the 41st Cong., 2d session.

A new mint bureau was created, with a director to be stationed at Washington.   The charge of ½ of 1 per cent on gold coinage was abolished.   The standard silver dollar was dropped from the list of coins.

The minor coinage provisions were, with some modifications, those which Linderman had presented in 1868.   There were the same three coins of 1, 3, and 5 cent denominations, with the same three weights of 1½, 3, and 5 grams, the coins to be made of the 75–25 copper-nickel alloy.   The earlier bill had specified an alloy of not less than 25 per cent nor more than 33 per cent of nickel.   There were the same provisions for redemption, for legal tender, for withdrawal of the current nickel and bronze coins, and for the discontinuance of the 10 cent paper note and the 3 cent and 5 cent silver coins.   It will be recalled that a bill establishing this plan for nickel coinage had passed the House in two Congresses, after a controversy between Kelley and the Missouri representatives, but had been rejected by the Senate.   The minor coin provisions were discussed at length by the critics to whom the bill was submitted.   Director Pollock was opposed to all the provisions, objecting especially to the substitution of a very small copper-nickel cent for his bronze pieces.   Snowden preferred the 88–12 nickel alloy which he had devised in 1857.   Some critics wanted only one minor coin, the 1 cent bronze piece, while others wished to retain the 3 cent and 5 cent silver coins when silver coinage should be revived.   No one of those consulted approved the creation of a 1½ gram copper-nickel cent.   But the bill as presented by Knox went to the Senate unchanged.   Apparently he was committed to an all-nickel minor coinage.

In the report which accompanied the bill Knox made a statement in connection with the discussion of the profits from minor coinage, as follows:

> The amount paid into the Treasury during the past twelve
> years from this source has been $4,225,000, so that the minor
> coinage has been manufactured at a cost of more than one-half
> of its nominal value. If the manufacture of this coinage had
> been under the supervision of an officer not influenced by the
> clamor for patronage, and independent of all local pressure, its
> cost would not probably have been more than one-third of its
> nominal value.

This frank statement referred, of course, to the purchase
of nickel from Wharton, and it clearly implied that the loss
to the government from the payment of prices above the
competitive market prices was about $1,500,000. The re-
markable feature of the matter was the identity of the persons involved. In the twelve year period since nickel coinage had been instituted by Snowden, there had been three
Directors, Snowden from 1857 to 1861, Pollock from 1861
to 1867, and Linderman from 1867 to 1869, and at the
time the report was written Pollock was again Director,
Linderman was assisting Knox in preparing the bill and the
report, and Snowden and Pollock were being consulted.
Finally, it should be noted, the bill proposed to abolish two
silver coins, two bronze coins, and a paper note in order
to make way for a large increase in nickel coinage, without any provision whatever for stopping the purchase of
nickel by secret arrangement.

It is clear from a study of the various documents and
drafts of the bill that Knox had failed to understand the
method by which the silver coinage had been illegally administered since 1853. The coinage provisions of the original draft were identical with the 1853 provisions. Some,
however, of the experts consulted were aware of the situation, among them Patterson, who had been Director before
Snowden. But the critic who most definitely condemned
the method was none other than Snowden, who was solely

responsible for the irregular procedure. He explained the matter in the following naive statement:

> When specie payments are resumed with us, or when the paper currency and the gold are rated at the same, or even nearly the same, value, unless some stringent restrictions are made upon the issues of reduced silver coins, as now authorized, there will be a plethora of them on the market, and their circulation will be not only an inconvenience but a loss.

This warning led Knox to examine the actual conditions of the coinage system he was revising, and he altered his original bill. He reworded the law of 1853 in such a manner that no director, however careless, could fail to carry out its instructions, and with the bill he submitted the following statement:

> It was evidently intended that these subsidiary or token coins should be issued only in exchange at par for gold coin. But the practice at the mint for many years has been to purchase all silver bullion offered at about $1.22½ per ounce, which is above the market price, paying therefor in silver coin. The effect of the mint practice has been to put in circulation silver coins without regard to the amount required for the purposes of "change," creating a discount upon silver coin, and bringing losses upon holders of any considerable amount.

It is worth noting that this public disclosure caused no alteration in the prevailing practice. It was unnecessary to reword the law of 1853. It would have been sufficient if Knox had merely submitted to his chief, Secretary Boutwell, a recommendation that he instruct Pollock to obey the law.

One other provision in Knox's bill calls for comment. His original draft reduced the silver dollar, still a standard unit under the law of 1837, to 384 grains gross, the weight

of $1 in subsidiary coins. He evidently intended to make
the coin subsidiary, although the provision was so ineffi-
ciently phrased that the intent was not disclosed by the
actual words. A number of the critics objected to the proposed change, and some of them suggested a special coin
for trade with the Far East. Knox thereupon dropped
the silver dollar entirely from the coinage system and in
his report suggested the possibility of the special trade coin.
His intention was simply to drop a coin which had been
in the list of permitted coins since 1837 but had been unknown to the people since 1806. It is not within the province of this book to discuss the bimetallic controversy that
tore the country asunder in the next three decades, but it
is permissible to note that neither Knox himself nor any
of the critics realized that the country was legally on the
double standard and that dropping the dollar would be
a vitally important action changing the country's organic
system.

The bill that Knox submitted was thus a measure that
restated the existing statutes, simplified mint administration,
formally but more or less unintentionally adopted the gold
standard, and proposed minor changes in the silver coins
below the dime and in the bronze and nickel pieces. The
measure made no attempt to restore gold coinage or subsidiary coinage. It ignored completely the vital problems
of eliminating fractional paper notes and bringing the greenbacks to parity with gold. The bill was essentially a simplified and clarified expression of laws already in force but
without present significance. The elimination of the silver
dollar and the abolition of bronze coinage in favor of nickel
were the only coinage proposals of serious consequence. It
is widely believed that Knox's revision was a work of great
importance, performed with marked skill and insight. As
a matter of historical fact it was a clumsy attempt to

simplify existing statutes, marked by a failure to understand existing conditions or to remedy existing evils.

The Senate Finance committee presented the bill, with various amendments, in January, 1871.[5] The section abolishing seigniorage charges on gold coinage had been changed to make the charge 3/10 of 1 per cent, and Western senators attacked the provision furiously. The bill was finally passed without a single reference to any one of the remaining seventy provisions. In the House the bill was long delayed, finally appearing in January, 1872. In the debate only two questions were discussed at length, the salaries of the mint officers and the propriety of minor coinage of the fiduciary type. One of these was a matter of no importance, the other a question settled by George Washington in 1795. The bitter feeling in connection with nickel was again evident, one member stating that the only purpose of nickel coinage was to give a Pennsylvania mine a monopoly profit. Once more representatives from Missouri demanded a provision requiring public bidding in the purchase of all nickel used in coinage. The bill was sent back to the House committee on coinage.

Representative Hooper presented the bill again on April 9. It had been amended in many particulars, and Hooper explained all the provisions, item by item. Three new provisions of importance had been incorporated. One of these provided for open bidding for nickel. Another created a new subsidiary coin, a silver dollar of 384 grains. The third was an odd provision which legalized the method of coining silver that had been in vogue since 1853. The practice was to continue for two years only. The commit-

---

[5] The legislative history of the bill extends over hundreds of pages in the Congressional Globe. The more important references in this chapter are taken from the Globe, 41st Cong., 3rd sess., 268, 394; 42nd Cong. 1st sess., 23; 2nd sess., 322, 326, 2304, 3882; and 3rd sess., 668, 721, 860, 1184.

tee had not only discovered the facts surrounding the coinage
and export of silver coins but had yielded to the demands
of bullion dealers that they be allowed to continue an arrangement under which the government gave them part of
the seigniorage belonging to the Treasury and assisted them
to export to Latin-America the entire output of United
States silver coins.   The discussion was distinctly personal
in tone.   Certain members declared that the bill was primarily in the interests of nickel.   Kelley retorted that opposition to the bill came from members supporting a ring of
silver exporters who were profiting by the illegal coinage
of silver.   Kelley denounced their traffic, but offered no
objection to the amendment which authorized its continuance.   Again the House refused to pass the bill.

On May 27 Hooper introduced a substitute bill, insisted that it be voted on without even a reading, and
finally obtained its passage.   Only one of its many changes
needs to be noted here.   The weight of the subsidiary
silver coins was altered.   The weight of the half-dollar,
quarter-dollar, and dime, which had been for each dollar's
worth 384 grains gross and 345.6 grains fine since the original law of 1853, was to be 25 grams gross and 22.5 grams
fine.   The Senate took the bill over and made further
amendments.   The most important of these was the elimination of the plan for an all copper-nickel minor coinage
system.   This plan had twice passed the House in a separate bill, had re-appeared in Knox's original bill of 1869,
and had then been approved by the House and by the Senate.
Just as in 1864, the nickel coinage plan was rejected by
a Senate committee.   After another wrangle over the
seigniorage on gold coinage the Senate passed the bill.   The
House refused the amendments, a conference committee
recommended a compromise, and a final bill emerged from
the committee, altered and reworded until no member out-

side the committees could possibly know its provisions. It was immediately passed by both houses and became the coinage law of February 12, 1873.

There were sixty-seven detailed sections. Fundamentally the measure was a rewriting of existing statutes. Antiquated, incomplete, and contradictory provisions of the past were eliminated or modernized. There were a few provisions that vitally altered the older statutes. The first of such changes provided for a reorganization of the mint establishment. The Director of the Mint, formerly stationed at Philadelphia, was now to head a Bureau of the Mint at Washington, with authority over all the mints. The duties of the officials and the details of operation were completely restated.

The silver dollar was dropped from the coinage system. The country had legally adopted the single gold standard. It will be recalled that the bill Knox sent to the Senate in 1869 simply dropped the silver dollar from the list of silver coins of the country, his original provision calling for a subsidiary silver dollar having been withdrawn when the critics objected. In his report Knox referred to his original suggestion of a subsidiary silver dollar and commented that some of those consulted had recommended a special type of silver dollar for use in trade with the Far East. In the first bill reported by the House committee in 1872 Knox's subsidiary dollar had again turned up, but the substitute bill presented a month later dropped the subsidiary coin and provided for the special trade piece. The coin was to weigh 420 grains, which was approximately the weight of the Mexican dollar with which it was to compete in the Orient. It was to be coined for any depositor of silver bullion. The section which listed the subsidiary coins and declared them legal tender in payments to $5 included this free coinage trade piece in the list. Thus the law created a new kind of silver dollar, granted it free coinage, and gave it a limited legal tender.

Every authority on our currency history, without exception, states that the trade dollar was created to encourage trade with the East and that the provision making it legal tender in domestic payments was solely due to a careless and unintentional inclusion of the piece in the list of legal tender coins.[6] This view rests on the two facts that at the time the piece was created a coin of 420 grains of standard silver, worth about $1.05 in gold, could not circulate and that giving a free coinage piece of the trade dollar type any legal tender quality was indefensible. The conclusion is hardly justified. The committee that interpolated the trade dollar into the provision listing the legal tender subsidiary silver coins could not possibly have failed to read the very short and explicit section. It is true that Linderman, urging the creation of the trade piece the previous year, had pointed out that it should have no legal tender power, as it was to be used only in foreign trade. But the interests behind the coin were anxious to promote its popularity. Some years later Linderman, in a casual comment not noticed by the historians, gave testimony on this point. He said that early in 1872 the silver interests, realizing that the metal was due to decline severely, had devised the trade coin as a support for the price of silver bullion.[7] It is probable that the House committee deliberately included the legal tender provision with the idea of giving the new coin a better standing. The silver interests, strong enough to obtain passage for the trade coin provision, were probably able to persuade the committee to insert the anomalous provision for legal tender. It would be incorrect, of course, to say that Congress as a body intended to make the coin a com-

---

[6] For example, see Hepburn, 274; Watson, 205.

[7] Annual Report on the Finances for 1875, 298

mon currency, for Congress as a whole did not know the provisions of the law.

This reference to the trade dollar throws light on the more important matter of the adoption of the gold standard. Laughlin and many others have demonstrated that this was not a corrupt or surreptitious action by the enemies of silver. The elimination of the standard silver dollar was simply in the interests of clarifying the coinage law. Exported before 1806, not coined from 1806 to 1836, and not in circulation from 1836 to 1873, the dollar was an unknown coin. There was nothing secret in the abolition of the piece. Pollock had been begging Congress to drop it since 1861, as Snowden had been before that. Knox accepted these recommendations, giving the reasons in his report. The silver interests made no objection to the proposal. Instead, they accepted the law, with its provision for a trade dollar, as a measure in their behalf. This fact is the key to the situation. Not one party to the passage of the law of 1873 recognized the significance of the abolition of the legally existing double standard. Laughlin's view that it was a deliberate, reasoned action of Congress is as untenable as his earlier contention that Congress intended to adopt the gold standard in 1853. It is quite as far from the truth as the popular belief of the time that the law of 1873 was the result of a sinister plot. Snowden, Pollock, and Knox in the years from 1853 to 1869, the critics of the bill in 1868 and 1869, and Congress from 1871 to 1873 had considered this measure, and not one person had commented that if the silver ratio should move to 16 to 1 the United States would revert to an actual double standard under the existing law. In their minds the fact that silver could not be coined under existing market conditions permanently eliminated silver coinage. In all the long discussion of the bill from 1870 to 1873 the dropping of the dollar was referred to only twice. In 1872 Kelley and Hooper discussed it at some length, stating clearly that the measure made the gold standard legal as well as actual. No one discussed the consequences of the provision. The merits of bimetallism were of no concern, and this Congress adjourned, a year passed, and the bill was altered, submitted, discussed, recommitted, and finally passed without reference to this issue. Congress adopted the gold standard, as it has adopted many other currency measures, with the majority of the members unaware of the meaning of their action. Francis A. Walker's idea that the measure was passed openly, but without the knowledge of the country at large is a correct interpretation, but it does not go far enough.[8] Neither the general public nor Congress realized what the law accomplished. If the silver mining interests had understood what the measure meant they would have aroused in Congress a storm of opposition.

The subsidiary coinage provisions of the law were the relatively unimportant changes originally proposed by Knox. The 3 cent silver piece and the silver half-dime were abolished. This was obviously a necessity if the 3 cent and 5 cent nickel pieces in circulation were to be continued after the revival of silver coinage. The essentials of the provisions of the law of 1853 governing the issue of subsidiary coins were in no way altered, but the wording was changed to make the new section a blunt and peremptory instruction to coin and issue the pieces in the way intended by the 1853 statute. Silver bullion was to be bought with the bullion fund and the coins were to be issued only by sales for gold at face value. But this section was followed by another clause providing that the mint at Philadelphia might continue for two years more its practice of accepting

[8] See Laughlin, Bimetallism, Chapter VII; and Walker, Bimetallism, Chapter V.

all silver bullion offered and paying for it with subsidiary coins at rates set by the Treasury. This was a legalization of the improper methods of issue followed since 1853, passed for the benefit of bullion dealers profiting by an unauthorized free coinage of subsidiary pieces. It was inserted by the House committee after that committee, as Kelley said, had gained an insight into the situation from the dealers themselves. Silver coins, of course, were not in circulation, and it was unlikely that silver would be brought back into circulation within two years. The committee, apparently, could see no impropriety in authorizing an irregular practice if there was a private interest clamoring for it. The amendment did not apply to the mints in San Francisco and New Orleans, possibly because dealers from those two cities did not appeal to the committee.

The remaining provision affecting the silver coins was even more remarkable. The weight of the subsidiary coins, 384 grains of standard silver per dollar, was changed to 25 grams per dollar, equal to 385.8 grains. The fine weight of two half-dollars or ten dimes was increased from 345.6 grains to 347.22 grains. The silver coins would now weigh 6.47 per cent less than the standard silver dollar instead of 6.91 per cent, as originally determined in 1853. This provision was the result of the contention of Senator Sherman and Representative Kelley that such a measure would promote their plan for a universal coinage system. The weight chosen for the coins, 25 grams, was the weight of the French 5 franc piece.

Kelley and Sherman were correct in their belief that the greenback régime offered an opportunity for coinage reforms. But the application of the metric system to the subsidiary coins as a means of promoting a universal coinage was absurd. The value of subsidiary coins is independent of bullion weight, and they circulate only in countries where they are exchangeable at their face values for standard money. In the Senate Sherman proposed to drop the eagle design from the coins so that there would be space for a statement of the silver content. He urged this as necessary if United States silver coins were "to float all over the world." He actually believed that adoption of metric weights would lead European peoples to use our fiduciary coins. These coins were not redeemable even in the United States. To make the measure even more fantastic, there was the fact that France had only recently reduced the silver content of all her subsidiary coins below the fineness of the new United States pieces.

From the bullion standpoint the slight increase in silver content was of no consequence. The only effect of the provision was to give our subsidiary silver coins an awkward foreign weight.[9] It has never been changed, and our dime, quarter-dollar, and half-dollar are metric coins, along with the copper-nickel 5 cent piece, which was given a metric weight in the beginning. Our gold coins, silver dollar, and 1 cent piece have weights in grains of the English system. In our mint operations the meaningless metric weights are converted into the nearest equivalent in grains.

The minor coinage provisions were only slightly changed. The effort to create an all copper-nickel minor coinage system, which had been the original inspiration of the entire revision, had failed. The bronze cent was retained, and no change was made in the 3 cent nickel coin of 30 grains or the 5 cent piece of 5 grams (77.16 grains). The 2 cent bronze coin was abolished. The clumsy legal tender differentiations of 4 cents, 60 cents, and $1.00 for

[9] This change of weight in the subsidiary coins is frequently overlooked. Three successive editions of Taussig's widely used Principles of Economics have contained the incorrect statement that our subsidiary coins still have the weights of the 1853 law. See 3rd edition, Vol. 1, 268.

the three minor coins retained were simplified by a provision which made each of them legal tender in payments to 25 cents. The much-debated provision for the purchase of nickel by open bidding was finally included. The law of 1871, providing for redemption of the minor coins, was re-enacted, with a further provision that any of the discontinued minor coins, the copper cent and half-cent, the copper-nickel cent, and the bronze 2 cent piece, might be directly redeemed by exchange for the current minor coins. The manufacture of minor coins was restricted to the Philadelphia mint.

This consideration of the law of 1873 shows that three years of study, debate, and amendment had resulted in a measure which improved the wording of the old laws, effected some changes in administration, created a new and dubious trade coin, made trivial changes in the minor and subsidiary coins, and more or less unconsciously made legal and permanent a gold standard that was actually prevailing under a nominal bimetallic standard. The problems of specie resumption and stabilization of the greenbacks, of restoring subsidiary coinage, and of redeeming subsidiary coins were left unsolved.

The statute of 1873 remains to this day the fundamental coinage law, although amendments have been made from time to time. There was a general revision of all the statutes in 1874 which technically constituted a new draft of all existing laws, but this revision left the law of 1873 unchanged in all essentials. Professor Laughlin makes the point that the law of 1873, since it did not specifically repeal the law of 1837 which had made the standard silver dollar unlimited in legal tender, did not demonetize silver. It is true that the 1873 measure did not refer to the legal tender of the standard dollar. Probably it did not appear to be necessary to take such action in the case of a coin that had never been in general circulation and would no longer be coined. In any event the revision of 1874 settled the matter by a provision which gave legal tender power only to the silver coins that remained in the system, and these were the trade dollar and the subsidiary half-dollar, quarter-dollar, and dime. From 1874 to 1878 the silver dollar was not a legal tender. In all the years before and since that period it has had unlimited legal tender power.

CHAPTER XVII

THE REVIVAL OF SILVER COINAGE

SILVER COINAGE on the Pacific coast—Redemption of fractional notes—
Problem of reviving silver coinage—Fall in the value of silver—Its relation
to subsidiary coinage—Unauthorized issue of silver coins—The specie
resumption act of 1875—Subsidiary provisions unwise—Treasury's illegal
policy—Motives of the officials—Law compelling issue of coin in 1876—
Resolution of 1876—Silver coinage revived—Return of old silver coins from
abroad—Twenty-cent piece created in 1875 and withdrawn in 1876.

The law of 1873, with all its elaborate provisions, had
little effect on the currency situation. The Philadelphia mint
continued to turn out silver coins for bullion dealers to ship
to Latin-America. It will be recalled that this permission
to continue the irregular coinage had been extended only to
the Philadelphia mint. The San Francisco mint was now
to issue silver coins only in exchange for gold coins at par.
The mint had already adopted this procedure in the preceding year. From 1862 to 1872 silver coins had been
redundant on the Coast, and the mint officials, on their
own responsibility, had in 1872 refused to issue coins except
in exchange for gold. Their action was, of course, merely
a compliance with the law of 1853, which had been violated
from its passage, but it gave rise to an odd situation in
which silver coins were sold for gold at one United States
mint and exchanged for silver bullion at another. The
cessation of exchanges of silver coin for bullion, decreed
by the San Francisco officials in 1872 and made permanent
by the law of 1873, exerted an influence on the coinage

situation on the Coast.   The discount on the excessive silver
coin circulation, which had for many years been 2 per cent
or more, dropped to 1 per cent almost immediately, and
in 1875 the coins went to parity with gold.[1]   Thereafter
the Pacific Coast regions were on an actual gold standard,
with a genuine subsidiary silver currency issued in accord
with the law.

In the remainder of the country the people still struggled with the problem of an inflated paper currency.   This
problem was two-fold.   The forces favoring and opposing
specie resumption were locked in battle.   It was impossible
to foretell the result.   But the retail currency of the country
was made up of minor coins and fractional paper notes, the
latter generally regarded as an emergency currency to be
done away with at some time in the future.   The subsidiary
silver coins would automatically return to circulation when
greenbacks reached parity and gold payments were resumed.
But it was possible to restore silver coinage by special legislation without waiting until some problematic future date
when specie payments would be resumed.   There was thus
the general problem of restoring a specie standard, and
independent of that question the particular problem of
reviving the subsidiary coinage.

There were serious objections to the plan of waiting for
specie resumption.   The fractional notes could not withstand
the wear and tear of rapid circulation.   They were soon
ragged and dirty.   Although the volume of redemptions
was large and growing rapidly, the notes were in poor condition everywhere.   Remote sections were not supplied with
fresh notes.   Counterfeiting was still widely practiced.   The
Treasury had adopted the practice of redeeming mutilated

---

[1] Linderman, Report of the Examination of the Branch Mints, 24; Annual
Report of the Director of the Mint for 1873, 18.

notes at a discount in proportion to the parts missing, and in nearly all redemptions owners suffered loss.

Most important of all was the expense of redemption. The volume of notes in circulation had increased since the war, but the rate of redemption had increased even more rapidly. Hundreds of employees were required to count, sort, and record a volume of notes that poured into the Treasury at the rate of 500,000 pieces a day. The figures in the annual reports for the fiscal years from 1868 to 1875 disclose the nature of the problem:

Fiscal Year	Notes Officially Outstanding	Amounts Redeemed
1868	$32,700,000	$20,800,00
1869	32,100,000	23,300,000
1870	39,800,000	23,400,000
1871	40,600,000	30,200,000
1872	40,800,000	31,500,000
1873	44,800,000	34,600,000
1874	45,900,000	40,800,000
1875	42,100,000	40,400,000

These figures do not accurately portray the conditions. The amounts actually in circulation were far below the official figures. Millions of the notes had been lost. There were in circulation in 1874 and 1875 an amount less than $30,-000,000, as will be shown later. The annual redemptions after 1873, amounting to more than $40,000,000, meant that the Treasury was annually redeeming and reissuing about one-third more than the entire amount outstanding. The average life of a note was nine months and was growing shorter. After 1870 the expense of redemption was more than $1,000,000. In 1875 it was $1,400,000.[2] To redeem and retire the entire volume of notes actually outstanding would cost less than $30,000,000 in greenbacks. To keep them in circulation the government was paying annually

[2] Congressional Record, 44th Cong., 1st sess., 1478.

about 5 per cent of this sum. The "loan without interest" which had appealed to Secretary Chase in 1862 had become an unpaid debt drawing 5 per cent interest.

The problem of reviving the silver coinage was beset with complications both technical and fiscal. It was possible to adopt Pollock's plan of reducing the silver coins to the point where their metal value would be less than the gold value of the greenbacks. But Pollock's pleas for a reduction in the size of the coins had been ignored by his superiors, and bills introduced for this purpose had been buried in committee. Greenback values fluctuated widely, and the proper degree of reduction of the silver coins was an uncertain matter. The conception of subsidiary coins as standard coins with a bullion value approximating money value still prevailed widely, and reduction was in the minds of Congress a "debasement." The forces of growing population and economic expansion, despite the depression of 1873 and the shifting tides of trade, were slowly bringing the greenbacks to parity with gold, and this movement would in time bring the revival of silver coinage without reduction of the bullion values established by the law of 1873.

Mighty influences were at work to restore silver coinage even before greenbacks should go to parity with gold. Economic events of widely differing types had combined to exert an overwhelming pressure on the value of silver in terms of gold. For a generation the market ratio had been close to 15½ to 1, giving the standard silver dollar a value around $1.04 in gold and the subsidiary coins a value around 97 cents. A precipitate decline began in 1873. In September of that year the ratio was 16 to 1, at which point the silver in four quarters or ten dimes was worth about 93 cents in gold. With the gold value of greenbacks slowly rising and the gold value of silver rapidly declining a point would be reached where the silver in a dollar's worth of subsidiary coins would be worth less than a dollar in greenbacks. At this point the government could buy silver with greenbacks and sell the coins for greenbacks at a profit. The coins would remain in circulation. In other words, the fall in the market value of silver would make the silver coins subsidiary not only to gold but to greenbacks, and a revival of silver coinage to take the place of fractional notes would be practicable and profitable. The one doubtful feature was the hazard of a sudden rise in the gold value of silver or a sudden fall in the gold value of greenbacks, either of which would drive out the silver coins.

This possibility of resumption of silver coinage should be described as theoretical, for the issue of subsidiary coins in exchange for greenbacks was legally impossible. The law of 1873, for reasons previously explained, was most emphatic in its direction that silver coins should be issued only in exchange for gold coins at par, except for the temporary arrangement for continued coinage for bullion dealers. Since subsidiary silver coins were as currency exchangeable for greenbacks at par they could not be sold to the public for gold until the greenbacks were at par with gold. Without intending to do so, Knox had so framed the law of 1873 that subsidiary coinage could not be revived until specie resumption, whenever that might be. The value of silver in terms of gold could drop indefinitely, making possible a resumption of subsidiary coinage with a large profit to the Treasury, but nothing could be done without a revision of the law of 1873.

Linderman was the first to discover this possibility of a revival of silver coinage through a fall in the gold value of silver. He had in 1873 again displaced Pollock, becoming the first Director of all the mints under the new administrative plan which he had helped to devise. In his first annual report, written in October, 1873, he explained the situation

at length, pointing out that the three values, of silver, greenbacks, and gold, were already at the point where the government could issue subsidiary coins without loss. He suggested that the mint be permitted to coin subsidiary pieces
and pay them out in change at government offices. He did
not suggest that the coins be sold to the public for greenbacks, although payment of the coins as change was identical
with this procedure, nor did he discuss the fact that the
slightest rise in silver bullion value or the slightest fall in
the gold value of greenbacks would cause the disappearance
of the coins.

Under the circumstances any attempt to issue the coins
was unwise as well as illegal. It is difficult to understand
the motives that could have prompted such action. And yet
the mint, without any change in the law, undertook such
issue a few weeks after Linderman's report was written.
In his report for 1873, submitted December 1, Secretary
Richardson makes this statement:

> The recent fall in the price of gold, together with the de-
> preciation in the market value of silver as compared with gold,
> which has been going on for some time, has enabled the Direc-
> tor to coin silver, to be paid out instead of United States Notes
> to advantage. Availing himself of this opportunity, the Director
> caused to be purchased as much silver bullion as could be con-
> veniently used in giving employment to the mints, when not
> engaged in the more important business of coining gold, and
> the same was so coined and paid out.

On November 1 Richardson had instructed the sub-Treasury
offices to pay out subsidiary coin to government creditors
in sums not more than $5 to one person. It is not possible
to learn how much was coined or paid out, as all information regarding the matter was suppressed. It happened that
greenbacks suffered a relapse in December, and every coin

that had been issued disappeared. Richardson hastily revoked his instructions, Upton declares, "by verbal orders
and by private letters." [3] Laughlin says the issue of the
coins was "an evidence of extraordinary ignorance of a
finance minister." It was more than that. It was illegal.
Secretary Bristow, who had succeeded Richardson, avoided
reference to the incident in his annual report, but he urged
that "authority be given the Secretary to commence the manufacture" of subsidiary silver.

The unauthorized coinage and issue of the silver pieces
illustrated the difficulties of reviving subsidiary coinage. The
silver coins would not be added to the fractional paper notes
outstanding, but would take the place of them. As they
went into circulation the redemptions of paper notes would
increase. The issue of subsidiary coins in exchange for
greenbacks meant the eventual retirement of all the fractional paper notes, amounting to a total somewhere around
$30,000,000. Assuming that it was possible to issue the
subsidiary coins without loss on the coinage, the cost of the
retirement would be approximately $30,000,000. Secondly,
it was doubtful whether the coins would stay in circulation
even momentarily. In fact, the value of greenbacks fell while
the coins were being given out in December, and the government creditors who received them merely turned them over
to bullion dealers.

Unfortunately, the problem of retiring the fractional
notes and restoring silver coinage was not considered on
its merits as a distinct problem, but became entangled with
the question of resumption of specie payments. The leaders

[3] For the record of this particular episode see Laughlin, Bimetallism, 89;
Upton, Money in Politics, 146; Annual Reports of the Director of the Mint for
1873 and 1874; Annual Reports on the Finances for 1873, XXXIII, and
1874, XXII. See also Chart I, which shows the market situation at the time
the coins were issued.

of the movement for contraction of the currency and resumption of gold payments conceived the notion that a revival of subsidiary silver coinage would be a first step in
their plan. The silver interests of the West, well represented in Congress, were quite ready to support any measure
that revived silver coinage. During the latter part of
1874 the respective values of gold, silver, and greenbacks
were such that it was possible to manufacture and issue subsidiary coins for greenbacks without loss. In December,
1874, Senator Sherman introduced the bill that became the
famous "specie resumption act" of 1875. It contained three
important provisions, one directing that after January 1,
1879, greenbacks be redeemed at par in gold coin, another
providing that greenbacks be retired as the national bank-
note circulation increased, and the third directing the Secretary of the Treasury to coin and issue subsidiary silver in
exchange for fractional paper notes.

Sherman insisted on immediate consideration of the bill,
despite the protests of senators not ready to vote. The debate was partisan and bitter.[4] Some senators declared the
bill an inflationist measure in disguise. Sherman himself
refused to state whether the greenbacks and fractional notes
retired under the law could again be re-issued. Two members, Schurz of Ohio and Hamilton of Texas, explained
clearly that the issue of silver coins under the prevailing
market conditions was exceedingly unwise. The bill passed
the Senate by a vote divided on party lines. In the House
the Republican majority did not permit discussion, although
the committee on banking and currency had received a letter
from the economist Carey bitterly denouncing the measure
and predicting the immediate disappearance of the silver
coins. The measure was signed by the President on January
14, 1875.

[4] Congressional Record, 43rd Cong., 2nd sess., 186, 194, 317.

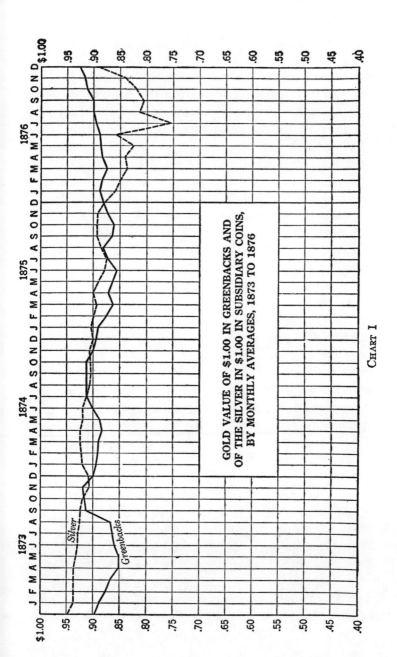

GOLD VALUE OF $1.00 IN GREENBACKS AND
OF THE SILVER IN $1.00 IN SUBSIDIARY COINS,
BY MONTHLY AVERAGES, 1873 TO 1876

CHART I

The subsidiary coinage section directed the Secretary of the Treasury "as rapidly as practicable" to coin subsidiary silver and issue it in redemption of fractional notes. He was authorized also to pay out the coins in change, cancelling equal amounts in fractional notes. The coins were to be issued until all the notes were retired. The measure thus called for the purchase of silver bullion with greenbacks and the immediate substitution of silver coins for fractional notes regardless of the cost of the silver or the possibility of keeping the coins in circulation. This process involved an outlay in greenbacks of a nominal total of more than $40,000,000. The only offset to this expense was a seigniorage profit on the coinage if silver went down in gold value without a corresponding fall in greenbacks. At the time the law was passed there was an almost exact equilibrium. A dollar in greenbacks would buy just the amount of silver contained in two half-dollars. Sherman admitted in the Senate that the government would have to pay the entire costs of coinage and of destroying the fractional notes.

The measure was an inexcusable blunder. A rise in silver or a fall in greenbacks would start an endless chain, with the mint buying silver and coining at a loss, the public eagerly redeeming fractional notes and selling the silver coins to bullion dealers, and the brokers melting the coins and selling the bullion to the mint. What was worse, the fractional notes would be withdrawn without a currency of silver coins to take their place. The specie resumption act provided by law for a repetition of the chaotic conditions of 1862.

There were some complex influences that tended to prevent silver coins from staying in circulation in the North and East even if the bullion value of silver remained below the greenback value. The discount on silver coins in the Pacific regions had long since been wiped out, and four quarters were worth exactly one dollar in gold. The South-West was also reluctant to accept fractional notes, and Texas as well as other southern states further East used subsidiary coins obtained either from the Pacific Coast or from Eastern bullion dealers engaged in coinage operations under the special permission of the law of 1873. Hamilton declared in the Senate that "all through the Southern States" subsidiary coins were worth almost as much as gold. Even before the specie resumption act was passed subsidiary coins were selling for more than their bullion values in the East. In his 1874 report Linderman said that the ruling price in greenbacks was $1.04, although the bullion value of a dollar in silver coins was almost exactly $1. With the expiration of the special free coinage privilege early in 1875, the demand for subsidiary coinage for export, for use in the Southwest, and for exchange for gold on the Pacific coast would probably give the coins a commodity value in the East above their value as money and keep them out of circulation.

The law had hardly been passed when a decided reaction in the value of greenbacks made it impossible for subsidiary silver either to be coined and issued without loss or to remain in circulation after it had been issued. Richardson had attempted to issue silver coins in exchange for greenbacks without authority of law, and Bristow and Linderman had urged Congress to grant them authority. They now had this authority, and it was an embarrassment. Compliance with the law meant a deficit on the Treasury books and the disappearance of fractional currency. Faced with this dilemma, the officials decided to obey part of the law and ignore another part. The mint bought silver bullion and coined it as rapidly as the facilities allowed, but the coins were not exchanged for fractional notes or issued in any other way. Before the end of 1875 the mint had invested more than $9,000,000 in silver bullion and converted it into subsidiary coins, all of which were stacked in the vaults. In his report for 1875 Bristow explains his action as follows:

> So much of the act of January 14, 1875, as relates to the purchase and coinage of silver for redemption of fractional currency, has been put into partial operation, and is now being executed as rapidly as the exigencies of the case will admit. . . . The Secretary has been urged to begin the work of redemption by issuing silver coin in redemption of outstanding currency, and it has been insisted that, under the first section of the act, he has no discretion, but must issue the silver coin as fast as it can be turned out from the mint. While the act requires the coinage to proceed as rapidly as practicable, it does not, in terms, require the Secretary to issue it at once; nor does it fix the period of time when the issue must begin. For obvious reasons, it has been, and yet is, impracticable to put or keep silver coins in circulation.

This statement was a mere quibbling over the wording of the law, the purpose of which was the retirement of fractional notes through the issue of silver coins. If the law was a foolish and impracticable measure, as it was, it was a mistake to obey that part of it which called for the purchase of bullion. The Treasury's procedure subjected the government to the expense involved in retiring the fractional notes without accomplishing any result of any sort, while the purchase of silver at prices which made a seigniorage profit impossible subjected the Treasury to further loss, whether the coins were issued or not.

The situation was aggravated by the conditions in the silver market. The slump in greenbacks was so great that the steady fall in the gold value of silver did not restore the equilibrium which would make it possible to issue the coins. But the decline of silver was none the less marked, and the loss on earlier purchases of silver increased with this decline. The mistake in Treasury policy became manifest when the millions of dollars in silver bought in the first half of 1875 at $1.11 in gold per ounce could be bought in December for $1.08 per ounce, while the coins still lay in stacks in the vaults. In his 1875 report Linderman refers to the problem, as follows:

> The coinage rate of the fractional coin being $124^{4108}/_{10000}$ cents per standard ounce, and the average cost of the bullion $111^{4}/_{100}$ cents, the seigniorage or gain on its coinage will be 13 cents per ounce, or about 12 per cent.

The price per ounce quoted here is the price paid in gold. If the subsidiary coins could have been sold for gold coin at par the profit of 13 cents per ounce could have been realized. But the specie resumption act required that the silver coins be exchanged for fractional notes. An ounce of silver in 1875 cost in greenbacks about $1.27, and to this cost there was to be added about 2 cents per ounce for the expenses of coinage and distribution. This ounce produced $1.24⅞ in subsidiary silver. The government incurred an actual loss of about 5 cents on each ounce of silver purchased and coined.

One aspect of the situation needs brief mention. The record of Congress and Treasury in connection with silver coinage after 1873 is so tainted with error and mal-administration that it provokes speculation. The law of 1873 authorized the continuance of an improper method of coining subsidiary silver for the benefit of bullion dealers. It gave legal tender power to a trade dollar not meant to circulate in the country. Shortly after the law was passed Richardson, without legal sanction, bought silver bullion, coined it, and issued it. In 1875 the specie resumption act, approved by the Treasury, provided for silver coinage under conditions that made such coinage an egregious stupidity. Bristow refused to obey that part of the law which was vital to its purpose and obeyed to the uttermost limit that part which

called for the purchase of silver bullion. He did this for
more than a year, with an outlay of $15,000,000 in govern-
ment money, in the face of bitter criticism. Consideration
of these facts forces the conclusion that certain members of
Congress and Treasury officials were moved by a desire to
promote the interests of silver. The Comstock Lode was
pouring out a steam of metal, and a flood of silver mining
stocks had appeared. Silver prices were falling relentlessly,
and the harried producers were desperately seeking, in Congress and out, every possible aid. That conception of government which deems it proper to use legislative and official
powers to promote private profits has in our history been
conspicuously evident in connection with silver bullion. It
is fair to conclude from the record that a desire to advance
the cause of the mine owners was a factor in financial legislation and administration from the date of the first slump in
the price of silver.[5]

The 1875 appropriation for the redemption and re-issue
of fractional notes was inadequate, and the Treasury asked
Congress for an additional sum of $250,000. The request
led the House committee to a consideration of the situation.
The Treasury had bought $15,000,000 worth of silver
bullion at prices well above the price then prevailing. It was
still buying silver, but no coins had been issued. The vaults
were piled high with new dimes, quarters, and half-dollars,
but the government was still spending more than $100,000 a
month for replacement of worn fractional notes. On March
2, 1876, the committee presented a bill which commanded
the Secretary to issue all the accumulated coins and to continue coinage for the redemption of all fractional notes that
reached the Treasury from any source.

[5] See, for example, Congressional Record, 44th Cong., 1st sess., 1769, 1987.
In 1876 it was openly charged on the floor of Congress that members of Congress and Treasury officials were personally interested in the price of silver.

The bill created an uproar in the House. The discussion runs over many pages in the Record.[6] Representative Wells presented a statistical study to prove that of the $45,000,000 in fractional notes officially outstanding, only $28,000,000 were actually in circulation. He showed that notes of the first three issues, of which there were more than $12,000,000 outstanding, were no longer presented for redemption, while notes of later issue were presented for redemption and replacement at least once a year. Obviously these older notes had disappeared. While there were minor errors in his calculations, Wells' estimate of $28,000,000 as the volume still in circulation was undoubtedly close to the actual figure. It followed from this that the government could retire the fractional notes by purchasing enough silver to make about $28,000,000 in subsidiary coins. At the current price $25,000,000 in gold would purchase the silver, and the interest on the investment would come to only $1,250,000 per year. This was less than the annual cost of redeeming and reissuing the fractional notes, even when the greenback costs were converted into costs in terms of gold.

The bill was assailed by Representative Hewitt, of New York, who said that it was presented for the partisan purpose of obtaining Democratic approval of the specie resumption act, which had been passed in the interests of silver mine owners and had resulted in the purchase of $15,000,000 worth of silver at prices $2,000,000 above its current value. Many members pointed out that the bill merely repeated the directions already given the Secretary by the specie resumption act. Kelley, siding with the Democrats, said that the coins would immediately disappear. His comments on the measure so exasperated James A. Garfield that he taunted Kelley with his activities in favor of nickel coinage. There

[6] Congressional Record, 44th Cong., 1st sess., 1414, 1762–1774, 1985, 2082.

were insinuations that opposition to the bill was inspired by
the Pennsylvania nickel interests and the New York bank-
note companies, both of which would be unfavorably affected
by the revival of silver coinage.

One amendment after another was proposed. One of
these called for the free coinage of silver at the subsidiary
coinage value of 347.22 grains of pure silver to the dollar.
Eventually the House adopted two amendments, both pre-
posterous. One raised the legal tender of silver coins "of a
denomination of $1" to $50 and of "other silver coins" to
$25. This amendment was an attempt to revive bimetallism
surreptitiously by raising the legal tender limit of the trade
dollar to a sum that would cause its unlimited coinage for
circulation in the United States. The other amendment provided that if bullion owners did not present sufficient silver
to provide the amount of subsidiary coins necessary to retire
the fractional notes the Treasury might purchase bullion.
This amendment is incomprehensible, and a House that
passed it could not have had even an elementary compre-
hension of the existing law or of the nature of subsidiary
coinage.

The Senate Finance Committee rejected the two amendments, but presented an amendment of equally startling character. It provided for a new silver dollar with a gross
weight of 412.8 grains. This proposed coin was nothing
less than the old standard silver dollar, with a trivial increase
in weight from 412.5 grains to make the coinage ratio exactly
16 to 1. It was provided that it should be legal tender to
$20. So much opposition developed that Sherman withdrew
the amendment. The Senate thereupon passed the bill, the
House agreed to accept it without its own amendments, and
the measure became the law of April 17, 1876. The act
was merely a repetition of the specie resumption act. It

was a point-blank order to Bristow to issue the $16,000,000 in silver coins stored in the vaults and to continue the coinage until all the fractional notes were withdrawn.

Issue of the accumulated stores was begun. The course of greenback and silver values had been such that the equilibrium point was reached early in 1876, and the coins remained in circulation, although the margin was so narrow that for a while the costs of silver plus the costs of coinage were more than the money value of the coins. The volume of fractional notes presented for exchange was very small. A peculiar situation had developed. The refusal of Congress to make extra appropriations for reprinting the notes had slowed down the processes of redemption. The Treasury staff had been reduced, and the machinery of issue had broken down. In the spring of 1876, while $16,000,000 in silver coins lay in the vaults, an acute shortage of fractional currency developed. Many complaints and memorials were sent to Congress. In some sections premiums as high as 3 per cent were paid for fractional notes.

Under such conditions the paper fractions, however worn, were kept in circulation.[7] By June 7, 1876, seven weeks after the issue of coins began, only $5,000,000 in notes had been presented for exchange. On May 1 a resolution was introduced in the House providing that the Secretary might issue the subsidiary coins in the vaults by direct sales for greenbacks as well as in redemption of fractional notes. A House committee amended the resolution by limiting the amount to be sold for greenbacks to $10,000,000. The Senate made other amendments and returned the resolution to the House, where it became involved in the controversy over bimetallism. It finally passed both houses and was signed by the President on July 22, 1876.

The resolution, which had the same force as a statute,

[7] See Congressional Record, 44th Cong., 1st sess., 3747.

directed the Secretary to sell subsidiary coins for greenbacks
up to a total sum not greater than $10,000,000 and to con-
tinue the redemption of fractional notes with silver coins.
The two operations could be continued so long as the combined total of silver coins and fractional notes in circulation
did not exceed $50,000,000. If it was necessary, more
bullion could be purchased, the total amount on hand at
any time not to exceed $200,000 in value. This resolution,
like the law of April 17, was a repetition of the specie resumption act. But the additional provision which permitted
direct sale for greenbacks was important. This meant an
actual resumption of specie payments. All the outstanding
notes could be replaced with silver, and additional coins
could be issued if the public needed more fractional currency. The limit of $10,000,000 on the amount to be sold
directly, as well as the limitation of the total coin and notes
outstanding, is difficult to explain, unless it was that Congress
feared to trust the Treasury's discretion in the purchases of
silver bullion. The restriction on the volume to be sold for
greenbacks was evidently determined on the assumption that
$10,000,000 in notes had been lost. The Treasury officials
had at last realized that their records of fractional notes
outstanding had little relation to the actual conditions. More
than $45,000,000 were officially in circulation. If $10,-
000,000 of these were lost, $35,000,000 in notes would be
redeemed and $10,000,000 more in coins could still be
issued. If an unexpectedly large volume of notes turned up
for redemption the limit of $50,000,000 would stop further
sales for greenbacks.

The effect of the resolution and the two statutes preceding was to restore the long absent silver fractional currency.
The coins were subsidiary, but subsidiary to greenbacks, not
to gold. They were made from bullion bought with greenbacks, and they were sold to the public in exchange for green-

backs. The gold value of greenbacks rose steadily after 1876 and the gold value of silver steadily declined. The coins were no longer in danger of disappearance, and a seigniorage profit on coinage became possible. It is a curious feature of the situation that the laws of 1875 and 1876 and the resolution of 1876 were all in direct conflict with the law of 1873, which required that silver coins be issued only in exchange for gold. No one of the three measures contained a provision for repeal of the 1873 statute.

The circumstances under which the San Francisco mint was selling silver coins for gold in 1873 while the Philadelphia mint was selling them for silver bullion were given a new turn by the legislation of 1876. The law authorizing the sale of silver coins for greenbacks applied, of course, to the entire country, but the San Francisco mint continued to sell the coins for gold, bringing about an absurd situation which certainly has no counterpart in the history of any other country. One mint was selling subsidiary coins at par for gold coins, while another was selling the same coins at par for greenbacks that sold at a material discount in gold.

By the end of 1876 more than $15,000,000 in fractional notes had been redeemed, and in October, 1877, the total reached $23,000,000. In addition, $13,000,000 in subsidiary coins had been sold for greenbacks, $3,000,000 in excess of the legal limit on such sales. Sherman, who had become Secretary of the Treasury, had asked the Treasury experts to estimate the volume of notes permanently lost. Their figure was about $8,000,000. Sherman ruled that the resolution was not intended to prevent the sale of coins to take the place of these lost notes.[8] This was, on the contrary, exactly what the resolution intended, as Sherman, chairman of the committee which framed the measure, should have known. On the other hand, business

[8] Annual Report on the Finances for 1877, XIX, 339.

was expanding, and the $10,000,000 to be issued in excess of the volume of fractional notes redeemed was hardly sufficient to take care of public needs. Sherman's interpretation permitted an issue of $18,000,000 in excess of the amount issued in redemption of the paper fractions.

The estimate of $8,000,000 as the amount lost was far too conservative. By the end of October, 1877, there were still officially outstanding $16,000,000 in fractional notes. More than $36,000,000 in silver coins had been issued, making a total $2,000,000 in excess of the $50,000,000 limit stipulated in the resolution. More than $6,000,000 additional coin had been produced and stored in the vaults.

Further sales were brought to a complete stop by an unexpected and dramatic development. In the winter of 1877 there suddenly reappeared in circulation literally hundreds of millions of the silver 3 cent pieces, 5 cent pieces, dimes, quarters, and half-dollars that had as suddenly departed in 1862. They streamed in from Canada, from Central America, from South America, and from the West Indies. A small quantity, probably, was brought out from domestic hoards. With the value of silver going down and the value of greenbacks rising toward parity with gold a point had been reached where these long absent coins were worth more at home than they were in foreign countries. The most interesting feature of this unexpected home-coming was the information it afforded as to the fate of the coins in 1862. It showed that they had not been melted or exported to Europe as bullion, although there was a definite profit in melting the coins at that time. They had gone to Latin-America, served as local currency for fifteen years, and then returned. Sherman in 1880 estimated the value of the coins returned in the preceding two years at $22,000,000, and a large amount came back after that time.

The immediate effect of this development was to stop

the sale of new coins. Sherman suspended subsidiary coinage in the last month of 1877. A later result was the gradual accumulation in the Treasury of an embarrassing volume of excess coins.[9] More than $10,000,000 was stored in the vaults by 1880. The coins came in through small tax payments, postal operations, and various change transactions at Treasury offices. Eventually they became a Treasury problem. The final disposition of this inert mass will be referred to in a subsequent chapter.

Specie payments were resumed on January 1, 1879. The discount on greenbacks disappeared, and the silver coins became subsidiary to gold. For the first time since the law of 1853 the relationship of silver coins to standard gold coins contemplated in that law was realized. Although one more step was necessary to complete the system, the fundamental requirements of an efficient subsidiary coinage were now met. After 1877 the fractional notes ceased to be used as a general currency. The large production of new coins by the mint and the influx of old coins from abroad gave the country a supply of small silver change greatly in excess of its needs, and the public preference for metal over paper led to a rapid withdrawal of the fractional notes. In one respect the notes were superior to coins. They were convenient and safe in remittances of small sums by mail. Many were retained for this use, banks keeping small supplies on hand for the accommodation of their customers. This explains the appearance in bank statements of holdings in fractional notes long after they had ceased to circulate. In June, 1884, the national banks reported in their assets almost $500,000 in fractional paper currency.[10]

---

[9] For references to the return of the coins and the excess holdings in the Treasury see the Annual Reports on the Finances for the years from 1878 to 1890.

[10] Annual Report of the Comptroller of the Currency for 1884, VII; see also Knox, 109.

Although the notes had generally disappeared by 1878, large amounts were still officially outstanding. Much the greater part of this outstanding total had been lost or destroyed. Conflagrations had accounted for a part, the great Chicago fire of 1873 alone destroying millions of notes. In the fifty years since 1878 redemptions have been very small, dwindling until in the present day they have almost ceased. Approximately $15,000,000 are still outstanding. A considerable amount is held by collectors, as much as $2,000,000 according to an estimate of the Treasury.[11] These souvenirs, now worth more as specimens than their face values, will never be presented for redemption. The remaining $13,-000,000 may be considered as permanently lost. The whole amount is carried on the Treasury books as an outstanding liability, and unless some accounting procedure is authorized to remove it, this item will remain as a perpetual reminder of an unhappy experience in financial mismanagement.

Even before silver coinage was restored in 1876 Congress added to the system of subsidiary coins a new denomination. In February, 1874, Senator Jones of Nevada introduced a bill providing for a 20 cent piece. Silver coins were circulating only in the Pacific states. In that part of the country the old Spanish valuations had given way very slowly. Although there were no Spanish reals in circulation prices were still commonly quoted in "bits." As explained in an earlier chapter, the customer who bought an article priced at one bit and gave a quarter-dollar in payment received a dime or "short-bit" in change. He should have received a Spanish real or a dime and 2 cents, but there were neither reals nor copper coins in circulation in the West. The 20 cent piece was suggested as a device to stop this practice of over-charging, which had been prevalent for more than forty years. Linderman supported the proposal,

[11] Annual Report on the Finances for 1925, 558.

recommending the 20 cent piece in his annual report for 1874. The bill passed the Senate in that year, but it did not become a law until March 3, 1875.[12]

The measure was a mistake. The creation of a 20 cent piece could hardly effect any reform in retail practices that two dimes could not as easily bring about. Competition between merchants and the increasing popularity of the 1 and 5 cent pieces would cure the evil. If, however, the 20 cent piece was to be created, it was necessary to abolish the quarter-dollar, as it was undesirable to have in circulation two silver coins so nearly alike in size and value. Senator Sherman, testifying before a House committee in 1878, said that the coin had been created only because Senator Jones asked for it. Linderman, in his Money and Legal Tender, admitted that it was a mistake to introduce the piece, but contended that it was the proper denomination between the dime and half-dollar and should have been adopted originally instead of the quarter-dollar.[13] It will be recalled that Jefferson had recommended the "fifth or pistreen" in preference to the quarter. The new piece was coined in small quantities. When it came into circulation its resemblance to the quarter-dollar caused confusion. A bill to withdraw it was introduced in July, 1876, permitted to go over to another Congress, and finally passed as the law of May 2, 1878.

---

[12] See Congressional Record, 43rd Cong., 1st sess., 1349, 5428.
[13] Linderman, Money and Legal Tender, 45.

Chapter XVIII

THE FRACTIONAL COINAGE SYSTEM COMPLETED

Coinage system in 1879—Oversupply of fractional silver—Sherman's recommendation—Subsidiary coin redemption law of 1879—Idle coin in the Treasury—Recoinage of old silver—Restrictions on issue of new coins—Refusal of Congress to remedy situation—Minor coins become popular—Three-cent piece discontinued.

The withdrawal of the fractional notes and the resumption of specie payments marked the establishment in both law and administration of our present day fractional coinage system. The subsidiary and minor coins were now genuine fiduciary currencies, with proper method of issue, satisfactory arrangement of denominations, and definite legal status. The system was not perfect. Some of the legislative provisions were badly in need of change, certain administrative processes had to be improved, and at least two important provisions were lacking. Between 1879 and 1905 nearly all of these improvements were effected. It is the purpose of this chapter to describe the measures which brought the system to its present efficient state.

The coins legally provided for at the time of specie resumption were as follows:

Coin	Material	Legal Tender	Redemption
Half-dollar	silver	to $5	not redeemable
Quarter-dollar	silver	to $5	not redeemable
Dime	silver	to $5	not redeemable
5 cent piece	copper-nickel	to 25 cents	in lawful money
3 cent piece	copper-nickel	to 25 cents	in lawful money
1 cent	copper-tin-zinc	to 25 cents	in lawful money

The table emphasizes the most important deficiency in the system. There was no redemption of subsidiary silver. The government was now selling the coins for gold, at a profit, without any provision for their return to the Treasury when they became redundant or unfit for circulation. Most of the coins were new, but the unexpected resurrection of millions coined before the war had put into circulation many pieces much the worse for wear. There were great numbers of the copper-silver 3 cent pieces of the law of 1851, discontinued in 1853 but never withdrawn, and many of the ordinary 3 cent and 5 cent silver coins of the 1853 statute.

The excess of silver coins, evident in 1877, became a serious problem even before specie resumption. The general public managed to get rid of the coins in various ways, chiefly through purchases of stamps, payments to the government wherever the Treasury offices would accept them, and deposits in the banks. They poured into the Treasury in a steady stream from 1876 to 1880. Meanwhile the Treasury was paying out new subsidiary coins in redemption of fractional notes. After the Bland-Allison Act began to add silver dollars in 1878, the country was called on to absorb in large numbers new subsidiary coins, old subsidiary coins from abroad, trade dollars, and new standard silver dollars.

The redundancy in silver coins was due to special conditions and to temporary legislation. In itself it did not call for a general and permanent redemption law. It was, rather, an illustration of the truth that a redemption law is a necessity in every subsidiary system in order to permit the prompt withdrawal of worn coins without loss to the holders. A provision making the coins acceptable in small government payments is neither an adequate nor an equitable arrangement for this purpose. Even this remedy was not available. There had never been a statute making subsidiary coins re-

ceivable in government transactions, and the post offices
arbitrarily refused to accept coins that they did not wish to
have accumulate in their hands. Some post offices, for example, refused to sell stamps for 3 cent pieces or 20 cent
silver coins. The failure of Congress to recognize the necessity for redemption is striking evidence of the tenacious
survival of the belief that subsidiary coins were merely a
modified form of standard money. Very slowly, one step
at a time, Congress had been driven to the enactment of
statutes providing for unlimited redemption of all the copper,
bronze, and nickel coins that had ever been produced at the
mint. From 1853 to 1878 no Treasury official or member
of Congress proposed a redemption privilege for the silver
subsidiary coins.

By the end of 1878 conditions were highly unsatisfactory. Wage-earners were receiving subsidiary coins and
trade dollars and forcing them on retailers. Small merchants everywhere were overburdened with silver coins.
Banks were refusing to accept them for deposit, and storekeepers had to dispose of them to brokers at discounts run-
ning as high as 3 per cent. On the Pacific Coast the discount
was at one time 8 per cent. Petitions and protests were
reaching Congress from many points.[1] Meanwhile the Treasury was still exchanging new coins for fractional notes,
although it was at the same time accumulating vast stores
of old coins through the various sub-Treasuries. In his annual report for 1878 Secretary Sherman made the following
recommendation:

> At times the fractional coins of the United States accumulate
> at certain places and are wanted at others. It is recommended
> that this Department be authorized to redeem them in United
> States notes . . . at the mint at Philadelphia, where they can
> be recoined, if necessary, and distributed.

[1] House Miscellaneous Document no. 37, 45th Cong., 1st sess.; **Annual
Report of the Director of the Mint for 1879**, 15.

This recommendation missed the point of the whole matter. Redemption was proposed, but only as a routine operation in the distribution of coin. The Secretary failed to see that unlimited redemption was an obligation, essential as a matter of fair dealing, necessary to prevent trouble, and serious in its financial aspects.

A redemption measure was introduced in the Senate late in 1878 and again presented in April, 1879. Tacked onto the redemption provisions was a clause raising the legal tender of subsidiary silver to $10. In the House an attempt was made to give subsidiary coins unlimited legal tender. The bill finally passed the House with two amendments, one raising the legal tender to $20, the other commanding the post offices to accept in sums up to $3 all United States coins of a denomination less than 25 cents. In the Senate the bill was passed, after a stormy debate, with the post office clause eliminated and the $20 legal tender reduced to $10.[2] After extended conferences the two houses agreed on the measure, and it became the law of June 9, 1879.

The act provided that the Treasury should redeem all subsidiary coins presented in multiples of $20 and that coins so redeemed should be again sold to the public on application. The legal tender power of subsidiary coins was raised from $5 to $10. This last provision had nothing in its favor. With an abundant currency of $1 and $5 notes in circulation, there was no need for an extension of the debt-paying power of fiduciary silver coins. It was passed as a concession to the clamorous silver interests, although it could be of no benefit to silver. Senator Sherman, conferring with the House committee, had said that he had no objection to an increase of the tender, although he saw no need for it. Chairman Stephens replied that its purpose was to enable shopkeepers to get rid of their large accumu-

[2] Congressional Record, 46th Cong., 1st sess., 483, 517, 675, 1356.

lations of coins.[3]   Apparently no member of the group, which included Linderman, realized that the provision for redemption they were considering would forever remove the necessity of forcing the coins on any reluctant creditor, while an increase of legal tender would enlarge the opportunity for such action and thereby increase the evil the law was intended to remedy.   The Senate committee reported, somewhat ironically, that they recommended an increase to $10 because the House had adopted $20 when the figure should have been left at $5.

This redemption law of 1879, intended by its framers to facilitate routine administration, was the final important step in the creation of our subsidiary system.   Without being aware of its action, Congress had committed the government to a permanent policy of redeeming without limit all the subsidiary coins that it had sold to the public, whether the pieces were worn beyond the circulation point, redundant in supply, or merely unpopular in circulation.   The long familiar phenomena of redundancy, depreciation, loss, and public annoyance were now impossible.   The loss from wear was to fall on the government.   And the mistakes of the government in choosing denominations, as in the cases of the 3 cent and 20 cent pieces, would no longer have any effect on the public, since there was now a means by which the people could determine what denominations they preferred.   In the previous history of the country the denominations had been determined largely by the arbitrary decisions of the Treasury, and there had been no adequate machinery for the elimination of undesirable coins.   Incidentally, the law had committed the Treasury to a contingent and indeterminable obligation of many millions of dollars.   There was already in circulation an excess of silver coins of at least $10,-

---

[3] House Miscellaneous Document no. 37, 45th Cong., 1st session.

ooo,ooo, and there were uncounted millions yet to return from foreign countries.

The immediate effect of the law was a very large movement of silver coins into the Treasury vaults. Sherman had suspended coinage in 1877, but old coins continued to pour into the Treasury for many years. On July 1, 1882, there was about $28,000,000 in the vaults. The estimated total in circulation was $50,000,000. This latter sum was about equal to the total of new coins produced and issued since 1875. The Treasury holdings, therefore, consisted almost entirely of the coins that had disappeared in 1862. The maximum was reached in 1885, when the total of idle coin in the Treasury reached $30,000,000. Of the more than $40,000,000 in subsidiary silver which had vanished from North and South in the summer of 1862 about $30,000,000 had returned from Latin-America fifteen years later and gone into the government vaults.

For nearly a generation this great hoard lay in the Treasury. When applicants for new coins appeared at the mint they were told to go to the Treasury offices and buy from the idle stocks. Except for certain special coinages, the mint produced no half-dollars from 1878 to 1892, no quarter-dollars until 1891. Secretary Sherman was so disturbed by the situation that he was led to recommend, in his annual report for 1890, the extraordinary expedient of abolishing subsidiary coinage.[4]

One result of Sherman's failure to understand the import of his redemption law was a Treasury deficit without a legislative provision for its reimbursement. The law au-

---

[4] This mass of idle coin was a matter of concern to the Treasury for many years. See Muhleman, Monetary and Banking Systems, 67, and the Annual Reports of the Treasurer of the United States from 1878 to 1900, especially that of 1899, 12.

thorized an indefinite expenditure of greenbacks in redemption of subsidiary coins. There was a heavy outlay of cash to be charged to current expenditures, and this expense could not be balanced by re-sale of the coins to the public for many years to come. But the books showed no loss, as the stored coins were carried at their face values. Millions of the coins, however, were so badly worn that they would not be acceptable to the public on any terms. All such pieces had to be melted. Recoinage meant a definite loss, amounting to the cost of the bullion required to replace the silver lost by wear, and this loss could be covered only by Congressional appropriations. Congress declined to consider the matter until 1882, in which year an appropriation of $25,000 was made. This sum was only a small fraction of the amount necessary, but it permitted a partial recoinage. From time to time other small appropriations were made. Secretary McCulloch in his annual report for 1884 made an urgent plea for a sum sufficient to cover the cost of a general recoinage, and in subsequent years the Mint directors and Treasury secretaries made similar requests. Congress was not finally persuaded to face the situation until 1891. By the act of March 31 in that year $150,000 was appropriated, and in subsequent years other large grants were made. The law of March 14, 1900, gave a blanket authorization for the recoinage of all worn or uncurrent silver as it comes into the Treasury. Free redemption, with the government taking all the loss from wear and bearing all the costs of recoinage, was thereby made a fixed and permanent part of the system.

Expansion of population and trade eventually exerted an influence on the vast stores of silver coins in the Treasury. The mints began to receive calls for new coins after 1885. The demand for dimes was insistent after 1886. From

1890 onwards the public demand absorbed all the new coins that the mints produced from the recoinages authorized. The $30,000,000 in storage melted away. In 1898, twenty years after Sherman stopped the coinage, the Director of the Mint reported that the subsidiary coin in hand was just sufficient to meet the current demand.

The Treasury, meanwhile, had become entangled in the meshes of legislation. The fundamental coinage law of 1873 had placed no limitations on the coinage and issue of subsidiary silver. As explained in the preceding chapter, the law of 1876 which restored silver coinage limited to $50,-000,000 the combined total of notes officially outstanding and new coins issued in redemption of fractional notes. The purpose of the provision is uncertain. It may have been intended to restrain the Treasury from abuse of the law in the interests of the silver market. More probably it was a general restraining clause passed by a Congress that still thought of subsidiary coins as "debased" standard coins. After the redemption measure of 1879 the limitation was wholly without point or purpose. As already related, Secretary Sherman nullified the law in part by a dubious interpretation which permitted an additional coinage of $8,000,000.

Even with this interpretation the Treasury approached the limit in 1877, and in his report for that year Sherman asked Congress to repeal the law. In the next year he was obliged to stop coinage. This action happened to coincide with the extraordinary influx of coins from Latin-America, and there was no need for new coins for many years. When, after 1885, the coinage was renewed, it was in violation of the restrictive law. The Treasury officials, uncertain as to their position, asked Congress to settle the matter. Director Kimball ably presented the situation in his annual report for 1886. For the next eighteen years all the coinage was produced in violation of the law, and year after year the officials begged Congress to relieve the situation.[5]

The so-called gold standard act of 1900 raised the limit to $100,000. This again was a wholly useless restriction, in conflict with the law of 1873. The new limit was soon attained. In March, 1903, a law was passed authorizing the use for subsidiary coinage of certain quantities of silver bullion left in the Treasury from the purchases under the Sherman act of 1890. The measure provided that the total bullion might be used even if the resulting coinage exceeded the limit of $100,000,000. This also was only a temporary extension of the limit. In 1905 the bullion was exhausted and the limit of $100,000,000 had been passed. The Director of the Mint laconically reported the result, as follows:

> This mint was practically idle, with the force on leave or furloughed without pay, in July, August, and September, 1905, owing to a lack of bullion on which to work.

As a last resort Secretary Shaw appealed to the Attorney General. He received an opinion to the effect that the law of 1873 took precedence over the laws of 1876, 1900, and 1903.[6] The opinion represented common sense rather than accurate interpretation, and was in itself a commentary on the ways of Congress in currency legislation. Coinage was resumed, and there has not been since that time any question of limitation on the issue of subsidiary coins, although the laws of 1900 and 1903 have not been repealed.

The stocks of idle coin in the Treasury after 1877

[5] The annual reports of the Secretary and of the Mint Director from 1880 to 1900 show how these officials struggled for two decades to persuade Congress to consider the problems of worn coin on the one hand and an arbitrary limit on new coinage on the other.

[6] See Annual Report of the Secretary of the Treasury and of the Director of the Mint for 1906.

created another administrative problem. Hitherto subsidiary coins had been sold directly to the public at the mints and the sub-Treasury offices. It was hoped that the accumulation would be reduced if shipments were made free of charge to customers at other points. In 1881 Congress appropriated $20,000 to pay for free distribution. Appropriations were made at irregular intervals thereafter, with the result that free distribution was made only part of the time. The officials urged Congress to provide for permanent free distribution or to discontinue the practice entirely. The matter was not finally settled until the Federal Reserve System took over the functions of the sub-Treasuries in 1920. Through these superior agencies the distribution of subsidiary and minor coins is now efficiently and inexpensively effected. New coins are obtained from the mints and the Treasury by the Federal Reserve Banks, which in turn distribute them to the banks within their respective districts. Member banks receive this service without charge, even for transportation, while non-member banks pay the costs of shipment. Through these same agencies as well as through the mints and Treasury offices redemption of mutilated, worn, or redundant coins is conveniently and inexpensively accomplished.

In the long period of redundancy in silver currency the minor coins were coming into their own. They had circulated throughout the war period and the greenback era. The 1 cent pieces were the first coins of the United States, and they are the only coins in our history that have been continuously in circulation, without interruption, since the first coinage law. The withdrawal of the 3 cent and 5 cent notes in the war years and the discontinuance of the 3 cent and 5 cent silver pieces in 1873 had left the field of circulation below 10 cents to the 1 cent bronze coins and the 3 cent and 5 cent copper-nickel coins. The 2 cent bronze coin and the 1857 copper-nickel cent still circulated, but the bulk of them drifted into the Treasury for redemption. The 3 cent copper-nickel piece was still coined, but very few were in circulation. Given a choice through unrestricted redemption the public chose the silver dime, the copper-nickel 5 cent piece, and the bronze 1 cent piece as the only coins required in transactions involving less than 25 cents.

A lively demand for 1 cent pieces developed after 1880. The period was marked by a large expansion of machine production and a rapid urbanization of the population. A great variety of small articles appeared in the markets, among them small match-boxes, postcards, one and two cent newspapers, toys, and small confections. The adoption of a 2 cent postal rate likewise increased the need for cent pieces. Somewhat later a similar increase in the demand for 5 cent pieces was reported by the mints. The excessive issues of bronze and nickel coins after the war had made the 3 cent and 5 cent coins greatly redundant, but the redemption measure and the growth of business turned the tide toward a renewal of coinage in the case of the 5 cent piece. Progress in metallurgy and mint processes eliminated the difficulties in coining nickel, and the attractive color and fine wearing qualities of the alloy made it a popular coinage material. After 1885 the mints had difficulty in keeping up with the demand. The street railway, the cheap cigar, the "notions counter," and the slot machine called for millions of the coins. The sale of toys, candies, gum, cigarettes, and soda waters requiring payments of 5, 10, or 15 cents very rapidly increased.

It will be recalled that the nickel 3 cent piece was forced into a circulation already over-burdened with 1 and 2 cent pieces. It should never have been authorized. After silver coins came back it became especially objectionable because of its resemblance to the silver dime. From 1880 onward the Treasury officials made annual appeals to Congress for the abolition of the coin. It was finally discontinued, along with the $1 and $3 gold pieces, by the law of September 26, 1890. This measure brought our fractional currency system to the 50 cent, 25 cent, 10 cent, 5 cent and 1 cent denominations of the present day.

The 1873 law created a minor coinage bullion fund of $50,000. With the growth of the coinage the amount was inadequate to meet the needs of the mint. After more than a decade of persistent nagging at Congress, the officials obtained by act of April 24, 1906, an increase to $200,000. The law included a provision repealing the clause in the 1873 law which restricted the coinage of 1 cent and 5 cent pieces to the Philadelphia mint. The West had at last adopted the 1 cent piece, and coinage at all the mints was a necessary measure of economy and convenience. By a law of December 2, 1918, the minor coinage bullion fund was increased to $400,000.

CHAPTER XIX

THE TRADE DOLLAR AND THE STANDARD
SILVER DOLLAR

HISTORY of the trade dollar—Its purpose—Comes into domestic circulation—Legal tender repealed in 1876—Coinage stopped in 1878—Redemption of the coin in 1887—Standard silver dollar dropped in 1873—The silver movement—Bland-Allison Act of 1878—Sherman Act of 1890—Repealed in 1893—Desirability of eliminating silver dollars.

By the definition of fractional currency in the first chapter the trade dollar and the standard silver dollar are excluded from the category of fractional silver coins. The history of these two coins in the years after 1873 might well be omitted, were it not for the fact that legislation made these two coins hybrids, neither standard money nor yet subsidiary, but invested with the qualities of both types of money. The history of the two coins is a part of the record of our subsidiary coins.

It will be recalled that the trade dollar was created by the law of 1873 ostensibly as a convenient coin for trade with the Orient. Knox had in his original bill proposed to make the standard silver dollar subsidiary. When the critics objected, Knox dropped the silver dollar entirely and in his report suggested the possibility of a trade dollar, a coin recommended by Linderman as a substitute for the Mexican dollars used in payments to China. The trade coin section was interpolated into the bill more than two years later, just before the measure was passed, in response to pressure by the silver interests.

The piece was to weigh 420 grains, $\frac{9}{10}$ fine, so that it would have a pure silver content of 378 grains, about 2 per cent above the amount in the standard dollar. It was to have free coinage, in the sense that any one could present bullion to the mint for conversion into trade dollars. Provision was made for a coinage charge equal to the costs of minting. The coin was made legal tender in payments to $5. As explained in an earlier chapter, this last provision was not an unintentional blunder in the wording of the law. More probably it was deliberately inserted in order to give the trade coin a standing in domestic use. In the general revision of the statutes in the year following the passage of the law the legal tender clause was re-enacted without objection from any source. In 1875 Linderman actually recommended that the legal tender power be increased to $10, and in 1876 the House passed an act which raised the tender to $50, although the wording of the clause was such as to disguise the intent. Only the refusal of the Senate to approve such a misguided measure prevented its enactment.[1]

At the time the law of 1873 was passed, a trade dollar was worth about $1.05 in gold and $1.15 in greenbacks. But silver was rapidly declining in gold value and greenbacks were going up. In the Pacific states silver coins were at par with gold. When silver declined to the point where 378 grains were worth less than one gold dollar, it would be profitable in California to take silver to the mint for coinage into trade dollars for domestic circulation. So far as the Pacific Coast was concerned, the provision for the free coinage of legal tender trade dollars was in effect a double standard measure at a ratio of about $16\frac{1}{3}$ to 1. In the remainder of the country, still on a greenback basis, the coinage and circulation of the trade dollar would be profit-

[1] See Chapters XVI and XVII.

able only when the silver in the coin was worth less than a dollar in greenbacks.

For a few years after 1873 there was a small coinage of trade dollars, chiefly at San Francisco, for shipment to China. Early in 1876 the price of silver reached the point where it was profitable to coin the pieces for circulation on the Pacific Coast. By the middle of that year the coins were flooding retail trade in California and shortly thereafter they were selling at a discount. Before the end of the year the rising value of greenbacks brought a similar development in the East. Trade dollars appeared in circulation all over the country.[2]

The coin was unlike any known to the people. The standard silver dollar itself was a tradition, not a currency. This new piece was not even like the standard coin. It was not redeemable, it was cumbrous in size and unfamiliar in design, and it entered into a circulation abundantly supplied with one dollar bills and oversupplied with fractional silver coins. But the trade coin was none the less forced into circulation by silver owners, and once there its $5 legal tender power kept it afloat. It circulated in retail trade, displacing subsidiary coins and intensifying the redundancy that was filling the Treasury vaults with silver coins.

The joint resolution of July 22, 1876, which increased the issue of subsidiary coins produced under the specie resumption act, contained a provision repealing the legal tender of the trade dollar and authorizing the Secretary to limit the coinage to the volume necessary to meet the demand for export. It was thought that this measure would drive the coins from circulation. Such was not the case. The con-

---

[2] Congressional Record, 44th Cong., 1st sess., 3749, 3745; Annual Report on the Finances for 1877, XX, 241, and for 1878, XXIII, 257. There is no satisfactory history of the trade dollar. Garnett's History, in the American Economic Review, is perhaps the best.

tinuous fall in silver made it increasingly profitable to circulate the coins, and in some way they were systematically forced into the channels of trade. Secretary Sherman said in 1878 that 4,000,000 pieces had been put into circulation by parties well aware of the nature of their action. In 1877 Sherman stopped the coinage, resumed it briefly a few months later, and stopped it finally in February, 1878. In his annual reports for both years he urged Congress to prohibit further coinage. This excellent recommendation would have come with better grace if Sherman's policy had been more in keeping with it. Millions were in circulation before the end of 1876, and coinage should have been suspended, under the law of that year, so long as any trade dollars remained in circulation. The Treasury continued to issue them, even though it refused to accept them in any sort of payments to the government. Some contemporary critics thought Sherman was influenced by the silver interests.[3] It is more likely that Sherman hesitated to use a power that was discretionary when it should have been mandatory. His discontinuance of the coinage in 1878 satisfied Congress, and the law authorizing the coinage was not repealed. In fact the silver interests presented a bill which commanded Sherman to resume coinage.

The withdrawal of legal tender failed to diminish the circulation of the coin. Five years after Sherman stopped their coinage as many trade dollars were in circulation as ever before. Unscrupulous employers bought the coins from brokers at a discount and paid them out as wages at their face value. Retailers supplying wage earners were obliged to accept them. Since the banks refused them in deposits, the merchants re-sold them to the brokers at a loss, doubtless recouping themselves in the prices they charged for their

[3] See Hallock's *Refusing its Own Coin*, a pamphlet accusing Sherman of bad faith and official misstatements.

goods. In his annual report for 1883 Director Burchard said:

> Probably from five to seven millions of these coins are now held in the country, mostly in the mining and manufacturing regions of Pennsylvania and contiguous states, and in the vicinity of New York, where they have been paid to workmen and laborers, and by them paid to and received from tradesmen in these localities.

Side by side with these trade dollars there were in circulation many Mexican dollars, imported and circulated by the same mean and unscrupulous sharpers who were circulating the trade coins. The victims of these operations were, of course, the poor and the unsophisticated. By 1883 the value of silver had fallen to a point where a trade dollar was worth as bullion about 85 cents. The coin had become so great a nuisance that concerted action to stop its circulation was taken by merchants and bankers. The bulk of the coins fell into the hands of speculators and brokers who paid bullion value or less.

There was continuous agitation for redemption of the coins from 1878 onwards. Memorials and petitions from many sources reached Congress, and bill after bill was introduced. But there was strenuous opposition to redemption, not because it would be an unjust measure for the benefit of speculators but because it would affect the silver market adversely. Redemption meant melting, and most of the bills provided for re-coinage of the metal into standard dollars under the Bland-Allison act. Such action would reduce the purchases of silver under that law, and the silver interests, which had been responsible for the trade dollar and had resisted the repeal of its legal tender, were now blocking the attempt to redeem the coins. They managed to prevent redemption for nine years.[4]

[4] Discussion of the trade dollar covers many pages in the Congressional Record. See especially 47th Cong., 1st sess., 1524, and 48th Cong., 1st sess., index, 80; also House Report 324, 48th Cong., 1st session.

Eventually the coins, long since out of circulation, fell into the hands of speculators and bankers powerful enough to force a redemption law. Ostensibly in the interests of the poor and ignorant, who no longer held the coins, Congress passed the law of February 19, 1887. It prohibited further coinage and directed the Secretary to redeem in standard silver dollars or in subsidiary coins all pieces not defaced or mutilated. This wording of the law was its one redeeming feature. Nearly 30,000,000 pieces had gone to China. To permit them to be brought back for redemption would have been a final blunder. The Chinese made a practice of "chopping" the coins as they arrived. The law refused redemption of chopped dollars, thus protecting both the silver interests and the government against the return of more than 25,000,000 pieces. Nearly 8,000,000 trade dollars were redeemed, of which, it is estimated, about 2,000,000 were unchopped pieces brought back from China. The average bullion value at the time of redemption was about 75 cents.

This book is not concerned with the details of the bitter struggle for bimetallism that was waged in the years from 1875 to 1900. The issue at stake was more than the choice of standards. After 1870 the need for money increased more rapidly than the supply of gold, not only in this country but the world over. The consequence was a relentless decline of general prices, depressing in its effects on industry and ruinous to many interests, more especially the impoverished South and the over-expanded Middle West. The people of these sections, led by those who had private interests in silver, seized upon bimetallism, national or international, as the key to the situation. Most of those who advocated the double standard sincerely believed that the remonetization of silver would lighten the stifling pressure exerted by the waning price level. Internationally adopted, the double standard would have done this very thing. As a policy for the United States alone the revival of the double standard at the old ratio of 16 to 1 would have been a grievous error.

As early as 1875 the silver interests had discovered what should have been clear when Knox presented the bill to Congress in 1870, that is, that the elimination of the one word "dollar" from the list of coins had changed this country from a legal double standard to a legal single gold standard nation. The movement for bimetallism was strengthened by the widespread belief that the abolition of the double standard was secretly accomplished by a Congressional committee, thus constituting a fraud upon a people sorely beset with economic difficulties. In preceding chapters it has been shown that the first moves to restore subsidiary coins were embarrassed by repeated attempts to tack on amendments reviving the double standard. Senator Sherman's Finance Committee recommended in 1876 the coinage of a silver dollar slightly increased in weight to bring the coinage ratio to exactly 16 to 1, and in the same year the House actually passed a bill restoring the double standard at the old ratio of 1837.

In the end Congress adopted the Bland-Allison act, passed over the veto of President Grant on February 28, 1878. The law directed the Secretary to purchase monthly from $2,000,000 to $4,000,000 worth of silver bullion, to be coined into standard silver dollars of the old weight and legal tender power. This famous law was not a free coinage measure, or a bimetallic measure, or a change of standard measure. It was a subsidiary coinage law. Bullion was to be bought on government account, coined into pieces worth less as bullion than as money, and sold to the public at a seigniorage profit to the government. There was no provision for direct sales to the public for gold, it is true, but this was only because the public obviously would not buy. The coins were to be paid out to government creditors at their face value, and this accomplished the same result as sales for gold. Two features distinguished the measure from an ordinary subsidiary coinage law. The public was required to accept a fixed amount of the coins, and the fiduciary pieces were given unlimited legal tender.

The law was a wretched compromise, without a single redeeming feature, carrying with it the dangers of a wrong-ratio bimetallism without establishing the double standard. By it the silver mine owners were bought off with a large market for silver, the bimetallists were deceived with a fictitious restoration of the double standard, and the single standard advocates were solaced with a last minute rescue of the gold standard when it appeared to be doomed. Its immediate effect was to add to the currency an unwieldy coin that had never circulated in the history of the country, too valuable for use as fractional currency, too bulky for large payments.

The Treasury bought the minimum amount possible under the law, $24,000,000 worth of silver bullion per year. The number of dollars produced was a variable, increasing with the decline in the value of silver and averaging about 28,000,000 dollars per year. The coins were, in general, very badly received. In two regions they were accepted in large numbers. In the South they circulated because of an interesting social situation. As a class the recently emancipated slaves were illiterate. There were no gold coins in circulation, and the colored population refused to use greenbacks with their printed symbols. They gladly accepted the new silver coins, and from this situation came the custom of using silver dollars in the South, a practice that is even today only slowly giving way. In the West the aversion to paper money and the general desire to support silver led to the acceptance of the silver dollar.

The North and East would have none of them. With the increasing annual coinage the volume returned to the Treasury in tax payments steadily increased. In 1886 Secretary Manning, anxious to keep them out of the Treasury assets, devised a clever scheme to transfer their ownership to the people even while they remained in the Treasury vaults. This was to issue silver certificates, then issued in large bills, in denominations small enough to insure wide circulation. At Manning's suggestion Congress passed the law of August 4, 1886, providing for the issue of $1 and $2 silver certificates. They were merely receipts entitling the holder to claim the dollars lying in the vaults. They were not legal tender, but they carried with them the ownership of silver dollars that were a tender. The notes were much like the familiar greenbacks and were readily accepted.

The Bland-Allison act was in force until 1890, steadily augmenting the volume of dollars in circulation or lying in the vaults against outstanding certificates. In 1890 renewed pressure was brought to bear on Congress, as a consequence of which the Bland-Allison act was repealed and replaced by the Sherman act, passed July 14. Under the new provisions the Treasury was to buy 4,500,000 ounces of silver per month, to be paid for with Treasury notes that were to be legal tender. The notes were to be redeemable in gold coin or in silver dollars coined from the bullion purchased. There was no provision for coinage beyond the amount called for by these redemptions, and none for the disposition in any other way of the large amount of bullion that would be left over.

Stripped of its technicalities, this measure provided for

a government subsidy for the benefit of silver miners, as a result of which the Treasury was to issue an indeterminate amount of fiat money redeemable in subsidiary coins worth less than their face value. The monthly purchases produced about 5,800,000 silver dollars, although the volume of notes issued was much smaller. The Treasury adopted the practice of redeeming the notes in gold. In 1893 a series of adverse economic developments brought disaster to the Treasury. It was involved in an "endless chain" situation in which it was paying out notes for bullion, redeeming the notes in gold, paying out the redeemed notes for current expenses and again redeeming in gold. This operation, which would eventually destroy the solvency of the government, was merely the process by which the excessive issues of silver dollars and paper money were displacing gold under the working of Gresham's law. The gold withdrawn from the Treasury was in the main exported to Europe.

The act of 1890 was hastily repealed. Eventually provision was made by law for the coinage of the surplus bullion into silver dollars and subsidiary coins. As a net result of the laws of 1878 and 1890 the country acquired approximately 570,000,000 silver dollars. A small proportion of these coins circulate in the South and West. The bulk of them are represented by $1, $2, and $5 silver certificates in general circulation. The "gold standard act" of 1900, which formally declared allegiance to the single standard, contradicted itself by re-affirming the fiction that the silver dollar is a standard coin. Although it is still unlimited in legal tender, it is a subsidiary coin. With the continued decline in silver the piece has become increasingly fiduciary. For years on end its gold value has been in the neighborhood of 50 cents. Except for its unrestricted legal tender and slightly larger weight in proportion to its money value, it differs in no respect from our subsidiary dimes, quarters, and half-dollars. Because of its pretended standard character it is not directly redeemable, although the government has declared itself responsible for maintenance of its parity with gold. There never was a reason for its coinage between 1878 and 1893. After the latter date there was not even a pretext for its further existence. There is none now. As a fiduciary coin it is too bulky for use. In circulation it merely displaces two half-dollars which weigh 6½ per cent less and are genuine subsidiary coins. The millions in the vaults are merely an undigested mass of stamped metal, of discreditable history and no present use. In any guise they represent an obligation of the government which may at some critical period embarrass the Treasury. They should be eliminated.

CHAPTER XX

THE PRESENT DAY

For more than twenty years there has been no material modification of the fractional coinage system. There has been no vitally important legislation since the redemption measure of 1879, if the silver dollar laws be excepted, and no important administrative developments since the Treasury obtained from the Attorney General in 1905 the authority for unlimited coinage which it had vainly sought from Congress for twenty-five years. The transfer of the function of distributing the coins from the sub-Treasuries to the Federal Reserve System in 1920 should, perhaps, be considered as an administrative development.

The system created before 1906 stood the strains of the war period from 1914 to 1919 without new legislation or irregular expedients. An early effect of the war, evident long before the United States became a participant, was to stimulate the demand for fractional coins. The prosperous years after 1900 had already brought the rate of issue to a volume hitherto unknown. Even these totals were dwarfed

by the production called forth by the extraordinary industrial activity in the years from 1916 to 1920. For many
weeks the mints ran day and night. Every possible improvement in equipment and processes was introduced.

The demand extended to all the coins, but it was most
insistent in the case of the 1 cent, 5 cent, and 10 cent pieces.
There were special conditions to account for the demand
for cents. The sumptuary taxes levied on drugs, cosmetics,
and various other small articles created an entirely new
demand for 1 cent coins. One cause of the unpopularity
of these taxes was the necessity of "odd sum" payments for
articles, such as soaps or perfumes, that were customarily
sold at prices quoted in multiples of 5 cents. The taxes on
amusements likewise enlarged the need for the 5 cent, 10
cent, and 25 cent coins. Still another factor was the rising
price level, which forced subway and street car companies,
cigarette manufacturers, and others to add one or two cents
to the ordinary prices of 5, 10, or 15 cents. The 1 cent
newspaper went to 2 cents or 3, the Sunday edition to 6 or
7 cents. The burdens of change making were so great that
Congress actually considered at different times during the
period proposals for the coinage of 2 cent, 2½ cent, 6
cent, 7 cent, 8 cent, and 15 cent coins. In the fiscal year
ending June 30, 1918, the mints produced more than
700,000,000 coins, and this tremendous total was again
reached in the fiscal year 1920.[1]

Despite the extraordinary demand there was no serious
deficiency of silver coins or 5 cent pieces. In the case of
the 1 cent piece there was a real shortage in the fall of
1917. In October the New York sub-Treasury's stock of
copper cents was completely exhausted and business concerns were unable to obtain adequate supplies. In Novem-

---

[1] The annual reports of the Mint Director from 1916 to 1920 give interesting accounts of mint operations in the war period.

ber Director Baker announced that the mints, although they were turning out 3,000,000 cent pieces every day, would not be able to avert a general scarcity. He urged that children stop putting cents in toy banks. He even went so far as to suggest the possibility of issuing fractional notes. Fortunately the shortage was relieved without resort to this type of currency.[2] The sale of war savings certificates by a method that brought millions of 1 cent pieces to the Treasury was a material factor in the solution of the problem.

The demand for coins ceased abruptly with the collapse of the post-war boom in 1920. Subsidiary coinage dropped from a total of $25,000,000 in the fiscal year 1920 to about $1,000,000 in 1921. It ceased entirely in 1922. The coinage of 1 cent and 5 cent pieces, which amounted to $8,000,000 in 1920, was about $70,000 in 1922. The familiar phenomenon of redundancy did not appear. Redemption took care of the surplus coins.

The most important development of the war period, from the standpoint of the student of currency principles, was one which attracted little attention at the time and has since been forgotten. The value of silver, which had been for many years in the neighborhood of 50 cents per fine ounce, rose to an average of 84 cents in 1917 and to 98 cents in 1918. In 1919 the average price was $1.12. The fluctuations were extreme, and in November the price reached a peak point of $1.38¼, with sales reported from San Francisco at even higher levels. The pure silver in $1.38⅕ in subsidiary coins weighs exactly one ounce. The price of silver in November, therefore, reached a point where the bullion value of four quarters or ten dimes was more than $1. The country was on the verge of a collapse of the fractional coinage such as that which paralyzed retail

[2] New York *Times* for Oct. 30, Nov. 3, Nov. 17, and Nov. 24, 1917.

trade in 1862. The price hovered about the disappearance point for some months, with a high mark of $1.36¾ in 1920, but it did not again pass the point. By good fortune the crisis did not materialize.

Secretary Houston and Director Baker discussed the situation in their annual reports for 1920.[3] There was nothing in their statements to indicate that they had any knowledge of the events of 1862 or any understanding of the way in which Secretary Chase and Director Pollock had failed in their responsibility under similar conditions. It was clear that neither Secretary Houston nor Director Baker had any plans for meeting the emergency. In fact they appeared to regard the perilous state of the silver currency as an extraordinary phenomenon outside their responsibility. If the price of an ounce of silver had risen a cent or so more in November, 1919, an economic calamity would have befallen the country, with the officials making no move to avert it.

A belated effort to provide for the emergency was made in Congress. On December 8, 1919, Representative Platt introduced a bill which reduced the weights of the subsidiary coins. The gross weight per dollar was to be reduced from 25 grams (385.8 grains) to 300 grains.[4] The plan was identical with that suggested by Chase as an alternative to his postage stamp plan. Like Chase's plan, it was introduced two weeks after the crisis had arrived and was inadequate and unscientific. The bill was referred to the committee on coinage and never heard from again, although the price of silver was near the disappearance point for many months.

In three emergencies of this kind Congress and Treas-

[3] Annual Report on the Finances for 1920, 182, 962.

[4] Congressional Record, 65th Cong., 1st sess., 6144, and 66th Cong., 2nd sess., 5713.

ury have ignored the approaching crisis and failed to take action after its arrival. In the period after 1853 the coins were close to the vanishing point for five years. In 1862 it was patent for six months that the coins would disappear. In 1919 the currency was permitted to reach the disappearance point without even a comment by the officials. Inertia and ineptitude, although they are factors, are not entirely responsible. Back of these is a failure to understand the nature of fiduciary currency, together with a not unnatural reluctance to alter an established coinage. The Platt bill of 1919 proposed a rather drastic reduction in coins that before the World War had been more than 50 per cent fiduciary. Congress hesitated to accept such a proposal, and it may be expected to hesitate under similar circumstances in the future. One reason is the unsatisfactory character of the remedy proposed. The Chase measure of 1862 and the Platt bill of 1919 called for a permanent alteration in the legal weights of the subsidiary coins, involving a reduction in both copper and silver content, new designs, and changes in mint processes. The plan is slow in application and unscientific in principle.

The proper remedy is to reduce the proportion of pure silver in the coins, with a proportionate increase in the copper. The size, design, and wording need not be changed. This plan involves no delays whatever. The only significant change in the coins is an alteration in color. In 1920 England adopted this method, delaying so long after the crisis had arrived that a law was hastily passed reducing the fineness of the silver coins from 92½ per cent to 50 per cent. The fall of silver since 1922 has been so great that the English coins have had a bullion value of about one-fifth of their money value.

The institution of this change in time of need should

not be left to the hazards of legislation, inevitably slow and
uncertain. Provision should be made in advance by a statute
authorizing the Treasury to reduce the silver content of subsidiary coins when conditions justify such action. Proper
safeguards to prevent uncalled-for changes could be incorporated. It might be desirable to require that the change
be initiated by the Director, recommended by the Secretary,
and approved by the President. A provision for a return
to the normal standard, made sufficiently flexible, might well
be included. Congress has already passed a law embodying
the principle of this proposed measure for the protection of
the Philippine silver coins.[5]

There is need for such a law now. While the value of
silver has declined to a point where the seigniorage on four
quarters is again around 50 cents, this value is wholly fortuitous. The course of silver prices is beyond prediction,
and a rapid appreciation is possible in time of peace or war.
The volume of our outstanding subsidiary coins is now so
great, approximating as it does 300,000,000 dollars, that
the withdrawal and marketing of the coins would in itself
counteract the forces causing the rise in the price of silver.
The sale as bullion of half a billion silver dollars, which
would disappear even before the first withdrawals of subsidiary coins, would also tend to stop the rise of silver. Pro-
tected by these economic forces, the subsidiary coins would
hardly disappear in the headlong fashion of 1862. But a
rising price of silver could cause a steady withdrawal of the
newer coins and bring about a tendency to hoarding that
would disorganize commerce. A law of the type suggested
here will enable the Treasury to anticipate the emergency
and accumulate coins for replacement. The mere existence
of such a law will tend to discourage hoarding and reduce

[5] Kemmerer, Modern Currency Reforms, 359.

premiums on the coins. It would be worth while to have the statute apply to the minor as well as the subsidiary coins.

The rising price of silver in the war period brought unexpected results in another quarter. The currency situation in India in 1918 forced the British government to appeal to the United States for silver bullion. At the time the silver in a standard dollar was worth nearly $1 in gold. Here was a providential opportunity to rid the country of a useless and dangerous element in the currency. It was necessary only to melt the coins in the vaults, sell the bullion to Great Britain, and cancel the silver certificates as they came into the Treasury. The unexpected rise in silver had made it possible to cancel without serious loss a contingent obligation of the government amounting to many millions of dollars. But this was not to be. The same forces that for twenty years after 1873 exerted every effort to foster their private interests at the expense of public welfare and eventually drove the country to financial collapse in 1893 mustered their strength and passed the Pittman act. In brief, the law provided for the sale of not more than 350,-000,000 silver dollars as bullion at not less than $1 per ounce, the purchase from American mine owners of an equal amount of bullion at the same price, and the recoinage of the pieces that had been sold. The purpose of the measure was to furnish the metal to Great Britain without interfering with the abnormal returns to the silver interests the war conditions had induced. In effect the law gave a subsidy from public taxation to protect the war profits of a private industry.

Some 260,000,000 dollars were sold. Since that time the Treasury has been buying bullion and recoining the dollars. All of it has been bought at the fixed price of $1

per ounce.[6] At the same time the Treasury has been buying bullion for subsidiary coinage at the current market
prices, which averaged 63 cents in 1921, 68 cents in 1922,
and 67 cents in 1924. These figures, significant as they are,
do not tell the whole story. These average market prices
around 65 cents were undoubtedly higher than they would
have been if the Treasury had not been buying large quantities at the artificial $1 price. To the direct losses of this
measure there should be added a loss on the seigniorage from
subsidiary coinage.

The present era has witnessed a gratifying improvement
in the mechanical efficiency of our mints. From this standpoint the mint establishment has come to be a model of its
kind, justifying a national pride in the perfection of its coinage. The way in which the mints met the demands of
the World War reflect credit on the Directors and their
assistants. By authority of Congress coinage for other
countries is permitted, and the establishment renders this
service to many nations. In earlier times our coins, though
mechanically well made, were inartistic to a degree. Changes
of design were frequent and sometimes arbitrary, the law
providing for certain permanent devices but leaving other
features to the decision of the officials. By a law of September 26, 1890, it was provided that changes in design,
approved by the Secretary, should not be made more frequently than every twenty-five years. Since that time new
designs have been adopted for the subsidiary and minor
coins. The half-dollar, quarter-dollar, and dime, designed
in 1916, are beautiful coins. The first design of the quarter-
dollar of this model was unsatisfactory, for reasons that
were apparently never publicly explained, and the Treasury

[6] See Annual Reports of the Director of the Mint for the years from 1918
to 1926.

was forced to the unusual and legally doubtful expedient of suspending coinage before Congress approved a new design by the act of July 9, 1917.[7] In the general revision of 1874 the provision of 1873 authorizing but not requiring the motto "In God We Trust" was omitted. The coins continued to bear the inscription. In 1907 a new design for the gold coins omitted the motto. Public opinion resented the change, and Congress by act of May 18, 1908, ordered the inscription restored on all the coins which had borne it in the past.

The silver coins and the 5 cent piece are attractive in appearance and satisfactory in use. Only one of our coins is physically deficient. The bronze cent is attractive when fresh from the mint, and it is convenient in size and durable in use. But it tarnishes quickly and turns dark. Director Roberts in his annual report for 1911 urged a new alloy, suggesting the 75–25 copper-nickel mixture of our 5 cent piece. Secretary MacVeagh approved the proposal, commenting that the condition of the cent pieces returned for redemption actually jeopardized the health of the Treasury employees. A bill changing the material and providing for scalloped edges on the coin to insure easy identification was considered by Congress and rejected, possibly because the measure included a provision for a ½ cent piece and a 3 cent piece. As far back as 1896 Congress had authorized a series of experiments to determine the qualities of various metals and alloys, among them aluminum, pure nickel, and various bronze combinations. The results were generally unfavor-

---

[7] The official records have an atmosphere of mystery. Secretary McAdoo's letter to Congress referred only to the artistic merit of the eagle design. The bill he forwarded referred to the stacking qualities of the coin. But the significant change actually made was an increase in the draperies of the beautiful but bold female figure on the original coin. See Congressional Record, 65th Cong., 1st sess., 1568, 4223. See also the attractive illustrations in the Annual Reports of the Director of the Mint for 1916 and 1917.

able. Since that time pure nickel coins and aluminum alloy coins have been successfully issued in various countries. Canada substituted a pure nickel 5 cent piece for the silver half-dime in 1921. The effort to change the material of our 1 cent piece will probably be revived in the future.

In this generation the mints have issued many gold and silver coins of special design commemorative of our historical and social development. Beginning with the Columbian Exposition half-dollar of 1892, a long series of souvenir coins have been issued. Many of them are beautiful examples of the art of coinage. The laws authorizing such coinages give the pieces the legal tender and redemption privileges of ordinary coins.

There are no longer any serious defects in our fractional currency system. The provisions for coinage, issue, redemption, legal tender, and recoinage are adequate. There are a few unsettled questions. Two of these, the elimination of the silver dollar and the desirability of a law permitting an administrative reduction of the silver content of the subsidiary coins, have been fully discussed. Another question has to do with the relation of subsidiary coins to the paper note circulation. It will be recalled that the use of $1 notes was largely the result of Secretary Manning's substitution of silver certificates for silver dollars in 1886. Before that time the issue of $1 greenbacks and $1 national bank-notes had been small. After 1916 war conditions greatly stimulated the demand for $1 bills, and the circulation of notes of this denomination increased rapidly. The demand has increased since the war. Popular explanations refer to the general expansion of business, to the public insistence on fresh new bills, and to the automobile, which has greatly increased the average "pocket money" requirements. The primary factor is the falling value of money. With the steady rise in the price level since 1896 the $1

bill has become a small change currency. The dollar bill
of 1900 has become a 50 cent note, and its velocity of circulation is that of a 50 cent piece of a generation ago.
Its increasing circulation and brief life are incurable conditions.

In the war period the Treasury was sorely distressed by
the increasing costs of issue, redemption and replacement
of the $1 bills. In 1924 the problem became acute, as the
Treasury found itself physically unable to make enough notes
to meet the demand. The situation was not unlike that in
the fractional currency after 1870. The notes wore out so
rapidly and returned in such volume for replacement that the
Treasury was overwhelmed. In the fall of 1924 Secretary
Mellon announced that the solution of the problem was to
force the people to use the silver dollar. This proposal
was predestined to failure. It was impossible to persuade
the public to use the coins. When the futility of this
plan was evident, another remedy was found. This was to
force into circulation enough $2 notes to reduce the $1 bills
outstanding by one-half. This proposal was approved by
the Bureau of Efficiency. Its only recommendation was that
it was not so objectionable as the silver dollar scheme.[8]
The circulation of the two denominations is undesirable.
They are confused in change operations, and their joint circulation is a cause of dispute, annoyance, and occasional
fraud. The $2 notes are accepted reluctantly, passed on
quickly, and driven back to banks and Treasury offices.

Through various improvements in Treasury methods the
problem has been in some measure solved. The reduction
in the size of all notes will still further relieve the situation. But the objectionable joint circulation of $1 and $2

[8] See article by Neil Carothers in the New York Times for March 13, 1926.
For details of Treasury policy in this connection see Commercial and Financial Chronicle for Oct. 4, 1924, and New York Times for Aug. 2, 1925.

bills is still promoted by the Treasury. There are two pos-sible solutions. One is to abolish the $2 note and provide an adequate number of $1 bills regardless of expense. The other solution, more drastic but more fundamental, is to abolish the $1 note.

There are many arguments in favor of this latter solu-tion. The $1 note is not, scientifically, the proper denomi-nation between the 50 cent piece and the $5 bill. It repre-sents a small change value, and its use calls for a volume of change operations in stores and ticket offices that seri-ously burdens business. If it were abolished retail trade would be carried on with subsidiary coins and $2 bills. Change operations would be much reduced. The average man would carry a larger amount in silver coins, and this would be an advantage in convenience and time for both customer and shopkeeper. The government would gain greatly from savings on the heavy costs of redeeming $1 bills as well as from seigniorage on a greatly increased coin-age of subsidiary silver.

The public has grown accustomed to the $1 bill, al-though it was but little used until recent times. A pro-posal to discontinue the note would probably be widely re-sented, and there would be a popular impression that busi-ness would be seriously disturbed by the change. The aboli-tion of the bill would cause no injury. Before the war Eng-land had no notes of less value than $25, and the smallest gold piece was a coin worth approximately $2.50. A note of a value as low as $1 would have been unthinkable in Eng-lish trade circles. If it should be unwise to discontinue the $1 note in view of public misunderstanding, the only alter-native is to abolish the $2 bill, which circulates in the face of popular dislike. The continued currency of both notes is wholly undesirable.

Another question relating to the function of subsidiary

coinage has to do with the failure of the system to meet a minor but definite need. There is no convenient method of making small remittances by mail. The postal money order service is available at certain times, but its use involves a trip to a post office and an over-elaborate routine procedure. Drawing checks for trivial sums is not good practice. Great numbers of exchanges by mail are effected by such makeshifts as postage stamps, due bills for merchandise, and slot devices for coins. Even the government attempts to meet the need by the sale of due-bills for its publications. It will be recalled that long after fractional notes disappeared from circulation banks kept supplies to enable customers to make mail remittances. The need for some similar device is much greater now. Mail-order houses and direct-sales advertisers have developed a very large volume of business in small articles. If the government could devise some form of note that would meet this need and at the same time not be used as a general circulating medium it would be a distinct service to trade. Some type of ungummed postage stamp, to be sold at a slight advance over face value, available for postage but not redeemable at the post offices, might serve the purpose.

The present arrangement of denominations, 1, 5, 10, 25, and 50 cents, is satisfactory. It was developed from the experience of a century. It accords with the principles governing the denominations in a decimal system, although the 5 and 25 cent pieces are not strictly decimal. From time to time bills are presented in Congress providing for additions to the present system. Unusual conditions, such as those arising in war time, call forth proposals of this kind, but they appear in normal times as well, prompted by some theory of currency or some temporary need for a coin of non-decimal denomination. The favorite denominations in these proposed measures are the ½ cent piece, the 2 cent piece, the 2½ cent piece, and the 3 cent piece. In 1911 Mayors Brand Whitlock of Toledo and Newton D. Baker of Cleveland sent a joint memorial to Congress urging the coinage of a 3 cent piece. In 1912 Director Roberts, Secretary MacVeagh, and a House committee approved a bill which included provision for a ½ cent piece and a 3 cent piece, in the form of copper-nickel coins with scalloped edges. In his annual report for 1916 Director Woolley urged the coinage of a 2½ cent piece, and in 1920 a bill providing for the issue of a 2 cent piece, to bear the likeness of Roosevelt, passed the Senate and received the strong approval of a House committee. Reference has already been made to the bills proposing the coinage of 6, 7, or 8 cent pieces.[9]

Similar proposals may be expected in the future. None of them should be accepted. The denominations now in use meet all our needs efficiently. Coins of 2, 2½, 3, 6, 7, or 15 cent values would complicate the system and serve little purpose. Our 1 cent piece is a very useful coin, but a ½ cent piece would be of little value. It is economically undesirable, on the principle that articles sold at any such vanishing point value as a half-cent carry an overhead cost of handling out of proportion to the utility of the article. Coins of tiny values are common in many countries, especially in those with a very low standard of living. They probably work actual harm to the very poor. In past years the people of this country have tried and rejected a ½ cent copper coin, a 2 cent bronze coin, a 3 cent nickel piece,

[9] For interesting details of the various proposals see Congressional Record, 66th Cong., 2nd sess., 6452; 67th Cong., 1st sess., 741; House Reports 636, 62nd Cong., 2nd sess., and 1204, 66th Cong., 3rd session. Examination of such proposals usually discloses their temporary purpose. Mayors Baker and Whitlock, for example, were obviously asking for a 3 cent coin in connection with the 3 cent street-car fare movement, now in the limbo of forgotten things.

a 3 cent silver coin, a 3 cent note, a 15 cent note, and a 20 cent silver coin.

The decline of silver, which brought the gold value of the metal in four quarters from 93 cents in 1873 to less than 50 cents in 1896, resulted in large seigniorage profits on subsidiary coinage. From 1894 to 1916, inclusive, the value of the silver in a dollar's worth of subsidiary coins was less than 50 cents, and it has again fallen below that figure since the war. After the accumulated stocks of the eighties dwindled away through recoinages and coinage was renewed on a large scale, the annual profits became a matter of millions. In 1902, for example, the mint report showed seigniorage profits of almost $2,500,000. The profits on subsidiary and minor coinage in the fiscal year 1916 were more than $4,000,000, and in 1921 they reached the un-heard-of total of $7,900,000. In the following year, when the business depression curtailed coinage, the returns were less than $170,000.[10]

The law requires the mint to account for these profits immediately. The total costs of coinage, including bullion, wastage, and certain distribution expenses, are deducted from the selling value of the coins and the difference is paid into the Treasury. This practice results in the charging off immediately of the entire gross profit on coinage, without any accounting for the obligations incurred through the issue of the coins. The Treasury is legally obligated to buy back at the selling price all the coins that have been issued. In theory, all the coins will in due time become so worn that they will be returned for redemption. They cannot be re-issued because of their condition, and the mints must melt them and recoin the metal. The worn pieces will not pro-duce the original sum, and the Treasury must buy sufficient

[10] The profits from seigniorage are given in the annual reports of the Director of the mint.

bullion to make up the loss from wear. Since the profit originally made has long since been charged to mint profits, there is a deficit equal to the cost of replacing the lost metal, as well as an expense for recoining. These losses must be made up by annual appropriations. Year after year the annual reports record the losses on recoinage. In reality they are not losses, but deductions from fictitious profits reported many years earlier.

In other words, the seigniorage profits from subsidiary coinage, universally regarded as net gains and so reported officially, are in a sense illusory and imaginary. When the Treasury purchases $1,000 worth of silver bullion, coins it into $2,000 in quarter-dollars, and sells the coins for $2,000 in gold, it reports a profit of $1,000. Years later it redeems these coins with $2,000 in gold and buys $100 worth of silver to replace the loss from wear. The outlay for bullion is now $1,100. The coins are again sold for $2,000 and in due time return to cause another expense of $100. In time the original cost of the bullion, the costs of coinage, and the losses on recoinage will exceed the $2,000 received for the coins. The process is slow and almost imperceptible. In a growing country such as the United States the gains from seigniorage may exceed the expenses and losses indefinitely, although the actual profits are never so large as those reported by the Treasury. In a country of static population and trade the gains from seigniorage disappear entirely, and the mint establishment is a source of expense. With a probable decline in the rate of population growth this country will show a decrease in the returns from seigniorage and an increase in the losses on recoinage. It is questionable whether this economic condition in seigniorage should not be recognized by an accounting procedure which would credit the mint annually with the gross seigniorage less the losses on recoinage.

Certain factors are present to offset the inevitable decline of seigniorage profits. One of these is a small return from interest. The government has the use of the original seigniorage gain until the coins return for redemption. There is a second offset in the gain from redemption of coins mutilated or defaced artificially. Coins that have become uncurrent from causes other than natural wear are bought as bullion, and the difference betwen face value and bullion value is net gain. The largest item is the gain from coins that never return. Many thousand pieces disappear, lost in fire, flood, shipwreck, and the ordinary affairs of life. Many find their way into collections, and some, such as the special memorial coins, are kept as souvenirs.

The percentage of loss in minor coins is very high. The law of 1873 and earlier statutes provided for the redemption of all discontinued minor coins, including the cent and half-cent of copper, the copper-nickel cent, and the bronze 2 cent piece. To this day less than half of the original number issued have been returned. There are still officially outstanding 118,000,000 pure copper cents, 120,000,000 nickel cents, 30,000,000 bronze 2 cent pieces and 20,000,000 nickel 3 cent coins. According to the annual reports of the Director of the Mint not one of the 8,000,000 copper half-cents issued was ever redeemed.[11] Some of these many mil-

---

[11] In the judgment of the writer the Mint reports are in error. As explained in Chapter XI, the law of 1857 provided for redemption of the pure copper cents and half-cents. The annual reports of Director Snowden for the years from 1857 to 1860 stated the value of "cents redeemed." The present-day Mint reports construe this as referring to cent pieces only. Snowden's figures must have included both cents and half-cents. In fact Snowden declares in Ancient and Modern Coins, a book written in 1860, that almost the entire coinage of half-cents in 1857 was withheld from issue and melted after the law of 1857 was passed. The annual statements of the Mint report this amount as well as all other half-cents issued as still outstanding. With Snowden's figures including both cents and half-cents it is impossible to determine the number of cents or half-cents that have been redeemed.

lions of copper, bronze, and nickel minor coins went abroad, and some are held in collections. But the majority have been lost in use.

Subsidiary and minor coins, always an integral and important element in the currency, have in our time come to be vital instruments of economic life. The development of large-scale production in the manufacture of hundreds of small necessities and luxuries, the growth of transportation, communication, and amusement enterprises that charge low rates, and the great enlargement in the number and variety of commodities sold across the counter have expanded their field of use. Narrower margins of profit in retail prices, the development of chain stores, the practice of "marking down," the growth of "cut-price" stores, and the tendency to quote special prices on "leaders" have been further influences. The great increase in the use of slot machines of various kinds, from simple vending machines for confections to gas-dispensing machines and subway slot devices has enormously increased the use of the smaller coins. It is estimated that all the cent pieces in the country, upward of 3,000,000,000, go through slot machines at least once a year. The world's largest financial enterprise is dependent upon a five cent telephone charge, the structure that was for many years the world's tallest building was built on five and ten cent sales, and the world's greatest passenger transportation system rests on a five cent subway fare.

CHAPTER XXI

CONCLUSION

ECONOMIC STATUS of fractional coins—General principles of subsidiary and minor coinage—Discreditable record of Congress and Treasury.

The story of our fractional currency is not without its lessons for the student of finance. It furnishes convincing evidence of the importance of fractional coins in the development of our currency system. It shows that the need for fractional currency was decisive in determining the original coinage standard, that the disappearance of fractional coins in 1852 led to the first steps in the transition to the gold standard, that the most painful monetary experiences of the Civil War grew out of the loss of the fractional coins, and that the most complex currency problem after the war was the restoration of silver coinage.

The story demonstrates that there is a most delicate relationship between the need for fractional coins and the volume in circulation, a slight over-issue giving rise to redundancy and discount, a small shortage causing distress and giving rise to a premium. It shows further that the people at large exercise keen discrimination in the selection of the type and denominations of the coins used in retail trade, rejecting unsatisfactory types and refusing unsuitable denominations such as half-cents and non-decimal coins.

The general principles of subsidiary and minor coinage are fairly well known. In the light of the experience of this country it is possible to amplify and restate these principles. They may be summarized as follows:

1. *Coinage should be solely on government account.*

The bullion should be bought in the open market as raw material. There should be no restrictions on these purchases. Assignments of bullion from special sources should be avoided. For more than a century our coinage was embarrassed by restrictions on the mint's supplies of bullion and inadequate provision for purchase in advance of public demand for coins.

2. *The coins should be issued only through sales to the public at their face values in exchange for standard money.*

Payment of subsidiary coins for bullion is unnecessary and unwise, even to the negligible extent permissible under the present law which authorizes the mints to give subsidiary coins for silver found mixed with gold presented for coinage. A very limited issue in change transactions at government offices is unobjectionable, though unnecessary.

3. *Total coinage, total issue, and total circulation should be unrestricted.*

These volumes should be determined solely by public demand. A provision authorizing the Treasury to restrict or stop the coinage can do little harm, but it serves no purpose. In the unlikely event that new coins are still being asked for in the face of an existing redundancy, redemptions will remedy the situation without official interference. Official attempts to influence the public choice of coins or denominations are unwise.

4. *The market value of the metal in the coins should be well below the face values.*

There is no fixed percentage for this fiduciary proportion. Two half-dollars have in the past twenty years ranged

in bullion value from 40 cents to $1. There is no definite
limit below which the bullion value should not go. The English silver coins have been 80 per cent fiduciary since the war.
There is no basis for the fear that private manufacturers
will make and circulate exact duplicates of the coins. Because of the psychological habits of the public it is desirable
that the bullion value be somewhat in accord with the money
value, at least to the extent that the more valuable coins
have greater bullion values. It is, therefore, justifiable to
use silver for the larger coins, and nickel, copper or other
cheap metals for the smaller.

*5. The coins should be redeemable without charge, with-
out delay, and without limit, at the issue price, in standard
money, regardless of the extent of wear.*

Redemption serves five purposes, each one important.
First, it permits the prompt removal of any excess of fiduciary coins as a whole or in any denomination, thus preventing public annoyance and loss through the development
of a discount. Secondly, it enables the public to exercise a
choice in the denominations of the coins. Thirdly, it facili-
tates proper distribution of the coins by enabling banks and
enterprises such as chain stores to turn excess supplies over
to the Treasury for redistribution. Fourthly, it prevents the
holders of coins too much worn for further circulation from
suffering unmerited loss. And finally, it keeps the coins in
good condition by encouraging a continuous flow of old coins
into the Treasury. In all the years before the redemption
measure of 1879 United States silver coins were in de-
plorable physical condition.

It is not sufficient for these five ends that the coins be
made receivable for tax payments to the government. The
common European practice of withholding redemption and
permitting payments in taxes is neither adequate nor equita-

ble. Even in the best regulated systems special conditions, such as widespread business depression, may make the supply of fractional coins excessive. Sometimes changes in the denominations of paper money will have the same result. Redemption will prevent depreciation regardless of the extent of redundancy. Coins mutilated artificially or worn by unnatural uses should be redeemed only as bullion.

6. *The coins should be a legal tender in private and public payments.*

The importance of legal tender is commonly exaggerated. It normally has little influence on circulation. In our history there has been free circulation of coins without a tender and public rejection of coins with legal tender power. The reduction of the legal tender power of the 1 and 2 cent pieces in 1865 was as ineffective in results as it was petty in aim. The essential purpose of legal tender is public convenience, through its provision for a certain means of paying small debts and fractional remainders of large debts. It also enables the general public to pass the coins on to banks or other institutions in a position to redeem them or redistribute them.

7. *The legal tender power should be limited to sums representing a proper maximum use of the coins.*

Here again the objective is public convenience. No coin should be legal tender to an amount so large that the payment can cause inconvenience to the creditor. For sixty years of our history a tiny 5 cent silver coin had unlimited legal tender power, and for an even longer period no one knew whether copper cents and half cents were unlimited in tender or without any power whatever. The scientific basis of limitation is the number of coins rather than the amount of the payment. Our law might well read that all the fiduciary coins, from the 1 cent piece to the half-dollar, should be legal tender in payments requiring 20 pieces or less. But in the interests of simplicity and definiteness it is permissible to fix a given sum for different denominations, and our practice of fixing a given sum for the silver pieces and a smaller sum for the minor coins is satisfactory. A $5 tender for the silver coins would be preferable to the present limit of $10, which permits a debtor to pay 100 dimes, but there is no serious objection to the larger figure. The 25 cent limit for 1 and 5 cent pieces is entirely satisfactory.

8. *The denominational system should be decimal, with intermediate coins in multiples of five.*

A purely decimal system with coins of 1, 10, and 100 units is impracticable. There should be intermediate pieces. Hamilton failed to recognize this in his report of 1791. Determination of the proper denominations is a matter of statistical analysis, with special consideration of such factors as the size of the smallest coin, the value of the standard unit, and the general level of prices. Every addition to the number of coins in a given series reduces the average number of pieces required to effect individual transactions in trade. In other words, the greater the number of denominations the less the number of pieces required for the average transaction. With three coins on a purely decimal basis it would require nine dimes and nine one-cent pieces to make a 99 cent purchase, whereas our present system of denominations calls for eight coins. There should be a sufficient number of intermediate pieces to permit payment of any fractional sum with a reasonably convenient number of coins. There is no mathematical formula for the determination of the number required, but it is possible to adopt as a rough-and-ready rule the principle that no coin should be more than five times as valuable as the coin next below it.

On the other hand, there is a point where the advantages of many pieces are over-balanced by the evils of over-lapping values. With too large a number of coins there is difficulty in identification and confusion in making change. Here again it is possible to devise a rule, to the effect that in the entire series every coin should be worth more than the sum of all the coins below it.

Our present currency system, from the 1 cent piece to the $10,000 gold certificate, accords with both rules. It has always been in accord with the rule for the minimum denominations necessary, but the rule for the maximum number has been repeatedly broken. It was violated in the simultaneous issue of 1, 2, 3, and 5 cent pieces, in the fractional note issues of 3, 5, 10, 15 and 25 cents, in the issue of 10, 20, and 25 cent silver coins, in the coinage of 1, 2½, 3, and 5 dollar gold pieces, and even in our own day in the issue of 1, 2, and 3 dollar bills. It is a striking fact that in every instance of violation of the rule suggested here the Treasury has been forced to withdraw the superfluous coins or notes.

Our present system of fractional coins is satisfactory. It is possible to make any payment from 1 cent to 99 cents with a maximum of eight coins, and the average number required for all payments in the series is a fraction above four. Most of the European countries have the series 1, 5, 10, 20, and 50, the arrangement advocated by Jefferson in 1783 and by Linderman in 1877. The American series, 1, 5, 10, 25, and 50, calls for a smaller average number of coins to make all payments from 1 to 99 cents. Either series is acceptable, and there is no advantage in the 20 cent denomination that would justify a change. In fact the 25 cent denomination is somewhat more desirable as the intermediate coin between 10 cents and 50 cents. There is no need for any additional coins in our system.

9. *The coins should be convenient in size, attractive in appearance, durable in use, and individual in feature.*

These qualities are obviously necessary, so that the coins will not be disagreeable to handle, will not require frequent redemption, and will not be confused with one another. The psychological reaction of the general public to unpleasant, unsightly, or unpopular coins is a definite factor in coinage administration. A striking illustration is afforded by British experience with the silver coins hastily reduced in silver content in 1920. The fineness was reduced from 92½ per cent to 50 per cent, with the result that the coins had an unusual coppery-yellow color. The coins were rejected by the people, and the government was driven to the extraordinary expedient of plating them with an extremely thin coating of pure silver. Since then the British subsidiary coins have consisted of a 50–50 copper-silver mixture coated with pure silver solely to meet the prejudices of the people.[1] Our subsidiary and minor coins are physically satisfactory, with two exceptions. The silver dollar is too large for convenient use, and the 1 cent piece, attractive when it leaves the mint, soon acquires a disagreeable color.

10. *There should be a legal provision for administrative reduction of the proportion of the more valuable metal in any coin.*

The desirability of such a measure had been discussed in the preceding chapter. Its application to the silver coins is much more important, but a provision permitting a change in the base metal components of the minor coins would be unobjectionable. At the present time the absence of a law of this type is the only important deficiency in our entire system.

[1] See Barton, History of Nickel Coinage, IV.

There is a final conclusion to be drawn from the annals of our fractional currency. The story shows that the control of this type of money calls for intelligence in legislation and talent in administration. It is an unpleasant truth that these two requisites have been lacking throughout our history. A careful consideration of the measures and policies that have controlled our fractional money forces the conclusion that our political system failed to place in authority officials capable of administering this currency. The history outlined in these pages is a depressing story of unnecessary economic distress and avoidable currency evils. Throughout much more than half our existence as a nation there has been either a burdensome excess of fractional currency or an acute scarcity. After a century of ill-conceived and badly administered measures that brought economic loss and disturbance our government muddled through to an efficient fractional money.

APPENDICES

APPENDIX A

COINAGE SYSTEM OF THE UNITED STATES

Coin	Material	Gross Weight, Grains	Fine Weight, Grains	Legal Tender	Authorized
Double eagle..	gold	516.0	464.4	unlimited	Mar. 3, 1849
Eagle........	gold	258.0	232.2	unlimited	Jan. 18, 1837
Half-eagle....	gold	129.0	116.1	unlimited	Jan. 18, 1837
Quarter-eagle..	gold	64.5	58.05	unlimited	Jan. 18, 1837
Half-dollar....	silver	192.9 (12½ grams)	173.61	to $10	Feb. 12, 1873
Quarter-dollar.	silver	96.45 (6¼ grams)	86.805	to $10	Feb. 12, 1873
Dime........	silver	38.58 (2½ grams)	34.722	to $10	Feb. 12, 1873
Five cents....	copper-nickel	77.16 (5 grams)	....	to 25 cents	May 16, 1866
One cent.....	copper-tin-zinc	48.0	....	to 25 cents	April 22, 1864

APPENDIX B

SILVER COINAGE CHRONOLOGY

Coin	Authorized	Discontinued	Gross Weight, Grains	Fine Weight, Grains	Fineness
Dollar	Apr. 2, 1792	Jan. 18, 1837	416	371.25	.8924
Dollar *..........	Jan. 18, 1837	Feb. 12, 1873	412.5	371.25	.9
Trade dollar.......	Feb. 12, 1873	Feb. 19, 1887	420	378	.9
Half-dollar........	Apr. 2, 1792	Jan. 18, 1837	208	185.625	.8924
Half-dollar........	Jan. 18, 1837	Feb. 21, 1853	206.25	185.625	.9
Half-dollar........	Feb. 21, 1853	Feb. 12, 1873	192	172.8	.9
Half-dollar........	Feb. 12, 1873	....	192.9 (12½ grams)	173.61	.9
Quarter-dollar.....	Apr. 2, 1792	Jan. 18, 1837	104	92.8125	.8924
Quarter-dollar.....	Jan. 18, 1837	Feb. 21, 1853	103.125	92.8125	.9
Quarter-dollar.....	Feb. 21, 1853	Feb. 12, 1873	96	86.4	.9
Quarter-dollar.....	Feb. 12, 1873	....	96.45 (6¼ grams)	86.805	.9
Twenty cents......	Mch. 3, 1875	May 2, 1878	77.16 (5 grams)	69.444	.9
Dime.............	Apr. 2, 1792	Jan. 18, 1837	41.6	37.125	.8924
Dime.............	Jan. 18, 1837	Feb. 21, 1853	41.25	37.125	.9
Dime.............	Feb. 21, 1853	Feb. 12, 1873	38.4	34.56	.9
Dime.............	Feb. 12, 1873	....	38.58 (2½ grams)	34.722	.9
Half-dime........	Apr. 2, 1792	Jan. 18, 1837	20.8	18.5625	.8924
Half-dime........	Jan. 18, 1837	Feb. 21, 1853	20.625	18.5625	.9
Half-dime........	Feb. 21, 1853	Feb. 12, 1873	19.2	17.28	.9
Three cents........	Mch. 2, 1851	Mch. 3, 1853	12.375	9.28125	.75
Three cents........	Mch. 3, 1853	Feb. 12, 1873	11.52	10.368	.9

* A limited coinage of silver dollars was authorized by the acts of Feb. 28, 1878, and July 14, 1890. The act of April 13, 1918, authorized the melting and later recoinage of a part of the outstanding total.

APPENDIX C

MINOR COIN CHRONOLOGY

Coin	Authorized	Discontinued	Material	Weight, Grains
Five cents....	May 16, 1866	....	Copper, 75% / Nickel, 25%	77.16 (5 grams)
Three cents...	Mar. 3, 1865	Sept. 26, 1890	Copper, 75% / Nickel, 25%	30.0
Two cents....	Apr. 22, 1864	Feb. 12, 1873	Copper, 95% / Tin and zinc, 5%	96.0
One cent.....	Apr. 2, 1792	Jan. 14, 1793	Copper	264.0
	Jan. 14, 1793	Dec. 27, 1795	Copper	208.0
	Dec. 27, 1795	Feb. 21, 1857	Copper	168.0
	Feb. 21, 1857	Apr. 22, 1864	Copper, 88% / Nickel, 12%	72.0
	Apr. 22, 1864	....	Copper, 95% / Tin and zinc, 5%	48.0
Half-cent.....	Apr. 2, 1792	Jan. 14, 1793	Copper	132.0
	Jan. 14, 1793	Dec. 27, 1795	Copper	104.0
	Dec. 27, 1795	Feb. 21, 1857	Copper	84.0

APPENDIX D

SILVER COINAGE OF THE UNITED STATES,
BY CALENDAR YEARS

Year	Dollars	Half-Dollars	Quarter-Dollars	Dimes	Half-Dimes	Three Cents
1793–95	$204,791	$161,572.00	....	....	$4,320.80	
1796	72,920	....	$1,473.50	$2,213.50	511.50	
1797	7,776	1,959.00	63.00	2,526.10	2,226.35	
1798	327,536	....	....	2,755.00		
1799	423,515					
1800	220,920	....	....	2,176.00	1,200.00	
1801	54,454	15,144.50	....	3,464.00	1,695.50	
1802	41,650	14,945.00	....	1,097.50	650.50	
1803	66,064	15,857.50	....	3,304.00	1,892.50	
1804	19,570	78,259.50	1,684.50	826.50		
1805	321	105,861.00	30,348.50	12,078.00	780.00	
1806	....	419,788.00	51,531.00			
1807	....	525,788.00	55,160.75	16,500.00		
1808	....	684,300.00				
1809	....	702,905.00	....	4,471.00		
1810	....	638,138.00		635.50		
1811	....	601,822.00	....	6,518.00		
1812	....	814,029.50				
1813	....	620,951.50				
1814	....	519,537.50	....	42,150.00		
1815	....	....	17,308.00			
1816	....	23,575.00	5,000.75			
1817	....	607,783.50				
1818	....	980,161.00	90,293.50			
1819	....	1,104,000.00	36,000.00			
1820	....	375,561.00	31,861.00	94,258.70		
1821	....	652,898.50	54,212.75	118,651.20		
1822	....	779,786.50	16,020.00	10,000.00		
1823	....	847,100.00	4,450.00	44,000.00		
1824	....	1,752,477.00				
1825	....	1,471,583.00	42,000.00	51,000.00		
1826	....	2,002,090.00				
1827	....	2,746,700.00	1,000.00	121,500.00		
1828	....	1,537,600.00	25,500.00	12,500.00		
1829	....	1,856,078.00	....	77,000.00	61,500.00	
1830	....	2,382,400.00	....	51,000.00	62,000.00	
1831	....	2,936,830.00	99,500.00	77,135.00	62,135.00	
1832	....	2,398,500.00	80,000.00	52,250.00	48,250.00	
1833	....	2,603,000.00	39,000.00	48,500.00	68,500.00	
1834	....	3,206,002.00	71,500.00	63,500.00	74,000.00	
1835	....	2,676,003.00	488,000.00	141,000.00	138,000.00	
1836	1,000	3,273,100.00	118,000.00	119,000.00	95,000.00	
1837	....	1,814,910.00	63,100.00	104,200.00	113,800.00	
1838	....	1,773,000.00	208,000.00	239,493.40	112,750.00	
1839	300	1,748,768.00	122,786.50	229,638.70	108,285.00	
1840	61,005	1,145,054.00	153,331.75	253,358.00	113,954.25	

316

SILVER COINAGE OF THE UNITED STATES,
BY CALENDAR YEARS—*Continued*

Year	Dollars	Half-Dollars	Quarter-Dollars	Dimes	Half-Dimes	Three Cents
1841	$ 173,000	$ 355,500.00	$ 143,000.00	$ 363,000.00	$ 98,250.00	
1842	184,618	1,484,882.00	214,250.00	390,750.00	58,250.00	
1843	165,100	3,056,000.00	403,400.00	152,000.00	58,250.00	
1844	20,000	1,885,500.00	290,300.00	7,250.00	32,500.00	
1845	24,500	1,341,500.00	230,500.00	198,500.00	78,200.00	
1846	169,600	2,257,000.00	127,500.00	3,130.00	1,350.00	
1847	140,750	1,870,000.00	275,500.00	24,500.00	63,700.00	
1848	15,000	1,880,000.00	36,500.00	45,150.00	63,400.00	
1849	62,600	1,781,000.00	85,000.00	113,900.00	72,450.00	
1850	47,500	1,341,500.00	150,700.00	244,150.00	82,250.00	
1851	1,300	301,375.00	62,000.00	142,650.00	82,050.00	$185,022.00
1852	1,100	110,565.00	68,265.00	196,550.00	63,025.00	559,905.00
1853	46,110	2,430,354.00	4,146,555.00	1,327,301.00	785,251.00	342,000.00
1854	33,140	4,111,000.00	3,466,000.00	624,000.00	365,000.00	20,130.00
1855	26,000	2,288,725.00	857,350.00	207,500.00	117,500.00	4,170.00
1856	63,500	1,903,500.00	2,129,500.00	703,000.00	299,000.00	43,740.00
1857	94,000	1,482,000.00	2,726,500.00	712,000.00	433,000.00	31,260.00
1858	....	5,998,000.00	2,002,250.00	189,000.00	258,000.00	48,120.00
1859	636,500	2,074,000.00	421,000.00	97,000.00	45,000.00	10,950.00
1860	733,930	1,032,850.00	312,350.00	78,700.00	92,950.00	8,610.00
1861	78,500	2,078,950.00	1,237,650.00	209,650.00	164,050.00	14,940.00
1862	12,090	802,175.00	249,887.50	102,830.00	74,627.50	10,906.50
1863	27,660	709,830.00	48,015.00	17,196.00	5,923.00	643.80
1864	31,170	518,785.00	28,517.50	26,907.00	4,523.50	14.10
1865	47,000	593,450.00	25,075.00	18,550.00	6,675.00	255.00
1866	49,625	899,812.50	11,381.25	14,372.50	6,536.25	681.75
1867	60,325	810,162.50	17,156.25	14,662.50	6,431.25	138.75
1868	182,700	769,100.00	31,500.00	72,625.00	18,295.00	123.00
1869	424,300	725,950.00	23,150.00	70,660.00	21,930.00	153.00
1870	445,462	829,758.50	23,935.00	52,150.00	26,830.00	120.00
1871	1,117,136	1,741,655.00	53,255.50	109,371.00	82,493.00	127.80
1872	1,118,600	866,775.00	68,762.50	261,045.00	189,247.50	58.50
1873	296,600	1,593,780.00	414,190.50	443,329.10	51,830.00	18.00
1874	....	1,406,650.00	215,975.00	319,151.70		
1875	....	5,117,750.00	1,278,375.00	2,406,570.00		
1876	....	7,451,575.00	7,839,287.50	3,015,115.00		
1877	....	7,540,255.00	6,024,927.50	1,735,051.00		
1878	22,495,550	726,200.00	849,200.00	187,880.00		
1879	27,560,100	2,950.00	3,675.00	1,510.00		
1880	27,397,355	4,877.50	3,738.75	3,735.50		
1881	27,927,975	5,487.50	3,243.75	2,497.50		
1882	27,574,100	2,750.00	4,075.00	391,110.00		
1883	28,470,039	4,519.50	3,859.75	767,571.20		
1884	28,136,875	2,637.50	2,218.75	393,134.90		
1885	28,697,767	3,065.00	3,632.50	257,711.70		
1886	31,423,886	2,943.00	1,471.50	658,409.40		
1887	33,611,710	2,855.00	2,677.50	1,573,838.90		

SILVER COINAGE OF THE UNITED STATES,
BY CALENDAR YEARS—*Continued*

Year	Dollars	Half-Dollars	Quarter-Dollars	Dimes	Half-Dimes	Three Cents
1888	$31,990,833	$ 6,416.50	$ 306,708.25	$ 721,648.70		
1889	34,651,811	6,355.50	3,177.75	835,338.90		
1890	38,043,004	6,295.00	20,147.50	1,133,461.70		
1891	23,562,735	100,300.00	1,551,150.00	2,304,671.60		
1892	6,333,245	1,652,136.50	2,960,331.00	1,695,365.50		
1893	1,455,792	4,003,948.50	2,583,837.50	759,219.30		
1894	3,093,972	3,667,831.00	2,233,448.25	205,099.60		
1895	862,880	2,354,652.00	2,255,390.25	225,088.00		
1896	19,876,762	1,507,855.00	1,386,700.25	318,581.80		
1897	12,651,731	2,023,315.50	2,524,440.00	1,287,810.80		
1898	14,426,735	3,094,642.50	3,497,331.75	2,015,324.20		
1899	15,182,846	4,474,628.50	3,994,211.50	2,409,833.90		
1900	25,010,912	5,033,617.00	3,822,874.25	2,477,918.20		
1901	22,566,813	3,119,928.50	2,644,369.25	2,507,350.00		
1902	18,160,777	4,454,723.50	4,617,589.00	2,795,077.70		
1903	10,343,755	3,149,763.50	3,551,516.00	2,829,405.50		
1904	8,812,650	2,331,654.00	3,011,203.25	1,540,102.70		
1905	....	1,830,863.50	2,020,562.50	2,480,754.90		
1906	....	5,426,414.50	2,248,108.75	2,976,504.60		
1907	....	5,825,587.50	3,899,143.75	3,453,704.50		
1908	....	5,819,686.50	4,262,136.25	2,309,954.50		
1909	....	2,529,025.00	4,110,662.50	1,448,165.00		
1910	....	1,183,275.50	936,137.75	1,625,055.10		
1911	....	1,686,811.50	1,410,535.75	3,359,954.30		
1912	....	2,610,750.00	1,277,175.00	3,453,070.00		
1913	....	663,313.50	493,853.25	2,027,062.20		
1914	....	558,305.00	2,388,652.50	3,136,865.50		
1915	....	1,486,440.00	1,969,612.50	658,045.00		
1916	....	1,065,200.00	2,095,200.00	5,720,400.00		
1917	....	10,751,700.00	9,464,400.00	9,196,200.00		
1918	....	10,434,549.00	8,173,000.00	6,865,480.00		
1919	....	1,839,500.00	3,776,000.00	5,452,900.00		
1920	....	6,398,570.00	9,456,600.00	9,202,100.00		
1921	87,736,473	611,062.50	479,000.00	231,000.00		
1922	84,275,000	50,030.50				
1923	56,631,000	1,226,038.50	2,769,000.00	5,657.000.00		
1924	13,539,000	71,040.00	4,223,000.00	3,794,000.00		
1925	11,808,000	1,338,518.00	3,070,000.00	3,657,700.00		
1926	11,267,700	574,306.50	3,933,000.00	4,050,800.00		
1927	2,982,900	1,216,017.00	3,321,100.00	3,766,200.00		
Total...	$846,593,947	$229,000,835.50	$155,265,691.00	$131,539,579.70	$4,880,219.40	$1,282,087.20

NOTE.—In addition, there were 35,965,924 trade dollars coined in the years 1873 to 1883 and $271,000 in 20 cent pieces in the years 1875 to 1878.

APPENDIX E

MINOR COINAGE OF THE UNITED STATES, BY CALENDAR YEARS

Year	Five Cents	Three Cents	Two Cents	Cents	Half Cents
1793–95	....	....	....	$10,660.33	$712.67
1796	....	....	....	9,747.00	577.40
1797	....	....	....	8,975.10	535.24
1798	....	....	....	9,797.00	
1799	....	....	....	9,045.85	60.83
1800	....	....	....	28,221.75	1,057.65
1801	....	....	....	13,628.37	
1802	....	....	....	34,351.00	71.83
1803	....	....	....	24,713.53	489.50
1804	....	....	....	7,568.38	5,276.56
1805	....	....	....	9,411.16	4,072.32
1806	....	....	....	3,480.00	1,780.00
1807	....	....	....	7,272.21	2,380.00
1808	....	....	....	11,090.00	2,000.00
1809	....	....	....	2,228.67	5,772.86
1810	....	....	....	14,585.00	1,075.00
1811	....	....	....	2,180.25	315.70
1812	....	....	....	10,755.00	
1813	....	....	....	4,180.00	
1814	....	....	....	3,578.30	
1815	....	...,....	....	....	....
1816	....	....	....	28,209.82	
1817	....	....	....	39,484.00	
1818	....	....	....	31,670.00	
1819	....	....	....	26,710.00	
1820	....	....	....	44,075.50	
1821	....	....	....	3,890.00	
1822	....	....	....	20,723.39	
1823	....	....	....	....	....
1824	....	....	....	12,620.00	
1825	....	....	....	14,611.00	315.00
1826	....	....	....	15,174.25	1,170.00
1827	....	....	....	23,577.32	
1828	....	....	....	22,606.24	3,030.00
1829	....	....	....	14,145.00	2,435.00

319

MINOR COINAGE OF THE UNITED STATES, BY CALENDAR YEARS—*Continued*

	Five Cents	Three Cents	Two Cents	Cents	Half Cents
1830	....	....	....	$ 17,115.00	
1831	....	....	....	33,592.60	$ 11.00
1832	....	....	....	23,620.00	
1833	....	....	....	27,390.00	770.00
1834	....	....	....	18,551.00	600.00
1835	....	....	....	38,784.00	705.00
1836	....	....	....	21,110.00	1,990.00
1837	....	....	....	55,583.00	
1838	....	....	....	63,702.00	
1839	....	....	....	31,286.61	
1840	....	....	....	24,627.00	
1841	....	....	....	15,973.67	
1842	....	....	....	23,833.90	
1843	....	....	....	24,283.20	
1844	....	....	....	23,987.52	
1845	....	....	....	38,948.04	
1846	....	....	....	41,208.00	
1847	....	....	....	61,836.69	
1848	....	....	....	64,157.99	
1849	....	....	....	41,785.00	199.32
1850	....	....	....	44,268.44	199.06
1851	....	....	....	98,897.07	738.36
1852	....	....	....	50,630.94	
1853	....	....	....	66,411.31	648.47
1854	....	....	....	42,361.56	276.79
1855	....	....	....	15,748.29	282.50
1856	....	....	....	26,904.63	202.15
1857	....	....	....	177,834.56	175.90
1858	....	....	....	246,000.00	
1859	....	....	....	364,000.00	
1860	....	....	....	205,660.00	
1861	....	....	....	101,000.00	
1862	....	....	....	280,750.00	
1863	....	....	....	498,400.00	
1864	....	....	$396,950.00	529,737.14	
1865	....	$341,460.00	272,800.00	354,292.86	
1866	$737,125.00	144,030.00	63,540.00	98,265.00	

MINOR COINAGE OF THE UNITED STATES, BY CALENDAR YEARS—*Continued*

Year	Five Cents	Three Cents	Two Cents	Cents	Half Cents
1867	$1,545,475.00	$117,450.00	$58,775.00	$ 98,210.00	
1868	1,440,850.00	97,560.00	56,075.00	102,665.00	
1869	819,750.00	48,120.00	30,930.00	64,200.00	
1870	240,300.00	40,050.00	17,225.00	52,750.00	
1871	28,050.00	18,120.00	14,425.00	39,295.00	
1872	301,800.00	25,860.00	1,300.00	40,420.00	
1873	227,500.00	35,190.00	....	116,765.00	
1874	176,900.00	23,700.00	....	141,875.00	
1875	104,850.00	6,840.00	....	135,280.00	
1876	126,500.00	4,860.00	....	79,440.00	
1877	....	....	....	8,525.00	
1878	117.50	70.50	....	57,998.50	
1879	1,455.00	1,236.00	....	162,312.00	
1880	997.75	748.65	....	389,649.55	
1881	3,618.75	32,417.25	....	392,115.75	
1882	573,830.00	759.00	....	385,811.00	
1883	1,148,471.05	318.27	....	455,981.09	
1884	563,697.10	169.26	....	232,617.42	
1885	73,824.50	143.70	....	117,653.84	
1886	166,514.50	128.70	....	176,542.90	
1887	763,182.60	238.83	....	452,264.83	
1888	536,024.15	1,232.49	....	374,944.14	
1889	794,068.05	646.83	....	488,693.61	
1890	812,963.60	....	....	571,828.54	
1891	841,717.50	....	....	470,723.50	
1892	584,982.10	....	....	376,498.32	
1893	668,509.75	....	....	466,421.95	
1894	270,656.60	....	....	167,521.32	
1895	498,994.20	....	....	383,436.36	
1896	442,146.00	....	....	390,572.93	
1897	1,021,436.75	....	....	504,663.30	
1898	626,604.35	....	....	498,230.79	
1899	1,301,451.55	....	....	536,000.31	
1900	1,362,799.75	....	....	668,337.64	
1901	1,324,010.65	....	....	796,111.43	
1902	1,574,028.95	....	....	873,767.22	
1903	1,400,336.25	....	....	850,944.93	

MINOR COINAGE OF THE UNITED STATES, BY CALENDAR YEARS—*Continued*

Year	Five Cents	Three Cents	Two Cents	Cents	Half Cents
1904	$1,070,249.20	....	....	$ 613,280.15	
1905	1,491,363.80	....	....	807,191.63	
1906	1,930,686.25	....	....	960,222.55	
1907	1,960,740.00	....	....	1,081,386.18	
1908	1,134,308.85	....	....	334,429.87	
1909	579,526.30	....	....	1,176,862.63	
1910	1,508,467.65	....	....	1,528,462.18	
1911	1,977,968.60	....	....	1,178,757.87	
1912	1,747,435.70	....	....	829,950.60	
1913	3,682,961.95	....	....	984,373.52	
1914	1,402,386.90	....	....	805,684.32	
1915	1,503,088.50	....	....	559,751.20	
1916	4,434,553.30	....	....	1,902,996.77	
1917	3,276,391.45	....	....	2,841,697.85	
1918	2,266,515.70	....	....	3,706,146.34	
1919	3,819,750.00	....	....	5,889,350.00	
1920	4,110,000.00	....	....	4,056,650.00	
1921	611,000.00	....	....	544,310.00	
1922	....	....	....	71,600.00	
1923	2,092,850.00	....	....	834,230.00	
1924	1,415,750.00	....	....	893,940.00	
1925	2,313,555.00	....	....	1,889,090.00	
1926	2,565,050.00	....	....	1,896,580.00	
1927	2,357,050.00	....	....	1,858,860.00	
Total..	$72,357,188.10	$941,349.48	$912,020.00	$53,782,374.27	$39,926.11

APPENDIX F

(1) Annual Average Ratio of Silver to Gold, 1830 to 1879.
(2) Annual Average Gold Value of the Silver in a Dollar in Fractional Coins, 1830 to 1879.
(3) Annual Average Gold Value of Greenbacks, 1862 to 1879.

Year	Ratio	Value of Fractional Silver	Gold Value of Greenbacks	Year	Ratio	Value of Fractional Silver	Gold Value of Greenbacks
1830	15.82	$0.950	......	1854	15.33	$0.971	......
1831	15.72	0.961	......	1855	15.38	0.968	......
1832	15.73	0.960	......	1856	15.38	0.968	......
1833	15.93	0.941	......	1857	15.27	0.974	......
1834	15.73	1.016*	......	1858	15.38	0.968	......
1835	15.80	1.012	......	1859	15.19	0.979	......
1836	15.72	1.017	......	1860	15.29	0.973	......
1837	15.83	1.010	......	1861	15.50	0.960	......
1838	15.85	1.009	......	1862	15.35	0.969	$0.883
1839	15.62	1.024	......	1863	15.37	0.967	0.689
1840	15.62	1.024	......	1864	15.37	0.967	0.492
1841	15.70	1.018	......	1865	15.44	0.963	0.636
1842	15.87	1.008	......	1866	15.43	0.964	0.710
1843	15.93	1.003	......	1867	15.57	0.956	0.724
1844	15.85	1.009	......	1868	15.59	0.955	0.716
1845	15.92	1.005	......	1869	15.60	0.954	0.752
1846	15.90	1.006	......	1870	15.57	0.956	0.870
1847	15.80	1.012	......	1871	15.57	0.955	0.895
1848	15.85	1.009	......	1872	15.63	0.952	0.890
1849	15.78	1.013	......	1873	15.92	0.938	0.879
1850	15.70	1.018	......	1874	16.17	0.925	0.899
1851	15.46	1.034	......	1875	16.59	0.888	0.870
1852	15.49	1.026	......	1876	17.88	0.842	0.898
1853	15.33	{ 1.043– / 0.971†	....	1877	17.22	0.869	0.954
				1878	17.94	0.834	0.992
				1879	18.40	0.813	1.00

* This figure gives the value after the passsage of the law of 1834.
† The second figure gives the value after the silver coins were made subsidiary in 1853.

323

APPENDIX G

LAWS OF THE UNITED STATES RELATING TO
FRACTIONAL MONEY [1]

April 2, 1792

Establishing the Coinage System

Sec. 1. *Be it enacted by the Senate and House of Representatives of the United States of America in Congress assembled and it is hereby enacted and declared,* That a Mint for the purpose of a national coinage be, and the same is established; to be situate and carried on at the seat of the Government of the United States, for the time being: And that for the well conducting of the business of the said Mint there shall be the following officers and persons, namely,—a Director, an assayer, a chief coiner, an engraver, a treasurer.

Sec. 9. *And be it further enacted,* That there shall be from time to time struck and coined at the said Mint, coins of gold, silver, and copper, of the following denominations, values, and descriptions, viz. Eagles—each to be of the value of ten dollars or units, and to contain two hundred and forty-seven grains and four eighths of a grain of pure, or two hundred and seventy grains of standard gold. Half-eagles—each to be of the value of five dollars, and to contain one hundred and twenty-three grains and six eighths of a grain of pure, or one hundred and thirty-five grains of standard gold. Quarter Eagles—each to be of the value of two dollars and a half dollar, and to contain sixty-one grains and seven eighths of a grain of pure, or sixty-seven grains and four eighths of a grain of standard gold,

---

[1] This appendix is a compilation of all the important laws relating to the fractional coins and the fractional paper money. Statutes relating exclusively to gold coins and to the silver dollar are omitted, as are also sections of fractional currency statutes of unimportant or purely routine character.

Dollars or Units—each to be of the value of a Spanish milled dollar as the same is now current, and to contain three hundred and seventy-one grains and four sixteenth parts of a grain of pure, or four hundred and sixteen grains of standard silver. Half-Dollars—each to be of half the value of the dollar or unit, and to contain one hundred and eighty-five grains and ten sixteenth parts of a grain of pure, or two hundred and eight grains of standard silver. Quarter Dollars—each to be of one fourth the value of the dollar or unit, and to contain ninety-two grains and thirteen sixteenth parts of a grain of pure, or one hundred and four grains of standard silver. Dismes—each to be of the value of one tenth of a dollar or unit, and to contain thirty-seven grains and two sixteenth parts of a grain of pure, or forty-one grains and three fifth parts of a grain of standard silver. Half Dismes—each to be of the value of one twentieth of a dollar, and to contain eighteen grains and nine sixteenth parts of a grain of pure, or twenty grains and four fifth parts of a grain of standard silver. Cents—each to be of the value of the one hundredth part of a dollar, and to contain eleven penny-weights of copper. Half-Cents—each to be of the value of a half a cent, and to contain five penny-weights and half a penny-weight of copper.

SEC. 10. *And be it further enacted,* That, upon the said coins respectively, there shall be the following devices and legends, namely: Upon one side of each of the said coins there shall be an impression emblematic of liberty, with an inscription of the word Liberty, and the year of the coinage; and upon the reverse of each of the gold and silver coins there shall be the figure or representation of an eagle with this inscription, "United States of America" and upon the reverse of each of the copper coins, there shall be an inscription which shall express the denomination of the piece, namely, cent or half cent, as the case may require.

SEC. 11. *And be it further enacted,* That the proportional value of gold to silver in all coins which shall by law be current as money within the United States, shall be as fifteen to one according to quantity in weight of pure gold or pure silver; that is to say, every fifteen pounds weight of pure silver shall be of equal value in all payments, with one pound weight of pure gold, and so in pro-portion as to any greater or less quantities of the respective metals.

SEC. 12. *And be it further enacted,* That the standard for all gold coins of the United States shall be eleven parts fine to one part alloy; and accordingly that eleven parts in twelve of the entire weight of each of the said coins shall consist of pure gold and the remaining one twelfth part of alloy; and the said alloy shall be composed of silver and copper in such proportions not exceeding one half silver as shall be found convenient; to be regulated by the Director of the Mint, for the time being, with the approbation of the President of the United States, until further provision shall be made by law. And to the end that the necessary information may be had in order to the making of such further provision it shall be the duty of the Director of the Mint, at the expiration of a year after commencing the operations of the said Mint, to report to Congress the practice thereof during the said year, touching the composition of the alloy of the said gold coins, the reasons for such practice, and the experiments and observations which shall have been made concerning the effects of different proportions of silver and copper in the said alloy.

SEC. 13. *And be it further enacted,* That the standard for all silver coins of the United States, shall be one thousand four hundred and eighty-five parts fine to one hundred and seventy-nine parts alloy; and accordingly that one thousand four hundred and eighty-five parts in one thousand six hundred and sixty-four parts of the entire weight of each of the said coins shall consist of pure silver, and the remaining one hundred and seventy-nine parts of alloy; which alloy shall be wholly of copper.

SEC. 14. *And be it further enacted,* That it shall be lawful for any person or persons to bring to the said Mint gold and silver bullion, in order to their being coined; and that the bullion so brought shall be there assayed and coined as speedily as may be after the receipt thereof, and that free of expense to the person or persons by whom the same shall have been brought. And as soon as the said bullion shall have been coined, the person or persons by whom the same shall have been delivered, shall upon demand receive in lieu thereof coins of the same species of bullion which shall have been so delivered, weight for weight, of the pure gold or pure silver therein contained: Provided nevertheless, That it shall be at the mutual option of the party or parties bringing such bullion, and of the Director of the said Mint to make an immediate exchange of coins for standard bullion with a deduction of one half per cent from the weight of the pure gold, or pure silver contained in the said bullion, as an indemnification to the Mint for the time which will necessarily be required for coining the said bullion, and for the advance which shall have been so made in coins. And it shall be the duty of the Secretary of the Treasury to furnish the said Mint from time to time whenever the state of the Treasury will admit thereof, with such sums as may be necessary for effecting the said exchanges, to be replaced as speedily as may be out of the coins which shall have been made of the bullion for which the monies so furnished shall have been exchanged; and the said deduction of one half per cent shall constitute a fund towards defraying the expenses of the said Mint.

SEC. 15. *And be it further enacted,* That the bullion which shall be brought as aforesaid to the Mint to be coined, shall be coined and the equivalent thereof in coins rendered, if demanded, in the order in which the said bullion shall have been brought or delivered, giving priority according to priority of delivery only, and without preference to any person or persons: and if any preference shall be given contrary to the direction aforesaid, the officer by whom such undue preference shall be given, shall in each case forfeit and pay one thousand dollars; to be recovered with costs of suit. And to the end that it may be known if such preference shall at any time be given, the assayer or officer to whom the said bullion shall be delivered to be coined shall give to the person or persons bringing the same, a memorandum in writing under his hand, denoting the weight, fineness and value thereof, together with the day and order of its delivery into the Mint.

SEC. 16. *And be it further enacted,* That all the gold and silver coins which shall have been struck at, and issued from the said Mint, shall be a lawful tender in all payments whatsoever, those of full weight according to the respective values herein before declared, and those of less than full weight at values proportional to their respective weights.

SEC. 17. *And be it further enacted,* That it shall be the duty of the respective officers of the said Mint, carefully and faithfully to use their best endeavours that all the gold and silver coins which shall be struck at the said Mint shall be, as nearly as maybe, conformable to the several standards and weights aforesaid, and that the copper whereof the cents and half cents aforesaid may be composed, shall be of good quality.

SEC. 20. *And be it further enacted,* That the money of account of the United States shall be expressed in dollars or units, dismes or tenths, cents or hundredths, and milles or thousandths, a disme being the tenth part of a dollar, a cent the hundredth part of a dollar, a mille the thousandth part of a dollar, and that all accounts in the public offices and all proceedings in the courts of the United States shall be kept and had in conformity to this regulation.

May 8, 1792

PROVIDING FOR COPPER COINAGE

SEC. 1. *Be it enacted* . . . , That the Director of the Mint, with the approbation of the President of the United States, be authorized to contract for and purchase a quantity of copper, not exceeding one hundred and fifty tons, and that the said Director, as soon as the needful preparations shall be made, cause the copper by him purchased to be coined at the Mint into cents and half cents, pursuant to "the act establishing a mint, and regulating the coins of the United States"; and that the said cents and half cents, as they shall be coined, be paid into the Treasury of the United States, thence to issue into circulation.

SEC. 2. *And be it further enacted,* That after the expiration of six calendar months from the time when there shall have been paid into the Treasury by the said Director, in cents and half cents, a sum not less than fifty thousand dollars, which time shall forthwith be announced by the Treasurer in at least two gazettes or newspapers, published at the seat of the Government of the United States, for the time being, no copper coins or pieces whatsoever, except the said cents and half cents, shall pass current as money, or shall be paid, or offered to be paid or received in payment for any debt, demand, claim matter or thing whatsoever; and all copper coins or pieces, except the said cents and half cents, which shall be paid or offered to be paid or received in payment contrary to the prohibition aforesaid, shall be forfeited, and every person by whom any of them shall have been so paid or offered to be paid or received in payment, shall also forfeit the sum of ten dollars, and the said forfeiture and penalty shall and may be recovered with costs of suit for the benefit of any person or persons by whom information of the incurring thereof shall have been given.

January 14, 1793

REDUCING WEIGHTS OF COPPER COINS

Be it enacted . . . , That every cent shall contain two hundred and eight grains of copper, and every half cent shall contain one hundred and four grains of copper; and that so much of the act, entitled "An act establishing a Mint, and regulating the coins of the United States," as respects the weight of cents and half cents, shall be, and the same is hereby repealed.

February 9, 1793

REGULATING THE VALUES OF FOREIGN COINS

SEC. 1. *Be it enacted* . . . , That, from and after the first day of July next, foreign gold and silver coins shall pass current as money within the United States, and be a legal tender for the payment of all debts and demands, at the several and respective rates following, and not otherwise, viz: . . . Spanish milled dollars, at the rate of one hundred cents for each dollar the actual weight whereof shall not be less than seventeen pennyweights and seven grains; and in proportion for the parts of a dollar. Crowns of France, at the rate of one hundred and ten cents for each crown, the actual weight thereof shall not be less than eighteen pennyweights and seventeen grains, and in proportion for the parts of a crown.

SEC. 2. *Provided always, and be it further enacted,* That at the expiration of three years next ensuing the time when the coinage of gold and silver, agreeably to the act, entitled "An act establishing a Mint, and regulating the coins of the United States," shall commence at the mint of the United States, (which time shall be announced by the proclamation of the President of the United States,) all foreign gold coins and all foreign silver coins, except Spanish milled dollars and parts of such dollars, shall cease to be a legal tender, as aforesaid.

SEC. 3. *And be it further enacted,* That all foreign gold and silver coins, (except Spanish milled dollars, and parts of such dollars,) which shall be received in payment for monies due to the

United States, after the said time, when the coining of gold and silver coins shall begin at the Mint of the United States, shall, previously to their being issued in circulation, be coined anew, in conformity to the act, entitled "An act establishing a Mint and regulating the coins of the United States."

March 3, 1795

Giving President Power to Reduce Copper Coins

Sec. 8. *And be it further enacted,* That the President of the United States be, and he is hereby authorized, whenever he shall think it for the benefit of the United States, to reduce the weight of the copper coin of the United States: Provided, Such reduction shall not, in the whole, exceed two pennyweights in each cent, and in the like proportion in a half cent; of which he shall give notice by proclamation, and communicate the same to the then next session of Congress.

Sec. 9. *And be it further enacted,* That it shall be the duty of the Treasurer of the United States, from time to time, as often as he shall receive copper cents and half cents from the treasurer of the Mint, to send them to the bank or branch banks of the United States, in each of the States where such bank is established; and where there is no bank established, then to the collector of the principal town in such State (in the proportion of the number of inhabitants of such State) to be by such bank or collector paid out to the citizens of the State for cash, in sums not less than ten dollars value; and that the same be done at the risk and expense of the United States, under such regulations as shall be prescribed by the Department of the Treasury.

January 26, 1796

Proclamation Reducing Weights of Copper Coins

. . . Whereas, on account of the increased price of copper and expense of coinage, I have thought it would be for the benefit of the United States to reduce the weight of the copper coin of the United States 1 pennyweight and 16 grains in each cent and in like proportion in each half cent, and the same has since the 27th day of December last been reduced accordingly: I hereby give notice thereof and that all cents and half cents coined and to be coined at the Mint of the United States from and after the said 27th day of December are to weigh, the cents each 7 pennyweights and the half cents each 3 pennyweights and 12 grains. . . .

G. WASHINGTON.

April 24, 1800

Creating Bullion Fund for Copper Coinage

Sec. 1. *Be it enacted* . . . , That a sum equal to the amount of the cents and half cents, which shall have been coined at the Mint and delivered to the Treasurer of the United States, subsequent to the third day of March, in the year one thousand seven hundred and ninety-nine, shall be, and the same is hereby appropriated for the purchase of copper for the further coinage of cents and half cents; and that a sum equal to the amount of cents and half cents, which shall be hereafter coined at the Mint, and delivered to the Treasurer of the United States in any one year, shall be, and the same is hereby appropriated for the annual purchase of copper for the coinage of cents and half cents, which sums shall be payable out of any monies in the Treasury not otherwise appropriated.

April 10, 1806

Renewing the Legal Tender of Foreign Coins

Be it enacted . . . , That from and after the passage of this act, foreign gold and silver coins shall pass current as money within the United States, and be a legal tender for the payment of all debts and demands, at the several and respective rates following, and not otherwise, viz: . . . Spanish milled dollars, at the rate of one hundred cents for each, the actual weight whereof shall not be less than seventeen pennyweights and seven grains, and in proportion for the parts of a dollar. Crowns of France at the rate of one hundred and ten cents, for each crown, the actual weight whereof shall not be less than eighteen pennyweights and seventeen grains, and in proportion for the parts of a crown.

SEC. 2. *And it is further enacted,* That the first section of the act intitled "An act regulating foreign coins, and for other purposes," passed the ninth day of February, one thousand seven hundred and ninety-three, be, and the same is hereby repealed. And the operation of the second section of the same act shall be, and is hereby suspended for, and during the space of, three years from the passage of this act.

April 21, 1806

PROVIDING PENALTIES FOR COUNTERFEITING

Be it enacted . . . , That if any person shall falsely make, forge or counterfeit, or cause or procure to be falsely made, forged, or counterfeited, or willingly aid or assist, in false making, forging or counterfeiting, any gold or silver coins, which have been or which hereafter shall be coined at the Mint of the United States, or who shall falsely make, forge or counterfeit, or cause, or procure to be falsely made, forged, or counterfeited, or willingly aid or assist in falsely making, forging, or counterfeiting any foreign gold or silver coins, which, by law now are or hereafter shall be made current, or be in actual use and circulation as money within the United States; or who shall utter, as true, any false, forged, or counterfeited coins of gold or silver, as aforesaid, for the payment of money, with intention to defraud any person or persons knowing the same to be falsely made, forged or counterfeited: any such person, so offending, shall be deemed and adjudged guilty of felony, and being thereof convicted according to the due course of law, shall be sentenced to imprisonment, and kept at hard labor for a period not less than three years, nor more than ten years; or shall be imprisoned not exceeding five years, and fined not exceeding five thousand dollars.

April 29, 1816

RENEWING LEGAL TENDER OF FOREIGN COINS

Be it enacted . . . , That from the passage of this act and for three years thereafter, and no longer, the following gold and silver coins shall pass current as money within the United States, and be a legal tender for the payment of all debts and demands, at the several and respective rates following, and not otherwise, videlicet: . . . the crowns of France, at the rate of one hundred and seventeen cents and six-tenths per ounce, or one hundred and ten cents for each crown weighing eighteen pennyweights and seventeen grains; the five franc pieces at the rate of one hundred and sixteen cents per ounce, or ninety-three cents and three mills for each five-franc piece, weighing sixteen pennyweights and two grains.

June 25, 1834

REVISING THE LEGAL TENDER OF FOREIGN COINS

Be it enacted . . . , That from and after the passage of this act, the following silver coins shall be of the legal value, and shall pass current as money within the United States, by tale, for the payments of all debts and demands, at the rate of one hundred cents the dollar, that is to say, the dollars of Mexico, Peru, Chili, and Central America, of not less weight than four hundred and fifteen grains each, and those re-stamped in Brazil of the like weight of not less fineness than ten ounces fifteen pennyweights of pure silver, in the troy pound of twelve ounces of standard silver: and the five franc pieces of France, when of not less fineness than ten ounces and sixteen pennyweights in twelve ounces troy weight of standard silver, and weighing not less than three hundred and eighty-four grains each at the rate of ninety-three cents each.

June 28, 1834

REVISING THE COINAGE RATIO

Be it enacted . . . , That the gold coins of the United States shall contain the following quantities of metal, that is to say: each eagle shall contain two hundred and thirty-two grains of pure gold, and two hundred and fifty-eight grains of standard gold: each half eagle one hundred and sixteen grains of pure gold, and one hundred and twenty-nine grains of standard gold; each quarter eagle shall contain fifty-eight grains of pure gold, and sixty-four and a half grains of standard gold; every such eagle shall be of the value of ten dollars; every such half eagle shall be of the value of five dollars; and every such quarter eagle shall be of the value of two dollars and fifty cents; and the said gold coins shall be receivable in all payments, when of full weight, according to their respective values; and when of less than full weight, at less values, proportioned to their respective actual weights.

SEC. 2. *And be it further enacted,* That all standard gold or silver deposited for coinage after the thirty-first of July next, shall be paid for in coin under the direction of the Secretary of the Treasury, within five days from the making of such deposit, deducting from the amount of said deposit of gold and silver one-half of one per centum: *Provided,* That no deduction shall be made unless said advance be required by such depositor within forty days.

SEC. 5. *And be it further enacted,* That this act shall be in force from and after the thirty-first day of July, in the year one thousand eight hundred and thirty-four.

January 18, 1837

GENERAL REVISION OF THE COINAGE LAWS

SEC. 8. *And be it further enacted,* That the standard for both gold and silver coins of the United States shall hereafter be such that of one thousand parts by weight, nine hundred shall be of pure metal, and one hundred of alloy; and the alloy of the silver coins shall be of copper; and the alloy of the gold coins shall be of copper and silver, provided that the silver do not exceed one-half of the whole alloy.

SEC. 9. *And be it further enacted,* That of the silver coins, the dollar shall be of the weight of four hundred and twelve and one-half grains; the half dollar of the weight of two hundred and six and one-fourth grains; the quarter dollar of the weight of one hundred and three and one-eight grains; the dime, or tenth part of a dollar, of the weight of forty-one and a quarter grains; and the half dime or twentieth part of a dollar, of the weight of twenty grains, and five-eighths of a grain. And that dollars, half dollars, and quarter dollars, dimes, and half dimes, shall be legal tenders of payment according to their nominal value, for any sums whatever.

SEC. 10. *And be it further enacted,* That of the gold coins, the weight of the eagle shall be two hundred and fifty-eight grains; that of the half eagle one hundred and twenty-nine grains; and that of the quarter eagle sixty-four and one-half grains. And that for all sums whatever, the eagle shall be a legal tender of payment for ten dollars; the half eagle for five dollars; and the quarter eagle for two and a half dollars.

SEC. 11. *And be it further enacted,* That the silver coins heretofore issued at the Mint of the United States, and the gold coins issued since the thirty-first day of July, one thousand eight hundred and thirty-four, shall continue to be legal tenders of payment for their nominal values, on the same terms as if they were of the coinage provided for by this act.

SEC. 12. *And be it further enacted,* That of the copper coins, the weight of the cent shall be one hundred and sixty-eight grains, and the weight of the half-cent eighty-four grains. And the cent shall be considered of the value of one hundredth part of a dollar, and the half cent of the value of one two-hundredth part of a dollar.

SEC. 13. *And be it further enacted,* That upon the coins struck at the Mint there shall be the following devices and legends: upon one side of each of said coins there shall be an impression emblematic of liberty, with an inscription of the word Liberty, and the year of the coinage: and upon the reverse of each of the gold and silver coins, there shall be the figure or representation of an eagle with the inscription United States of America, and a designation of the value of the coin; but on the reverse of the dime and half dime, cent and half cent, the figure of the eagle shall be omitted.

SEC. 33. *And be it further enacted,* That copper bullion shall be purchased for the Mint, from time to time by the treasurer, under instructions from the Director; that the cost shall be paid from the fund hereinafter provided for; and that the copper bullion shall be of good quality, and in form of planchets fit for passing at once into the hands of the chief coiner.

SEC. 35. *And be it further enacted,* That it shall be the duty of the treasurer of the Mint to deliver the copper coins, in exchange for their legal equivalent in other money, to any persons who shall apply for them; *Provided,* That the sum asked for be not less than a certain amount, to be determined by the Director, and that it be not so great as, in his judgment, to interfere with the capacity of the Mint to supply other applicants.

SEC. 36. *And be it further enacted,* That the copper coins may, at the discretion of the Director, be delivered in any of the principal cities and towns of the United States, at the cost of the Mint for transportation.

SEC. 37. *And be it further enacted,* That the money received by the treasurer in exchange for copper coins shall form a fund in his hands, which shall be used to purchase copper planchets, and to pay the expense of transportation of copper coins; and that if there be a surplus, the same shall be appropriated to defray the contingent expenses of the Mint.

March 3, 1843

REVISING THE LEGAL TENDER OF FOREIGN COINS

SEC. 2. *And be it further enacted,* That from and after the passage of this act, the following foreign silver coins shall pass current as money within the United States, and be receivable by tale, for the payment of all debts and demands at the rates following, that is to say: The Spanish pillar dollars, and the dollars of Mexico, Peru, and Bolivia, of not less than eight hundred and ninety-seven thousandths in fineness, and four hundred and fifteen grains in weight, at one hundred cents each; and the five franc pieces of France, of not less than nine hundred thousandths in fineness, and three hundred and eighty-four grains in weight, at ninety-three cents each.

March 3, 1851

CREATING A 3 CENT SILVER COIN

SEC. 11. *And be it further enacted,* That from and after the passage of this act, it shall be lawful to coin at the Mint of the United States and its branches, a piece of the denomination and legal value of three cents, or three hundredths of a dollar, to be composed of three fourths silver and one fourth copper, and to weigh twelve grains and three eighths of a grain; that the said coin shall bear such devices as shall be conspicuously different from those of the other silver coins, and of the gold dollar, but having the inscription United States of America, and its denomination and date; and that it shall be a legal tender in payment of debts for all sums of thirty cents and under. And that no ingots shall be used for the coinage of the three-cent pieces herein authorized, of which the quality differs more than five thousandths from the legal standard; and that, in adjusting the weight of the said coin the following deviations from the standard weight shall not be exceeded, namely, one-half of a grain in the single piece, and one pennyweight in a thousand pieces.

February 21, 1853

ESTABLISHING SUBSIDIARY COINAGE

Be it enacted . . . , That from and after the first day of June, eighteen hundred and fifty-two, the weight of the half dollar or piece of fifty cents shall be one hundred and ninety-two grains, and the quarter dollar, dime, and half dime, shall be, respectively, one half, one fifth, and one tenth of the weight of said half dollar.

SEC. 2. *And be it further enacted,* That the silver coins issued in conformity with the above section, shall be legal tenders in payment of debts for all sums not exceeding five dollars.

SEC. 3. *And be it further enacted,* That in order to procure bullion for the requisite coinage of the subdivisions of the dollar authorized by this act, the treasurer of the Mint shall, with the approval of the Director, purchase such bullion with the bullion fund of the Mint. He shall charge himself with the gain arising from the coinage of such bullion into coins of a nominal value exceeding the intrinsic value thereof, and shall be credited with the difference between such intrinsic value and the price paid for said bullion, and with the expense of distributing said coins as hereinafter provided. The balances to his credit, or the profit of said coinage, shall be, from time to time, on a warrant of the Director of the Mint transferred to the account of the Treasury of the United States.

SEC. 4. *And be it further enacted,* That such coins shall be paid out at the Mint, in exchange for gold coins at par, in sums not less than one hundred dollars; and it shall be lawful, also, to transmit parcels of the same from time to time to the assistant treasurers, depositaries, and other officers of the United States, under general regulations, proposed by the Director of the Mint, and approved by the Secretary of the Treasury: *Provided,* however, That the amount coined into quarter dollars, dimes, and half dimes shall be regulated by the Secretary of the Treasury.

SEC. 5. *And be it further enacted,* That no deposits for coinage into the half dollar, quarter dollar, dime, and half dime, shall hereafter be received, other than those made by the treasurer of the Mint, as herein authorized, and upon account of the United States.

March 3, 1853

REVISING THE LAW OF MARCH 3, 1853

SEC. 7. *And be it further enacted,* . . . And the Secretary of the Treasury is hereby authorized to regulate the size and devices of the new silver coin, authorized by an act entitled "An act amendatory of existing laws relative to the half dollar, quarter dollar, dime, and half dime," passed at the present session; and that, to procure such devices, as also the models, moulds, and matrices or original dies for the coins, disks, or ingots authorized by said act, the Director of the Mint is empowered, with the approval of the Secretary of the Treasury, to engage temporarily for that purpose the services of one or more artists, distinguished in their respective departments, who shall be paid for such services from the contingent appropriation for the Mint: And that hereafter the three cent coin now authorized by law shall be made of the weight of three fiftieths of the weight of the half dollar, as provided in said act, and of the same standard of fineness. And the said act, entitled "An act amendatory of existing laws relative to the half dollar, quarter dollar, dime, and half dime," shall take effect and be in full force from and after the first day of April, one thousand eight hundred and fifty-three, any thing therein to the contrary notwithstanding.

February 21, 1857

CREATING A COPPER-NICKEL CENT AND WITHDRAWING FOREIGN COINS

Be it enacted . . . , That the pieces commonly known as the quarter, eighth, and sixteenth of the Spanish pillar dollar, and of the Mexican dollar, shall be receivable at the Treasury of the United States, and its several officers, and at the several post-offices and land-offices, at the rates of valuation following,—that is to say, the fourth of a dollar, or piece of two reals, at twenty cents; the eighth of a dollar, or piece of one real, at ten cents; and the sixteenth of a dollar, or half real, at five cents.

SEC. 2. *And be it further enacted,* That the said coins, when so received, shall not again be paid out, or put in circulation, but shall be recoined at the Mint. And it shall be the duty of the Director of the Mint, with the approval of the Secretary of the Treasury, to prescribe such regulations as may be necessary and proper, to secure their transmission to the Mint for recoinage, and the return or distribution of the proceeds thereof, when deemed expedient, and to prescribe such forms of account as may be appropriate and applicable to the circumstances; *Provided,* That the expenses incident to such transmission or distribution, and of recoinage, shall be charged against the account of silver profit and loss, and the net profits, if any, shall be paid from time to time into the Treasury of the United States.

SEC. 3. *And be it further enacted,* That all former acts authorizing the currency of foreign gold or silver coins, and declaring the same a legal tender in payment for debts, are hereby repealed; but it shall be the duty of the Director of the Mint to cause assays to be made, from time to time, of such foreign coins as may be known to our commerce, to determine their average weight, fineness, and value, and to embrace in his annual report a statement of the results thereof.

SEC. 4. *And be it further enacted,* That from and after the passage of this act, the standard weight of the cent coined at the Mint shall be seventy-two grains, or three twentieths of one ounce troy, with no greater deviation than four grains in each piece; and said cent shall be composed of eighty-eight per centum of copper and twelve per centum of nickel, of such shape and device as may be fixed by the Director of the Mint, with the approbation of the Secretary of the Treasury; and the coinage of the half cent shall cease.

SEC. 5. *And be it further enacted,* That the Treasurer of the Mint, under the instruction of the Secretary of the Treasury, shall, from time to time, purchase from the bullion fund of the Mint the materials necessary for the coinage of such cent piece, and transfer the same to the proper operative officers of the Mint to be manufactured and returned in coin. And the laws in force relating to the

Mint and the coinage of the precious metals, and in regard to the
sale and distribution of the copper coins, shall, so far as applicable,
be extended to the coinage herein provided for: *Provided;* That the
net profits of said coinage, ascertained in like manner as is prescribed in the second section of this act, shall be transferred to the
Treasury of the United States.

Sec. 6. *And be it further enacted,* That it shall be lawful to
pay out the said cents at the Mint in exchange for any of the gold
and silver coins of the United States, and also in exchange for the
former copper coins issued; and it shall be lawful to transmit parcels
of the said cents, from time to time, to the assistant treasurers, depositaries, and other officers of the United States, under general
regulations proposed by the Directors of the Mint, and approved
by the Secretary of the Treasury, for exchange as aforesaid. And it
shall also be lawful for the space of two years from the passage of
this act and no longer, to pay out at the Mint the cents aforesaid for
the fractional parts of the dollar hereinbefore named, at their nominal value of twenty-five, twelve-and-a-half, and six-and-a-quarter
cents, respectively.

Sec. 7. *And be it further enacted,* That hereafter the Director
of the Mint shall make his annual report to the Secretary of the
Treasury, up to the thirtieth of June in each year, so that the same
may appear in his annual report to Congress on the finances.

March 3, 1859

Extending Period for Exchange of Cents

Sec. 2. *And be it further enacted,* That the authority given by
the sixth section of the act entitled "An act relating to foreign coins
and to the coinage of cents at the Mint of the United States," approved February twenty-one, eighteen hundred and fifty-seven, to pay
out at the Mint the cents authorized and directed by said act to be
coined, in exchange for the fractional part of a dollar therein named,
at their nominal values of twenty-five, twelve-and-a-half, and six-and-
a-quarter cents, respectively, shall be, and the same hereby is, extended to two years from and after the twenty-first day of February,
eighteen and fifty-nine, and no longer.

June 25, 1860

REPEALING PROVISION FOR EXCHANGE OF CENTS

SEC. 3. *And be it further enacted,* That the second section of the act making appropriations for the legislative, executive and judicial expenses of the Government for the year ending the thirtieth of June, eighteen hundred and sixty, approved the third of March, eighteen hundred and fifty-nine, shall be, and the same is hereby, repealed.

July 17, 1862

PROVIDING FOR THE USE OF POSTAGE STAMPS FOR MONEY

Be it enacted . . . That the Secretary of the Treasury be, and he is hereby, directed to furnish to the Assistant Treasurers, and such designated depositaries of the United States as may be by him selected in such sums as he may deem expedient, the postage and other stamps of the United States, to be exchanged by them, on application, for United States notes; and from and after the first day of August next such stamps shall be receivable for all dues to the United States less than five dollars, and shall be exchanged for United States notes when presented to any Assistant Treasurer or any designated depositary selected as aforesaid in sums not less than five dollars.

SEC. 2. *And be it further enacted,* That from and after the first day of August, eighteen hundred and sixty-two, no private corporation, banking association, firm, or individual shall make, issue, circulate, or pay any note, check, memorandum, token, or other obligation, for a less sum than one dollar, intended to circulate as money or to be received or used in lieu of lawful money of the United States; and every person so offending shall, on conviction thereof in any district or circuit court of the United States, be punished by fine not exceeding five hundred dollars, or by imprisonment not exceeding six months, or by both, at the option of the court.

March 3, 1863

PROVIDING FOR THE ISSUE OF FRACTIONAL NOTES, ETC.

SEC. 4. *And be it further enacted,* That in lieu of postage and revenue stamps for fractional currency, and of fractional notes, commonly called postage currency, issued or to be issued, the Secretary of the Treasury may issue fractional notes of like amounts in such form as he may deem expedient, and may provide for the engraving, preparation, and issue thereof in the Treasury Department building. And all such notes issued shall be exchangeable by the assistant treasurers and designated depositaries for United States notes, in sums not less than three dollars, and shall be receivable for postage and revenue stamps, and also in payment of any dues to the United States less than five dollars, except duties on imports, and shall be redeemed on presentation at the Treasury of the United States in such sums and under such regulations as the Secretary of the Treasury shall prescribe: *Provided,* that the whole amount of fractional currency issued, including postage and revenue stamps issued as currency, shall not exceed fifty millions of dollars.

SEC. 7. *And be it further enacted,* all banks, associations, or corporations, and individuals issuing or reissuing notes or bills for circulation as currency after April first, eighteen hundred and sixty-three, in sums representing any fractional part of a dollar, shall be subject to and pay a duty of five per centum each half year thereafter upon the amount of such fractional notes or bills so issued.

April 22, 1864

CREATING BRONZE 1 AND 2 CENT COINS

Be it enacted . . . , That, from and after the passage of this act, the standard weight of the cent coined at the mint of the United States shall be forty-eight grains, or one-tenth of one ounce troy; and said cent shall be composed of ninety-five per centum of copper, and five per centum of tin and zinc, in such proportions as shall be determined by the Director of the Mint; and there shall be, from time to time, struck and coined at the mint a two-cent piece, of the same composition, the standard weight of which shall be ninety-six grains, or one-fifth of one ounce troy, with no greater deviation than four grains to each piece of said cent and two-cent coins; and the shape, mottoes, and devices of said coins shall be fixed by the Director of the Mint, with the approval of the Secretary of the Treasury; and the laws now in force relating to the coinage of cents and providing for the purchase of material and prescribing the appropriate duties of the officers of the mint and the Secretary of the Treasury be, and the same are hereby, extended to the coinage herein provided for.

SEC. 4. *And be it further enacted,* That the said coins shall be a legal tender in any payment, the one-cent coin to the amount of ten cents, and the two-cent coin to the amount of twenty cents; and it shall be lawful to pay out said coins in exchange for the lawful currency of the United States, (except cents or half cents issued under former acts of Congress,) in suitable sums, by the treasurer of the mint, and by such other depositaries as the Secretary of the Treasury may designate, under general regulations proposed by the Director of the Mint and approved by the Secretary of the Treasury; and the expenses incident to such exchange, distribution, and transmission may be paid out of the profits of said coinage; and the net profits of said coinage, ascertained in like manner as is prescribed in the second section of the act to which this is a supplement, shall be transferred to the Treasury of the United States.

SEC. 5. *And be it further enacted,* That if any person or persons shall make, issue, or pass, or cause to be made, issued, or passed, any coin, card, token, or device whatsoever, in metal or its compounds, intended to pass or be passed as money for a one-cent piece or a two-cent piece, such person or persons shall be deemed guilty of a misdemeanor, and shall, on conviction thereof, be punished by a fine not exceeding one thousand dollars, and by imprisonment for a term not exceeding five years.

June 8, 1864

PROVIDING PENALTIES FOR COUNTERFEITING AND FOR PRIVATE COINAGE

Be it enacted . . . , That if any person or persons, except as now authorized by law, shall hereafter make, or cause to be made, or shall utter or pass, or attempt to utter or pass, any coins of gold or silver or other metals or alloys of metals, intended for the use and purpose of the United State or of foreign countries, or of original design, every person so offending shall, on conviction thereof, be punished by fine not exceeding three thousand dollars, or by imprisonment for a term not exceeding five years, or both, at the discretion of the court according to the aggravation of the offence.

June 30, 1864

Revising the Fractional Currency Law

Sec. 5. *And be it further enacted,* That the Secretary of the Treasury may issue notes of the fractions of a dollar as now used for currency, in such form, with such inscriptions, and with such safeguards against counterfeiting, as he may judge best, and provide for the engraving and preparation, and for the issue of the same, as well as of all other notes and bonds, and other obligations, and shall make such regulations for the redemption of said fractional notes and other notes when mutilated or defaced, and for the receipt of said fractional notes in payment of debts to the United States, except for customs, in such sums, not over five dollars, as may appear to him expedient; and it is hereby declared that all laws and parts of laws applicable to the fractional notes engraved and issued as herein authorized, apply equally and with like force to all the fractional notes heretofore authorized, whether known as postage currency or otherwise, and to postage stamps issued as currency; but the whole amount of all descriptions of notes or stamps less than one dollar issued as currency shall not exceed fifty millions of dollars.

March 3, 1865

Creating a 3 Cent Copper-nickel Coin

Be it enacted . . . , That as soon as practicable after the passage of this act, there shall be coined at the Mint of the United States a three-cent piece, composed of copper and nickel in such proportions, not exceeding twenty-five per centum of nickel, as shall be determined by the Director of the Mint, the standard weight of which shall be thirty grains, with no greater deviation than four grains to each piece, and the shape, mottoes, and devices of said coin shall be determined by the Director of the Mint, with the approval of the Secretary of the Treasury. And the laws now in force relating to the coinage of cents and providing for the purchase of material and prescribing the appropriate duties of the officers of the Mint, and of the Secretary of the Treasury be, and the same are hereby, extended to the coinage herein provided for.

Sec. 3. *And be it further enacted,* That the said coin shall be a legal tender in any payment to the amount of sixty cents. And it shall be lawful to pay out said coins in exchange for the lawful currency of the United States, (except cents or half-cents or two-cent pieces issued under former acts of Congress,) in suitable terms by the Treasurer of the Mint and by such other depositaries as the Secretary of the Treasury may designate, and under general regulations approved by the Secretary of the Treasury. And under the like regulations the same may be exchanged in suitable sums for any lawful currency of the United States; and the expenses incident to such exchange, distribution, and transmission, may be paid out of the profits of said coinage, and the net profits of said coinage, ascertained in like manner as is prescribed in the second section of the act entitled "An act relating to foreign coins, and the coinage of cents at the Mint of the United States," approved February twenty-first, eighteen hundred and fifty-seven, shall be transferred to the Treasury of the United States: *Provided,* That from and after the passage of this act, no issues of fractional notes of the United States shall be of a less denomination, than five cents, and all such issues of a less denomination at that time outstanding, shall, when paid into the Treasury or any designated depositary of the United States, or redeemed or exchanged as now provided by law, be retained and cancelled.

Sec. 5. *And be it further enacted,* That, in addition to the devices and legends upon the gold, silver, and other coins of the United States, it shall be lawful for the Director of the Mint, with the approval of the Secretary of the Treasury, to cause the motto "In God we trust" to be placed upon such coins hereafter to be issued as shall admit of such legend thereon.

Sec. 6. *And be it further enacted,* That the one and two cent coins of the United States shall not be a legal tender for any payment exceeding four cents in amount; and so much of the laws of the United States heretofore enacted as are in conflict with the provisions of this act, are hereby repealed.

May 16, 1866

CREATING A 5 CENT COPPER-NICKEL COIN

Be it enacted . . . , That, so soon as practicable after the passage of this act, there shall be coined at the Mint of the United

States a five-cent piece composed of copper and nickel, in such proportions, not exceeding twenty-five per centum of nickel, as shall be determined by the Director of the Mint, the standard weight of which shall be seventy-seven and sixteen hundredths grains, with no greater deviation than two grains to each piece; and the shape, mottoes and devices of said coin shall be determined by the Director of the Mint, with the approval of the Secretary of the Treasury; and the laws now in force relating to the coinage of cents, and providing for the purchase of material, and prescribing the appropriate duties of the officers of the Mint and the Secretary of the Treasury, be, and the same are hereby, extended to the coinage herein provided for.

SEC. 3. *And be it further enacted,* That said coin shall be a legal tender in any payment to the amount of one dollar, and it shall be lawful to pay out such coins in exchange for the lawful currency in the United States, (except cents, or half cents, or two-cent pieces, issued under former acts of Congress,) in suitable sums, by the treasurer of the Mint, and by such other depositaries as the Secretary of the Treasury may designate, and under general regulations approved by the Secretary of the Treasury. And under the like regulations the same may be exchanged in suitable sums for any lawful currency of the United States, and the expenses incident to such exchange, distribution, and transmission may be paid out of the profits of said coinage; and the net profits of said coinage, as ascertained in the manner prescribed in the second section of the act entitled "An act relating to foreign coins and the coinage of cents at the Mint of the United States," approved February twenty-first, eighteen hundred and fifty-seven, shall be transferred to the Treasury of the United States: *Provided,* That from and after the passage of this act no issues of fractional notes of the United States shall be of a less denomination than ten cents; and all such issues at the time outstanding shall, when paid into the Treasury or any designated depository of the United States, or redeemed or exchanged as now provided by law, be retained and cancelled.

SEC. 5. *And be it further enacted,* That it shall be lawful for the Treasurer and the several assistant treasurers of the United States to redeem in national currency, under such rules and regulations as may be prescribed by the Secretary of the Treasury, the coin herein authorized to be issued when presented in sums not less than one hundred dollars.

March 3, 1871

Providing for Redemption of Minor Coins

Be it enacted . . . , That the Secretary of the Treasury is hereby authorized and required to redeem in lawful money, under such rules and regulations as he may from time to time prescribe, all copper, bronze, copper-nickel, and base-metal coinage of every kind heretofore authorized by law, when presented in sums not less than twenty dollars; and whenever under this authority these coins are presented for redemption in such quantity as to show the amount outstanding to be redundant, the Secretary of the Treasury is authorized to discontinue or diminish the manufacture and issue of such coinage until otherwise ordered by him.

February 12, 1873

General Revision of the Coinage Laws

Be it enacted . . . , That the Mint of the United States is hereby established as a Bureau of the Treasury Department, embracing in its organization and under its control all mints for the manufacture of coin, and all assay-offices for the stamping of bars, which are now, or which may be hereafter, authorized by law. The chief officer of the said Bureau shall be denominated the Director of the Mint, and shall be under the general direction of the Secretary of the Treasury. He shall be appointed by the President, by and with the advice and consent of the Senate, and shall hold his office for the term of five years, unless sooner removed by the President, upon reasons to be communicated by him to the Senate.

Sec. 13. That the standard for both gold and silver coins of the United States shall be such that of one thousand parts by weight nine hundred shall be of pure metal and one hundred of alloy; and the alloy of the silver coins shall be of copper, and the alloy of the gold coins shall be of copper, or of copper and silver; but the silver shall in no case exceed one-tenth of the whole alloy.

Sec. 15. That the silver coins of the United States shall be a trade dollar, a half-dollar, or fifty-cent piece, a quarter dollar, or twenty-five cent piece, a dime, or ten-cent piece; and the weight of the trade dollar shall be four hundred and twenty grains troy; the weight of the half-dollar shall be twelve grams (grammes) and one-half of a gram, (gramme;) the quarter-dollar and the dime shall be, respectively, one-half and one-fifth of the weight of said half dollar; and said coins shall be a legal tender at their nominal value for any amount not exceeding five dollars in any one payment.

SEC. 16. That the minor coins of the United States shall be a five-cent piece, a three-cent piece, and a one-cent piece, and the alloy for the five and three-cent pieces shall be of copper and nickel, to be composed of three-fourths copper and one-fourth nickel, and the alloy of the one-cent piece shall be ninety-five per centum of copper and five per centum of tin and zinc, in such proportions as shall be determined by the Director of the Mint. The weight of the piece of five cents shall be seventy-seven and sixteen hundredths grains, troy; of the three-cent piece, thirty grains; and of the one cent piece, forty-eight grains; which coins shall be a legal tender, at their nominal value, for any amount not exceeding twenty-five cents in any one payment.

SEC. 17. That no coins, either of gold, silver, or minor coinage, shall hereafter be issued from the mint other than those of the denominations, standards, and weights, herein set forth.

SEC. 18. That upon the coins of the United States there shall be the following devices and legends: Upon one side there shall be an impression emblematic of liberty, with an inscription of the word "Liberty" and the year of the coinage, and upon the reverse shall be the figure or representation of an eagle, with the inscriptions "United States of America" and "E Pluribus Unum," and a designation of the value of the coin; but on the gold dollar and three-dollar piece, the dime, five, three, and one cent piece the figure of the eagle shall be omitted; and on the reverse of the silver trade-dollar the weight and the fineness of the coin shall be inscribed; and the Director of the Mint, with the approval of the Secretary of the Treasury, may cause the motto "In God we trust" to be inscribed upon such coins as shall admit of such motto: and any one of the foregoing inscriptions may be on the rim of the gold and silver coins.

SEC. 21. That any owner of silver bullion may deposit the same at any mint, to be formed into bars, or into dollars of the weight of four hundred and twenty grains, troy, designated in this act as trade-dollars, and no deposit of silver for other coinage shall be received;

but silver bullion contained in gold deposits, and separated therefrom, may be paid for in silver coin, at such valuation as may be, from time to time, established by the Director of the Mint.

SEC. 25. That the charge for converting standard gold bullion into coin shall be one-fifth of one per centum; and the charges for converting standard silver into trade-dollars for melting and refining when bullion is below standard, for toughening when metals are contained in it which render it unfit for coinage, for copper used for alloy when the bullion is above standard, for separating the gold and silver when these metals exist together in the bullion, and for the preparation of bars, shall be fixed, from time to time, by the Director, with the concurrence of the Secretary of the Treasury, so as to equal but not to exceed, in their judgment, the actual average cost to each mint and assay-office of the material, labor, wastage, and use of machinery employed in each of the cases aforementioned.

SEC. 27. That in order to procure bullion for the silver coinage authorized by this act, the superintendents, with the approval of the Director of the Mint, as to price, terms, and quantity, shall purchase such bullion with the bullion fund. The gain arising from the coinage of such silver bullion into coin of nominal value exceeding the cost thereof shall be credited to a special fund denominated the silver profit fund. This fund shall be charged with the wastage incurred in the silver coinage, and with the expense of distributing said coins as hereinafter provided. The balance to the credit of this fund shall be from time to time, and at least twice a year, paid into the Treasury of the United States.

SEC. 28. That silver coins other than the trade-dollar shall be paid out at the several mints, and at the assay-office in New York City, in exchange for gold coins at par, in sums not less than one hundred dollars; and it shall be lawful, also, to transmit parcels of the same, from time to time, to the assistant treasurers, depositaries, and other officers of the United States, under general regulations proposed by the Director of the Mint, and approved by the Secretary of the Treasury; but nothing herein contained shall prevent the payment of silver coins, at their nominal value, for silver parted from gold, as provided in this act, or for change less than one dollar in settlement for gold deposits: *Provided,* That for two years after the passage of this act, silver coins shall be paid at the mint in Philadelphia and the assay-office in New York City for silver bullion purchased for coinage, under such regulations as may be prescribed by the Director of the Mint, and approved by the Secretary of the Treasury.

SEC. 29. That for the purchase of metal for the minor coinage authorized by this act, a sum not exceeding fifty thousand dollars in lawful money of the United States shall be transferred by the Secretary of the Treasury to the credit of the superintendent of the Mint at Philadelphia, at which establishment only, until otherwise provided by law, such coinage shall be carried on. The superintendent with the approval of the Director of the Mint as to price, terms and quantity, shall purchase the metal required for such coinage by public advertisement, and the lowest and best bid shall be accepted, the fineness of the metals to be determined on the Mint assay. The gain arising from the coinage of such metals into coin of a nominal value, exceeding the cost thereof, shall be credited to the special fund denominated the minor-coinage profit fund; and this fund shall be charged with the wastage incurred in such coinage, and with the cost of distributing said coins as hereinafter provided. The balance remaining to the credit of this fund, and any balance of profits accrued from minor coinage under former acts, shall be, from time to time, and at least twice a year, covered into the Treasury of the United States.

SEC. 30. That the minor coins authorized by this act may, at the discretion of the Director of the Mint, be delivered in any of the principal cities and towns of the United States, at the cost of the Mint, for transportation, and shall be exchangeable at par at the mint in Philadelphia, at the discretion of the superintendent, for any other coins of copper, bronze, or copper-nickel heretofore authorized by law; and it shall be lawful for the Treasurer and the several assistant treasurers and depositaries of the United States to redeem, in lawful money, under such rules as may be prescribed by the Secretary of the Treasury, all copper, bronze, and copper-nickel coins authorized by law when presented in sums of not less than twenty dollars; and whenever, under this authority, these coins are presented for redemption in such quantity as to show the amount outstanding to be redundant, the Secretary of the Treasury is authorized and required to direct that such coinage shall cease until otherwise ordered by him.

SEC. 37. That in adjusting the weight of the silver coins the following deviations shall not be exceeded in any single piece: In the dollar, the half and quarter dollar, and in the dime, one and one-half grains; and in weighing large numbers of pieces together, when delivered by the coiner to the superintendent, and by the superintendent to the depositor, the deviations from the standard weight shall not exceed two-hundredths of an ounce in one thousand dollars, half-dollars, or quarter dollars, and one-hundredth of an ounce in one thousand dimes.

SEC. 38. That in adjusting the weight of the minor coins provided by this act, there shall be no greater deviation allowed than three grains for the five-cent piece and two grains for the three and one cent pieces.

January 14, 1875

PROVIDING FOR REDEMPTION OF FRACTIONAL NOTES WITH SILVER COINS

Be it enacted . . . , That the Secretary of the Treasury is hereby authorized and required, as rapidly as practicable, to cause to be coined, at the mints of the United States, silver coins of the denominations of ten, twenty-five, and fifty cents, of standard value, and to issue them in redemption of an equal number and amount of fractional currency of similar denominations, or, at his discretion, he may issue such silver coins through the mints, the sub-treasuries, public depositaries and post-offices of the United States; and, upon such issue, he is hereby authorized and required to redeem an equal amount of such fractional currency, until the whole amount of such fractional currency outstanding shall be redeemed.

March 3, 1875

CREATING A 20 CENT SILVER COIN

Be it enacted . . . , That there shall be, from time to time, coined at the mints of the United States, conformably in all respects to the coinage act of eighteen hundred and seventy-three, a silver coin of the denomination of twenty cents, and of the weight of five grams.

April 17, 1876

DIRECTING THAT FRACTIONAL NOTES BE REDEEMED WITH SILVER COIN

SEC. 2. *Be it enacted* . . . , That the Secretary of the Treasury is hereby directed to issue silver coins of the United States, of the denomination of ten, twenty, twenty-five, and fifty cents of standard value, in redemption of an equal amount of fractional currency, whether the same be now in the Treasury awaiting redemption, or whenever it may be presented for redemption; and the Secretary of the Treasury may, under regulations of the Treasury Department, provide for such redemption and issue by substitution at the regular sub-treasuries and public depositaries of the United States until the whole amount of fractional currency outstanding shall be redeemed. And the fractional currency redeemed under this act shall be held to be a part of the sinking-fund provided for by existing law, the interest to be computed thereon, as in the case of bonds redeemed under the act relating to the sinking-fund.

July 22, 1876

JOINT RESOLUTION PROVIDING FOR INCREASED ISSUE OF SILVER COIN

Resolved by the Senate and House of Representatievs of the United States of America in Congress assembled, That the Secretary of the Treasury, under such limits and regulations as will best secure a just and fair distribution of the same through the country, may issue the silver coin at any time in the Treasury to an amount not exceeding ten million dollars, in exchange for an equal amount of legal tender notes; and the notes so received in exchange shall be kept as a special fund separate and apart from all other money in the Treasury, and be reissued only upon the retirement and destruction of a like sum of fractional currency received at the Treasury in payment of dues to the United States; and said fractional currency, when so substituted, shall be destroyed and held as part of the sinking-fund, as provided in the act approved April seventeen, eighteen hundred and seventy-six.

SEC. 2. That the trade dollar shall not hereafter be a legal tender, and the Secretary of the Treasury is hereby authorized to limit from time to time the coinage thereof to such an amount as he may deem sufficient to meet the export demand for the same.

SEC. 3. That in addition to the amount of subsidiary silver coin authorized by law to be issued in redemption of the fractional currency it shall be lawful to manufacture at the several mints, and issue through the Treasury and its several offices, such coin, to an amount, that, including the amount of subsidiary silver coin and of fractional currency outstanding, shall, in the aggregate, not exceed, at any time fifty million dollars.

SEC. 4. That the silver bullion required for the purposes of this resolution shall be purchased, from time to time, at market rate, by the Secretary of the Treasury, with any money in the Treasury not otherwise appropriated; but no purchase of bullion shall be made under this resolution when the market-rate for the same shall be such as will not admit of the coinage and issue, as herein provided, without loss to the Treasury; and any gain or seigniorage arising from this coinage shall be accounted for and paid into the Treasury, as provided under existing laws relative to the subsidiary coinage: *Provided,* That the amount of money at any one time invested in such silver bullion, exclusive of such resulting coin shall not exceed two hundred thousand dollars.

May 2, 1878

DISCONTINUING 20 CENT COIN

Be it enacted . . . , That from, and after the passage of this act, the coinage of the twenty cent piece of silver, by the Government of the United States be, and the same is hereby prohibited. And all laws in conflict with this act are hereby repealed.

June 9, 1879

PROVIDING FOR REDEMPTION OF SUBSIDIARY SILVER COINS AND FOR INCREASE OF THEIR LEGAL TENDER POWER

Be it enacted . . . , That the holder of any of the silver coins of the United States of smaller denomination than one dollar, may, on presentation of the same in sums of twenty dollars, or any multiple thereof, at the office of the Treasurer or any assistant treasurer of the United States receive therefor lawful money of the United States.

SEC. 2. The Treasurer or any assistant treasurer of the United States who may receive any coins under the provision of this act shall exchange the same in sums of twenty dollars, or any multiple thereof, for lawful money of the United States, on demand of any holder thereof.

SEC. 3. That the present silver coins of the United States of smaller denominations than one dollar shall hereafter be a legal tender in all sums not exceeding ten dollars in full payment of all dues public and private.

August 4, 1886

PROVIDING FOR TRANSPORTATION OF SILVER COIN

. . . For transportation of silver coin, including fractional silver coin by registered mail or otherwise, forty thousand dollars; and in expending this sum the Secretary of the Treasury is authorized and directed to transport from the Treasury or subtreasuries, free of charge, silver coin when requested to do so; *Provided,* That an equal amount in coin or currency shall have been deposited in the Treasury or such subtreasuries by the applicant or applicants. And the Secretary of the Treasury shall report to Congress the cost arising under this appropriation.

February 19, 1887

PROVIDING FOR REDEMPTION OF THE TRADE DOLLAR

Be it enacted . . . , That for a period of six months after the passage of this act, United States trade-dollars, if not defaced, mutilated, or stamped, shall be received at the office of the Treasurer, or any assistant treasurer of the United States in exchange for a like amount, dollar for dollar, of standard silver dollars, or of subsidiary coins of the United States.

September 26, 1890

Providing for Changes of Design

Be it enacted . . . , That section thirty-five hundred and ten of the Revised Statutes of the United States be, and the same is hereby, amended so as to read as follows:
"Section 3510. The engraver shall prepare from the original dies already authorized all the working-dies required for use in the coinage of the several mints, and, when new coins, emblems, devices, legends, or designs are authorized, shall, if required by the Director of the Mint, prepare the devices, models, hubs, or original dies for the same. The Director of the Mint shall have power, with the approval of the Secretary of the Treasury, to cause new designs or models of authorized emblems or devices to be prepared and adopted in the same manner as when new coins or devices are authorized. But no change in the design or die of any coin shall be made oftener than once in twenty-five years from and including the year of the first adoption of the design, model, die, or hub for the same coin: *Provided,* That no change be made in the diameter of any coin: And provided further, That nothing in this section shall prevent the adoption of new designs or models for devices or emblems already authorized for the standard silver dollar and the five-cent nickel piece as soon as practicable after the passage of this act. But the Director of the Mint shall nevertheless have power, with the approval of the Secretary of the Treasury, to engage temporarily for this purpose the services of one or more artists, distinguished in their respective departments of art, who shall be paid for such service from the contingent appropriation for the mint at Philadelphia."

September 26, 1890

Discontinuing the 3 Cent Nickel Coin

Be it enacted . . . , That from and after the passage of this act the coinage of the three-dollar gold piece, the one dollar gold piece, and the three-cent nickel piece be, and the same is hereby, prohibited, and the pieces named shall not be struck or issued by the Mint of the United States.

March 3, 1891

Providing for Recoinage of Worn Silver Coins

Recoinage of Silver Coins: For recoinage of the uncurrent fractional silver coins abraded below the limit of tolerance in the Treasury, to be expended under the direction of the Secretary of the Treasury, one hundred and fifty thousand dollars: *Provided,* That the Secretary of the Treasury shall, as soon as practicable, coin into standard silver dollars the trade-dollar bullion and trade dollars now in the Treasury, the expense thereof to be charged to the silver profit fund.

June 11, 1896

Providing for Recoinage of Worn Minor Coins

Recoinage, Reissue, and Transportation of Minor Coins: The Secretary of the Treasury is authorized to transfer to the United States mint at Philadelphia, for cleaning and reissue, any minor coins now in, or which may be hereafter received at, the sub-treasury offices, in excess of the requirement for the current business of said offices; and the sum of four thousand dollars is hereby appropriated for the expense of transportation for such reissue. And the Secretary of the Treasury is also authorized to recoin any and all the uncurrent minor coins now in the Treasury.

March 14, 1900

Providing for the Coinage of Subsidiary Silver and the Recoinage of Worn Coin

Sec. 8. That the Secretary of the Treasury is hereby authorized to use, at his discretion, any silver bullion in the Treasury of the United States purchased under the Act of July fourteenth, eighteen hundred and ninety, for coinage into such denominations of subsidiary silver coin as may be necessary to meet the public requirements for such coin: *Provided,* That the amount of subsidiary silver coin outstanding shall not at any time exceed in the aggregate one hundred millions of dollars. Whenever any silver bullion purchased under the act of July fourteenth, eighteen hundred and ninety, shall be used in the coinage of subsidiary silver coin, an amount of Treasury notes issued under said act equal to the cost of the bullion contained in such coin shall be cancelled and not reissued.

SEC. 9. That the Secretary of the Treasury is hereby authorized and directed to cause all worn and uncurrent subsidiary silver coin of the United States now in the Treasury, and hereafter received, to be recoined, and to reimburse the Treasurer of the United States for the difference between the nominal or face value of such coin and the amount the same will produce in new coin from any moneys in the Treasury not otherwise appropriated.

March 3, 1903

PROVIDING FOR TRANSPORTATION OF SILVER COINS AND INCREASED ISSUE OF SUBSIDIARY SILVER COINS

. . . : For transportation of silver coin, including fractional silver coin, by registered mail or otherwise, one hundred thousand dollars; and in expending this sum the Secretary of the Treasury is authorized and directed to transport from the Treasury or subtreasuries, free of charge, silver coin, when requested to do so: *Provided,* That an equal amount of coin or currency shall have been deposited in the Treasury or such sub-treasuries by the applicant or applicants. *That the authority given to the Secretary of the Treasury to coin subsidiary silver coin by the eighth section of an act entitled "An act to define and fix the standard of value, to maintain the parity of all forms of money issued or coined by the United States, to refund the public debt, and for other purpose," approved March fourteenth, nineteen hundred, may hereafter be exercised without limitation as to the amount of such subsidiary coin outstanding.* And the Secretary of the Treasury shall report to Congress the cost arising under this appropriation.

April 24, 1906

PROVIDING FOR MINOR COINAGE BY THE BRANCH MINTS

Be it enacted . . . , That sections thirty-five hundred and twenty-eight and thirty-five hundred and twenty-nine of the Revised

Statutes be, and the same are hereby, amended so as to read as follows:

"Section 3528. For the purchase of metal for the minor coinage authorized by this act a sum not exceeding two hundred thousand dollars in lawful money of the United States shall, upon the recommendation of the Director of the Mint, and in such sums as he may designate, with the approval of the Secretary of the Treasury, be transferred to the credit of the superintendents of the mints at Philadelphia, San Francisco, Denver, and New Orleans, at which establishments, until otherwise provided by law, such coinage shall be carried on.

May 18, 1908

Restoring Motto on Gold Coins

Be it enacted . . . , That the motto "In God we trust," heretofore inscribed on certain denominations of the gold and silver coins of the United States of America, shall hereafter be inscribed upon all such gold and silver coins of said denominations as heretofore.

July 9, 1917

Changing the Design of the 1916 Quarter-Dollar

Be it enacted . . . , That for the purpose of increasing the artistic merit of the current quarter-dollar, the Secretary of the Treasury be, and he is hereby, authorized to make slight modifications in the details of the designs. . . . No changes shall be made in the emblems or devices used. The modifications shall consist of the changing of the position of the eagle, the rearrangement of the stars and lettering, and a slight concavity given to the surface. . . .

BIBLIOGRAPHY

The list below includes only general works. The government documents and newspapers cited in the text are referred to by title in such a way that they are identifiable without bibliographic listing.

AMERICAN ANNUAL CYCLOPEDIA AND REGISTER OF IMPORTANT EVENTS—New York, 1861–1895.

AMERICAN JOURNAL OF NUMISMATICS—New York, 1866—

BANKERS MAGAZINE—Baltimore, 1846–1852. New York, 1852—

BARTON, F. R.—Nickel Coinage. London, 1927.

BENTON, T. H.—Abridgement of the Debates of Congress from 1789 to 1856. New York, 1857–1861.

BLAKE, G. H.—United States Paper Money. New York, 1908.

BOLLES, A. S.—Financial History of the United States from 1861 to 1885. New York, 1883–1892.

BRECK, L.—Historical Sketch of Continental Paper Money. Philadelphia, 1863.

BRECKINRIDGE, S. P.—Legal Tender. Chicago, 1903.

BRONSON, H.—Historical Account of Connecticut Currency. New Haven, 1867.

BRUCE, P. A.—Economic History of Virginia. New York, 1907.

BULLOCK, C. J.—Essays on the Monetary History of the United States. New York, 1900.

BURNS, A. R.—Money and Monetary Policy in Ancient Times. New York, 1927.

CAJORI, FLORIAN—Evolution of the Dollar Mark, in Popular Science Monthly, Vol. 81.

CARROLL, R. B.—Historical Collections of South Carolina. New York, 1836.

CHALMERS, R.—History of Currency in the British Colonies. London, 1893.

COIN COLLECTORS JOURNAL—New York, 1876–1883.

COMMERCIAL AND FINANCIAL CHRONICLE—New York, 1865—

CROSBY, S. S.—Early Coins of America. Boston, 1878.

DAVIS, A. M.—Colonial Currency Reprints. Boston, 1911–1912.

———— Currency and Banking in the Province of Massachusetts Bay. New York, 1901.

DEL MAR, A.—History of Money in America. New York, 1899.

———— History of the Precious Metals. London, 1880.

DEWEY, D. R.—Financial History of the United States. New York, 1924.

———— State Banking Before the Civil War, in Publications of the National Monetary Commission, Vol. 4. Washington, 1911.

DICKESON, M. W.—The American Numismatic Manual. Philadelphia, 1865.

DROWNE, H. R.—United States Postage Stamps as Necessity War Money, in American Journal of Numismatics, Vol. 52.

ECKFELDT, J. R., and DuBOIS, W. E.—Manual of Gold and Silver Coins of All Nations. Philadelphia, 1842.

EDIE, L. D.—Economics: Principles and Problems. New York, 1926.

FALKNER, R. P.—The Private Issue of Token Coins, in Political Science Quarterly, Vol. 16.

FARMERS ALMANAC—Boston, 1793–1873.

FELT, J. B.—An Historical Account of Massachusetts Currency. Boston, 1839.

FERNOW, B.—Coins and Currency of New York, in Memorial History of New York, Vol. 4. New York, 1900.

FISKE, JOHN—Critical Period of American History. Boston, 1902.

GARNETT, P.—History of the Trade Dollar, in American Economic Review, March, 1917.

GOUGE, W. M.—An Inquiry into the Principles of the American Banking System. New York, 1840.

——— Short History of Paper-Money and Banking. New York, 1835.

GOULD, L. P.—Money and Transportation in Maryland. Baltimore, 1913.

HALLOCK, J. E., JR.—Refusing its Own Coin. Brooklyn, 1884.

HAMILTON, J. C. (Editor)—Works of Alexander Hamilton. New York, 1851.

HASELTINE, J. W.—Description of the Paper Money Issued by the Continental Congress of the United States and the Several Colonies. Philadelphia, 1872.

HEPBURN, A. B.—History of Currency in the United States. New York, 1924.

HICKCOX, J. H.—An Historical Account of American Coinage. Albany, 1858.

——— History of the Bills of Credit or Paper Money Issued by New York. Albany, 1866.

HISTORICAL COLLECTIONS OF LOUISIANA—New Orleans, 1846–1875.

HOLDSWORTH, G. T.—Money and Banking. New York, 1915.

HUNT'S MERCHANTS MAGAZINE AND COMMERCIAL REVIEW—New York, 1839–1863.

INTERNATIONAL MONETARY CONFERENCE OF 1878, REPORT OF PROCEEDINGS—Washington, 1879.

KEMMERER, E. W.—Modern Currency Reforms. New York, 1916.

——— Money and Credit Instruments in Their Relation to General Prices. New York, 1909.

——— Recent Rise in the Price of Silver, in Quarterly Journal of Economics, Vol. 26.

KNOX, J. J.—United States Notes. New York, 1885.

LAUGHLIN, J. L.—A History of Bimetallism in the United States. New York, 1881.

——— Principles of Money. New York, 1911.

LEE, F. B.—New Jersey as a Colony and as a State. New York, 1902.

LINDERMAN, H. R.—Money and Legal Tender in the United States. New York, 1877.

————— Report of the Examination of the Branch Mints. Washington, 1872.

LIVERPOOL, EARL OF—A Treatise on the Coins of the Realm. London, 1880.

LONG, E.—History of Jamaica. London, 1774.

LOW, L. H.—Hard Times Tokens, in American Journal of Numismatics, Vols. 33, 34, and 35.

MCFARLANE, C. W.—Pennsylvania Paper Currency, in Annals of the American Academy, Vol. 8.

MCLACHLAN, R. W.—Money of Canada from the Historical Standpoint, in Transactions of the Royal Society of Canada, June 1915.

MCMASTER, J. B.—History of the People of the United States from the Revolution to the Civil War. New York, 1901.

MADISON, JAMES—Letters and Other Writings of James Madison. New York, 1884.

MASSACHUSETTS REGISTER AND UNITED STATES CALENDAR—Boston, 1784–1877.

MERENESS, N. D.—Maryland as a Proprietory Province. New York, 1901.

MITCHELL, W. C.—Gold, Prices, and Wages under the Greenback Standard. Berkeley, Calif., 1908.

————— History of the Greenbacks. Chicago, 1903.

MONROE, A. E.—Monetary Theory before Adam Smith. Cambridge, 1923.

MORING, H. E.—Suggestions to Congress on the Finances of the United States. New York, 1869.

MUHLEMAN, M. L.—Monetary and Banking Systems of the World. New York, 1896.

————— Money of the United States. New York, 1894.

NICHOLSON, J. S.—Treatise on Money and Essays on Monetary Problems. London, 1901.

NILES' WEEKLY REGISTER—Baltimore, 1811–1847.

PALGRAVE, R. H. I.—Dictionary of Political Economy. London, 1925.

PHILLIPS, HENRY, JR.—Historical Sketch of the Paper Money Issued by Pennsylvania. Philadelphia, 1862.

————— Historical Sketches of the Paper Money of the American Colonies. Roxbury, 1865.

PORCUPINE'S GAZETTE AND UNITED STATES DAILY ADVERTISER—Philadelphia, 1797–1798.

POTTER, S. R., and RIDER, S. S.—Some Account of the Bills of Credit of Rhode Island. Providence, 1880.

RAGUET'S FINANCIAL REGISTER OF THE UNITED STATES—Philadelphia, 1837–1838.

RICHARDSON, J. D.—Compilation of the Messages and Papers of the Presidents. Washington, 1896–1899.

ROBERTSON, J. A.—Louisiana under Spain, France, and the United States. Cleveland, 1911.

ROOSEVELT, THEODORE—Gouverneur Morris. Boston, 1898.

SCHARF, J. T.—Chronicles of Baltimore. Baltimore, 1874.

———— History of Maryland. Baltimore, 1879.

SEAGER, H. R.—Principles of Economics. New York, 1925.

SHAW, W. A.—The History of Currency, 1252 to 1894. London, 1896.

SMYTHE, A. H. (Editor)—Writings of Benjamin Franklin. New York, 1905.

SPARKS, JARED—Life and Writings of Gouverneur Morris. Boston, 1832.

SNOWDEN, J. R.—Ancient and Modern Coins. Philadelphia, 1860.

SOUTH CAROLINA'S FIRST PAPER MONEY, IN SOUND CURRENCY, VOL. 5.

STANLEY, R. C.—Nickel Past and Present. Toronto, 1927.

STEWART, F. H.—History of the First United States Mint. Philadelphia, 1924.

SUMNER, W. G.—The Coin Shilling of Massachusetts Bay, in Yale Review, Vol. 7.

———— History of American Currency. New York, 1875.

———— The Financier and the Finances of the American Revolution. New York, 1892.

———— The Spanish Dollar and the Colonial Shilling, in American Historical Review, Vol. 3.

TAUSSIG, F. W.—Principles of Economics. New York, 1923.

WHIG ALMANAC (LATER TRIBUNE ALMANAC)—New York, 1843—

UPTON, J. K.—Money in Politics. Boston, 1884.

VALENTINE, D. W.—Fractional Currency of the United States. New York, 1924.

WALKER, F. A.—International Bimetallism. New York, 1896.

WASHINGTON, H. A. (editor)—Writings of Thomas Jefferson. New York, 1854.

WATSON, D. K.—History of American Coinage. New York, 1899.

WEBSTER, PELATIAH—Political Essays. Philadelphia, 1791.

WEEDEN, W. B.—Early Rhode Island. New York, 1910.

———— Economic and Social History of New England. Boston, 1890.

———— Indian Money as a Factor in New England Civilization. Baltimore, 1884.

WHARTON, JOSEPH—Memorandum Concerning Small Money and Nickel Alloy Coinage. Philadelphia, 1877.

———— Project for Reorganizing the Small Coinage of the United States of America. Philadelphia, 1864.

WHITE, C. A.—Archaic Monetary Terms of the United States, in Smithsonian Miscellaneous Collections, Vol. 50.

WHITE, HORACE—Money and Banking, New York, 1914.

———— New York's Colonial Currency, in Sound Currency, Vol. 5.

WOODFORD, A. B.—On the Use of Silver as Money in the United States. Baltimore, 1893.

WOODWARD, A.—Wampum. Albany, 1880.

INDEX

Board of Treasury, 52
Boudinot, Elias, Director, 72
Boutwell, George S., Secretary, 174,
    176, 212, 226
Bristow, Ben. H., Secretary:
    and silver policy, 247, 250–252
Bronze coinage:
    created, 199
    legal tender of, 199
Bullion content, 305
Bullion dealers:
    and law of 1857, 145
    and law of 1873, 236–237
    and Spanish coins, 145
    as exporters of coin, 230, 232
    in Civil War period, 157–158
Bullion fund:
    established, 94
    increased, 274
    proposed, 74
Bureau of Efficiency, 296
Bureau of the Mint, 233

C

California (see Pacific Coast)
Canada:
    and nickel coins, 218
    exports of coin to, 153, 155
Cent (bronze):
    created, 199–200
    legal tender of, 199, 202, 203
    lost, 302
    qualities of, 294–295
    usefulness of, 273
    volume of, 274
Cent (copper):
    abolished, 140
    altered, 65
    created, 64
    in Hamilton's plan, 59
    in Jefferson's plan, 51
    in Morris' plan, 47
    legal tender of, 86

Cent (copper):
    lost, 302
    origin of, 41
    redeemed, 302
    reduced by Washington, 71–72
    unpopularity of, 77, 103, 139
Cent (copper-nickel):
    abolished, 199
    as Civil War money, 160, 187
    bullion value of, 190–192
    created, 140
    excess supply of, 147
    legal tender of, 144–145
    lost, 302
    premium on, 187–192
    qualities of, 142
    use of, 148
Chalmers, 45
Chase, S. P., Secretary:
    and fractional notes, 180–185
    and postage currency, 171–180
    and Postmaster General Blair, 173–
        176
    estimates coin, 151–152
    policy of, 184–185
Cincinnati, 164
Coinage:
    Board of Treasury's report on, 50
    first United States, 49, 55
    Grand committee's report on, 51
    Hamilton's report on, 57–60
    in colonies, 29–30
    Jefferson's report on, 50–51
    mediaeval, 9–11
    Morris' report on, 46–50
Coins (see bronze, copper, fiduciary,
        minor, and silver coins)
Colonial currency:
    commodities used as, 20
    legal tender of, 18
    of non-British colonies, 31
    paper money as, 24, 30–31
    value of, 19
Colonial mints, 29–30